From the library of
Danny Doyle
Raised on songs and stories

VOICES
1870–1914

Peter Vansittart

FRANKLIN WATTS

NEW YORK 1985

Library of Congress Cataloging in Publication Data

Vansittart, Peter.
Voices, 1870–1914.

Bibliography: p.
Includes index.
1. Quotations, English. 2. Europe—History—
1871–1918—Miscellanea. I. Title.
PN6081.V3   1985   082   84-29146
ISBN 0-531-09793-5

First published in Great Britain in 1984
by Jonathan Cape Ltd

First published in the United States in 1985
by Franklin Watts, 387 Park Avenue South, New York, NY 10016

Introduction, arrangement and linking material
copyright © 1984 by Peter Vansittart
For details of other copyright material reproduced
see *Acknowledgments*

To
George and Brenda Rothery,
To
William and Gina

CONTENTS

INTRODUCTION

This is not an impartial historical survey but a collage, more quirky than partisan, a personal reaction to dynamic cross-currents of an extinct European order. It begins and ends in wholesale bloodshed, a big bang.

I myself have never had any ideas, at best only what Somerset Maugham, rather complacently and more than once, termed notions. Here, I mostly avoid direct interventions but the very act of selection is, of course, a judgment, a bias. My temperament follows Turgenev's words to Tolstoy: 'Those who bind themselves to systems are those incapable of understanding the whole truth and try to grab it by the tail; a system is like truth's tail in your fingers, but truth itself resembles a lizard: it leaves its tail in your fingers and runs off, knowing very well that in a second it will sprout a new one.'

These pages will present no real villains but some admirable figures. My motives are several. Those who wish to forget the past, a growing band, assume a dangerous trust in human goodwill, and forget that in much pain is much retribution. Work on *Voices from the Great War* made me reflect on pre-1914 life, whose survivors entertained my childhood with loving recollections of social equanimity, happy servants, amusing beggars and easy money. This provoked disrespectful, though indolent, scepticism.

Undeniably, these decades held thrilling achievements in art and science, experimental medicine and psychology, engineering and shipbuilding, in social reform. Even Russia was advancing, industrially, faster than rather stagnant Britain, and was scarcely

Trotsky's scarecrow land of 'ikons and cockroaches'. All proved insufficient to arrest or even foresee not perhaps a smash-up but the revolutionary effects of a total smash-up. Blatant portents are now visible. The naval masterpiece steers for the iceberg despite explicit warnings delivered by a most far-reaching invention, radio: the mammoth bridge sways ominously in the wind: machine-gun and barbed wire await the haughty, resplendent cavalry: the emperor rattles his sabre at the Yellow Peril, at the encircling enemies, boasting wars from which his spirit cowers.

Despite periodic international crises, people seemed more worried by poverty, strikes, birth control, H. G. Wells's Ann Veronica and Ibsen's Nora, sexual jealousy and free love ('Marriage', reflected Robert Louis Stevenson, 'is a sort of friendship recognised by the police'), than by the likelihood of abrupt extermination. The Siege of Paris was soon remoter than the Siege of Troy, and, in 1881, panic erupted not about policies in Germany or Ireland, but about the end of the world which had been predicted by Mother Shipton, who had died in 1561, to her great surprise. Andrew Flexner, discussing prostitution, in 1914, acknowledged the economic pressures and the collapse of families but added, 'Sheer loneliness, even among employed persons, is not infrequently a decisive factor.' This was overlooked in Shaw's lively but over-neat Mrs Warren's Profession, 1898.

The golden Edwardian afternoon! Osbert Sitwell ruminated in his autobiography, 'I had the fortune to be born towards the sunset hour of one of the great periodic calms of history . . . Everything was calm and still and kindly.'

The hellish enormities of the two world wars have obscured the blazing nastiness, even the very fact, of the Franco-Prussian war of 1870. A few weeks ago I was citing some lines of the late Philip Toynbee to illustrate his particular imaginative flavour.

> Even the Chassepot and the Mitrailleuse betrayed them.
> Whenever I read again this debacle of France and
> old Europe, I'm half-persuaded that Bazaine will suddenly
> turn and break them.

My listeners, highly intelligent friends of Philip's, were puzzled and slightly irritated by a subject so obviously perverse or arcane. What was Bazaine? Who was the Chassepot?

That war, as unnecessary and unexpected as most others, was the first in which the Press, and consequently street opinion, had a powerful role. A. J. P. Taylor adds that the railway time-table was the basis of Prussian success. One can exaggerate the importance of Cleopatra's nose and Helen's eyes, but the personalities of Bismarck and Napoleon III cannot here be ignored. Deaths exceeded 130,000. The Head of the French State surrendered at Sedan with a marshal, thirty-nine generals and over 80,000 men. Worse followed. The Siege of Paris, lasting 135 days, introducing Europe to ration cards, entailed thousands more casualties from shells, disease, hunger and battle. Alistair Horne mentions the recorded eating of 25,523 cats. After a triumphal march through Paris, Wilhelm of Prussia was proclaimed German Emperor at Versailles under the painting *The Glories of France*, with a brash Empire and a constitution disgraceful to the high intelligence of its chief architect, Bismarck. It was to be easily manipulated by political and military irresponsibles.

After royalist victory in the Third Republic's first elections and vehement disputes with the government, first at Bordeaux, then at Versailles, the Paris Commune, more anarchist and Jacobin than Marxist, declared itself independent, urging all other towns to do likewise. From March 18 to May 28, Government and Commune fought each other with mounting atrocities. In this civilized age, contemporary with Shaw and George Eliot, Tolstoy and Flaubert, the Commune shot, bayoneted and lynched some 500 hostages, suspects, private enemies and petty criminals, then, in defeat, attempted to burn down Paris. The Versailles troops in return killed over 18,000, usually after perfunctory trials or none, forerunning the 'People's Courts' of subsequent eras, and, in one week, outnumbering the total of those guillotined during the far longer and more famous Reign of Terror, 1793–4.

The causes of the outbreak of war in 1914 are outside my brief, I can discuss here only the human material that made war possible. Probably enough is included to ridicule, if still necessary, another belief popular in my youth, as expressed by the Socialist Patrick Gordon-Walker in 1939: 'The war of 1914–18 was essentially a war between imperialist powers for the control of colonies.' Even this, I suppose, improves upon W. B. Yeats's considered judgment: 'The First World War did not have much reality.'

Patterns of violence cross my pages, like a fire smouldering in walls and attics, lurking under floors, showing here a glint, there a smudge, exuding an acrid stench or ominous haze. Indeed, since 1789, continuous attempts to interpret the French Revolution and overturn the Vienna Treaty had been savage. Europe endured ugly strikes, agitations and repressions until 1913. On the verge of war, in 1870, menacing French strikes occurred, notably at the Creusot arms works, supported by the International, broken by the army. Violence, like religion, like the Dreyfus case, transcended nominal Party lines. The Socialist, Aristide Briand, cheerfully smashed a rail strike, 1910, by imposing martial law and threatening to conscript the strikers, an example imitated by General Franco, years later. The radical Clemenceau who, as Mayor of Montmartre during the Commune, had generous opportunity to assess human nature, was merciless towards strikers.

Camus refers to over 1,000 European dynamite outrages in 1892. Russian women terrorists included Dora Brilliant, Rachel Louriée and Sophia Perovskaya. Vera Zussulich shot the Governor of St Petersburg, 1878. Perovskaya was hanged for helping to murder Alexander II, 1881. The Russian minister Plehve and the Grand Duke Sergei were murdered, 1905, the year of the Winter Palace Massacre. Other assassinations were of the Russian statesman Stolypin, King Umberto of Italy, King Carlos of Portugal and his heir, Empress Elizabeth of Austria, the King and Queen of Serbia, Jean Jaurès, Leon Gambetta, President Carnot and many less illustrious. London has not quite forgotten the Latvian anarchist, Peter the Painter, whose burglar associates, having murdered three unarmed police, died with their guns and bombs in a burning house during the 'Siege of Sidney Street', watched by Winston Churchill with customary good appetite. French police charged a May Day procession, 1891, killing ten. Belgian troops killed twelve during the General Strike, 1893, and eight strikers at Louvain, 1902. French troops killed twenty strikers and wounded 667 at Nantes, 1908. Kipling's 'The Islanders', 1902, caustically attacked the British propensity to strike, and *The Times* attributed Britain's industrial decline partly to restrictive labour practices. In the Liverpool riots, 1911, which may have had racial undercurrents, a striker was killed by troops and 200 were wounded. Two were killed at Llanelli. Miners, dockers, seamen and railwaymen at Southampton, Liverpool, Hull and Cardiff attacked trains, looted, fired buildings, fought troops, of whom some 50,000 were used to break strikes and quell rioters. Churchill called the rail strike 'an abyss of horror which no man dared to contemplate'. Fierce strikes periodically convulsed British docks, mines, railways and factories from 1880 to 1913. Nor should the street-warfare between organized gangs, very brutal and of bizarre appearance, be forgotten.

This was the era of the murderous Russian Black Hundreds and the libellous and disruptive *Protocols of Zion*. Violence tormented Ireland: there were 500 acts of arson in 1880. Terrorists killed the Irish Secretary, Lord Frederick Cavendish, in Dublin, 1882, the year of some 2,500 rural assaults and 10,000 evictions. Systematic genocide against Armenians by Kurds and Turks was encouraged by the Turkish State, 1894. Anarchist threats and bombs terrorized Paris in 1892.

Ireland was scorched with too much history, much of it trouble-some, after its splendid beginnings independent of Rome and London. *Annals of Our Time* records, 19 November 1870, 'The Irish organs of disaffection congratulate their supporters on the threatened war with Russia, *The Nation* openly announcing that in the event of hostilities occurring, Irishmen mean to secure, in the first place, a settlement of the Irish question.'

Theoretical justifications for violence were widespread. Georges Sorel's *Reflections on Violence* praised proletarian violence in the class-war as fine and heroic. 'Condemnation of war is absurd and immoral,' his fellow-intellectual, Heinrich von Treitschke, consid-ered. Bernard Shaw applauded the Boer War. In *Germany's Fu-ture*, 1909, General Karl von Bernhardi, echoing Field-Marshal von Moltke, victor of 1870, insisted: 'War is the highest expression of culture, bringing into play the loftiest manifestations of human nature. Individual crudities and weaknesses vanish before the idealism of the whole – Only where the possibilities of war remain will the energies of a nation be preserved.' The Futurist, Marinetti, who ended as an insignificant Fascist flunkey, wanted, before 1914, to bomb Venice and destroy art galleries and museums, to let in fresh air.

Colonial atrocities make obvious targets, notoriously the de-population by floggings, torture, mutilation, killing for sport, by whites of the Arano Rubber Company in Putumayo; the shootings, crucifixions and enslavement in the Congo Free State appalled liberal Europe. Of the Congo, H. G. Wells commented in 1932, 'the originator, the mainstay and the chief beneficiary of a system which has killed more human beings than the European War, was King Leopold II of Belgium.'

In the Boer War, some 18,000 Boer civilians died in Kitchener's camps: British casualties were some 30,000, together with perhaps 13,000 Blacks, less scrupulously recorded. 350,000 horses perished as 'wastage'. Yet it was scarcely true that the British, by 1900 holding the largest empire in history, merely sought destruction of splendid civilizations. Though leaving unrestrained the greedy Indian moneylender and injuring much local industry, the British abolished banditry, widowburning and civil wars in India, introduced tea planting and an honest civil service, and taught Indians their own history. In Malaya they began rubber-planting and tin-mining, built Singapore, hospitals, roads, suppressed piracy. These benefits, as in Africa, are easy to forget, as indeed are the costs. Indigenous cruelties were also formidable. Winwood Read's *The Martyrdom of Man* shattered any belief in the Noble Savage. Still remembered are the piled Ashanti skulls, and skeletons nailed to trees; the Casembe of Mweru with his porch decorated with skulls, his courtiers with lopped ears and hands; King Mtesa of Uganda, with victims clubbed senseless before their heads were sawn off, for such crimes as coughing. His son attracted British intervention by burning alive thirty missionaries in 1889. The sadistic slaver, Tippu Tib, still alive in 1890, half-African, half-Arab, was as calculating as his conqueror, King Leopold. White slave contractors must share guilt with African rulers and Arab middlemen. Dr Livingstone saw the pointless massacre in Central Africa, by Arabs, of hundreds of peaceful Manyema Africans at market.

> As I write, I hear the loud wails on the left bank over those who are slain . . . oh let Thy kingdom come! No one will ever know the exact loss on this bright sultry summer morning, it gave the impression of being in hell.

To begin this selection from 1870 to 1914 with Robespierre, 1758–94, may seem whimsical, but his influence, like that of Dickens, did not die with him. It enlivened the French youth riots in 1968. George Sand hailed him 'the greatest man, not only of the Revolution, but of recorded history'.

I enjoy seeking precedents, which continually recede as if through mirrors. John Wesley wrote on 'gradual and elegantly varied' evolution, 'from a plant to a man'. Very early in this century, Kipling was agitated by 'the tyranny of the miners' union'. The Redl Affair, 1913, displayed Russian skills in blackmailing homosexuals. Catherine the Great imprisoned dissidents in madhouses. Ludwig Feuerbach wrote in 1839, 'Dreaming is the key to religious mysteries.' For Wagner, 'Today we have only to interpret the Oedipus myth in a way that keeps faith with its essential meaning to get a coherent picture from it of the whole history of man.' Nietzsche asserted, 'All instincts that cannot be released outwards will turn inwards.' The pre-1914 anti-semitic Austrian Nationalist, Georg von Schönerer, believed, 'Religion is only a mask – the foulness lies in the blood.' The Austrian *Ostara*, 1907, was an 'Aryan brotherhood' against Jews and 'inferior races', its founder sporting a swastika over his castle. Ernst Hasse, in 1895, advocated the deportation of Jews and Slavs, the annexation of Poland, Ruthenia, Serbia, Belgium, Romania, the Baltic states endorsing the 1891 Pan-German League: 'We want territory even if it belongs to aliens, so that we may fashion the future according to our own needs.' Von Treitschke had protested, in 1878, against the growing power of German Jewry. In Britain, where an Aliens Act was passed in 1905, Wyndham Lewis considered that the 'modern world owes everything to the Anglo-Saxons'. Theories of racial aristocracy were propounded by the Frenchman, Gobineau, and the Englishman, H. S. Chamberlain, Wagner's son-in-law, much admired by Wilhelm II and Adolf Hitler. *Cassell's Family Magazine*, 1877, had misgivings about a threatened import of cheap Chinese labour: 'It is certain that we, in our crowded community, could even less than in America afford to tolerate a horde of people whose habitual vices cast ancient Corinth into the shadow.'

William J. Fishman has written recently, 'The immigrant flood brought an inevitable reaction from nationalists in the form of the British Brothers League, from the trade-unionists led by Ben Tillet's dockers, and from the native-born Jewish middle-class who were afraid of a backlash from the unpopularity of the East End Jews against themselves.'

Yet Herzen may remain pertinent. 'The Englishman has no special love of foreigners, still less of refugees whom he regards as guilty of poverty, a vice he himself never forgives. But he clings to the right of asylum.'

Matthew Arnold, in 1869, deplored the insistence on perfecting only 'the moral side, the side of obedience and action', at the expense of the total human personality. Disraeli feared 'a despotism of the most formidable and dangerous character', were the Commons to eliminate Lords and Crown. Wilhelm II, like Khrushchev, demanded that Art should create 'an ideal of elevating character', and that 'the Theatre must induce respect for the highest traditions of our German Fatherland'. Bernard Shaw's view was not absolutely dissimilar. His theatre should be 'a factory of thought, a prompter of conscience, an armoury against despair and dullness, and a temple to the ascent of man'. Neither view was acclaimed by Irving, Tree, Bernhardt, Marie Lloyd, Dan Leno, Marya Delvard, though Shaw's beliefs are accepted today by all save audiences.

In *The World Set Free*, 1914, Wells forecast a proto-atomic bomb. In Turgenev's *A Month In The Country*, 1872, censorship forced the omission of the husband and the transformation of the wife into a widow.

All ages are contradictory. My period was of unusual women, amongst them Alma Werfel, Lou Andreas – Salomé, Cosima Wagner, Mary Kingsley, Isadora Duncan, Rebecca West, who conceived the idea that one of Thomas Hardy's ancestors must have been a weeping willow, Amber Reeves, Eleanor Marx, Olive Schreiner, Duse, Colette, Annie Besant, Marie Stopes, George Eliot, the Pankhursts, Berthe Morisot, Florence Nightingale, Gwen John, Käthe Kollwitz, Elizabeth Garrett Anderson, Rosa Luxemburg, Constance Lytton, Lady Gregory, Marie Curie, Beatrice Webb, Clara Zetkin, the strenuously vulgar and generous Marie Lloyd, Queen Victoria herself, who once rebuked a minister, 'My Lord, I have been taught to judge between right and wrong: expediency is a word I neither wish to hear again nor understand.' Mary Kingsley strode through Africa. Of 'the Divine Sarah', Shaw remarked that he could never do her justice or believe in her impersonations because she was so very like his aunt Georgina.

Simultaneously, masculinity was grossly rampant. Militarism, savaged by the Dreyfus case, was increasingly reckless, as if the officer caste, baited by intellectuals, sensed its own decline and, like the knights before it, covered it with arrogance, flamboyance and fantasy. Yet revolutionaries themselves would jib at women's rights; which Marx and Lenin usually lumped together with those of a generalized proletariat.

Traditionalist masculine governments were confronted with militant Nationalism in Bohemia, Hungary, Ireland, the Balkans, Poland. Everywhere, the emergent new was entangled with the old. The German Chancellor, von Bülow, never forgot his feudal background and language: 'Military prowess, national greatness, dynastic splendour, an Imperial future – these were the noble aspirations surrounding me as an adolescent.' He was no isolated freak as he quoted with relish: 'Only horses and warriors guard the steep height where the Princes stand. Not democrats, Jews, or bandits, for whoever trusts them has built on muck.' The German-born Queen Mother of Italy was to assess the Great War with him: 'What she most regretted about the war was that events would have made it very difficult for German princes and princesses to marry their social equals in France and Russia. A second disagreeable result of the War, the Queen suggested, was the possible danger of a serious spread of democracy.'

Incidentally, A. J. P. Taylor's suggestion interests me: 'In my opinion, most of the great men of the past were only there for the beer – the wealth, prestige and grandeur that went with the power.' As Disraeli said of the Commons, 'We're here for fame!'

Art that still stimulates was countered by stolid or vehement philistinism, at its most blatant in the hoots at the handcuffed Wilde on Clapham Junction platform, an outburst doubtless concealing fear. Enthralling scientific vitality had begun. Faraday had died, 1867, but Clerk Maxwell, Darwin, T. H. Huxley, Marconi, J. J. Thompson and Max Planck were analysing light, space, matter, discovering the electron, the quantum and changing the globe, but no more than the new Art was the new Science welcomed wholeheartedly.

Outwardly, Europe was hurrying in all directions, though not in all directions improving. Inwardly, much was static. Scientific evolution did not seriously impair superstition and make-believe. The *Cape Town Times*, 15 July 1896, aroused excitement with news of the arrival of Mr Sherlock Holmes and Dr Watson. The decline, not of religious temperament but of formal religion, was tempered by interest in spiritualism and occultism. Louis Blanc found Victorian London crammed with clairvoyants, astrologers, warlocks, attracting all classes. D. D. Home allegedly levitated from 15 Ashley Place, and round the drawing-room of Mr S. C. Hall. Dostoevsky held that man seeks not so much God as the miraculous. Clairvoyants assisted in the Jack the Ripper case, and, in 1882, 'a drum was beaten over the river Derwent in the hope of locating the corpse of a poor girl who had been drowned in its depths. It was actually believed that when the boat in which the drummer sat passed over the spot where the body sat submerged, the drum would cease to sound' (Lewis Spence). Gladstone once said that psychical research was 'by far the most important' work being done in the world, and consulted a medium, William Eglington. George V's tutor, Rev. J. N. Dalton and twelve others, at sea, in 1880, saw the *Flying Dutchman* 'all aglow'.

A fertility bull is reported buried alive in Scotland, 1870. Madame Blavatsky's hermetic *Isis Unveiled: A Master Key to the Mysteries of Ancient and Modern Science*, 1877, tapped considerable curiosity concerning the Occult Hierarchy, Elder Brethren, Adepts, mediumistic Tibetan Mahatmas, Blavatsky claiming herself the reincarnation of Paracelsus, 1493–1541. Freud and Zola, like Mussolini, had obsessions with numbers, Freud being agitated by 23, 28, 61 and 62. Henry James found special qualities in 23. Yvonne de Gaulle remembered being promised by a fortune-teller that she would be 'almost a queen'. During the 1906 General Election: 'Working-class audiences were told the Tories would introduce Chinese labour into England if they won, and pictures of a pig-tailed coolie in a straw hat were labelled "Tory British Working Man". Thrown on a London screen at political meetings, the pictures, reported Graham Wallas, a Liberal sympathiser, aroused "an instantaneous howl of indignation against Mr Balfour". The audience could not have told whether it howled from humanitarian indignation or fear of the competition of cheap labour. Underlying both these sentiments Wallas thought he detected a fear of the alien symbolized by the alien pigtail. The hideous yellow face aroused "an immediate hatred of the mongoloid racial type" and this hatred was transferred to the Conservative Party. In the hatred of the audience he heard the force of the irrational in public affairs' (Barbara Tuchman). A century after the Enlightenment saw the stirring efforts for the Rights of Man, the hysterical passions released by the Dreyfus affair reveal the shallowness of political revolution in effecting genuine 'change of heart'.

This was a dimension that socialism, with its bright hopes, often ignored. Meanwhile, Tolstoy, Dostoevsky, D. H. Lawrence condemned Science for warping live human awareness, detaching humanity from the warmly primitive, mysterious, intuitive: for surrendering to the inorganic, materialistic, mechanical. This may have prompted Alexander Blok: 'The sinking of the *Titanic* has made me indescribably happy; there is, despite everything, an ocean.'

D. H. Lawrence insisted, in 1912, 'We can go wrong in our minds, but what the blood feels, and believes, and says, is always true.' He retorted to Aldous Huxley, 'I don't care about evidence. Evidence doesn't mean a thing to me.'

The 'Spirit of the Age', elusive, perhaps imaginary, is perhaps best approached by artists. Before the *Titanic* sank, April 1912, Celia Thanter's poem, 'The Tryst', 1887, concerned the destruction of a giant liner, as did Morgan Robertson's novel, *Futility*, 1898, about the *Titan* wrecked by an iceberg on an April night. Yet another huge ship suffered catastrophe in Mayne Clew Garnett's story, *The White Ghost of Disaster*.

Always, even under Terror, children had to be fed, washed, taught, comforted, and told to trust in the Lord, without always realizing that this might refer to Lord Northcliffe. Much in my book shows traces of the fears and misunderstandings of childhood. 'I can still see the shadow of wolves if I lie in bed with a fire in the room,' wrote Ford Madox Ford. I myself would crouch on a table, from the wolves, and once saw a blue staring giant in the darkened garden. North Country children still fear Winnie with the Long Green Fingers, and Jennie Greenteeth, sitting in slime. The infant Rider Haggard 'suffered terrors from an old doll with boot-button eyes, black wool hair and a sinister leer on its painted face. An unkind nurse-maid playing on his fear of the doll, used to frighten him into obedience by brandishing it. This doll was known as She-who-must-be-obeyed' (Peter Beresford Ellis).

Victorian children were given 'Mother Bailey's quietening syrup', reinforced with opium. It may not have always sufficed. I remember two remarks by Dickens:

Force a child into a lonely bedroom at night, and you'd better murder it.

If we all knew our own minds, I suspect that we should find our nurses responsible for most of the dark corners we are forced to go back to against our will.

His own nurse, Miss Weller, captivated and terrorized him with her nightly tale of Captain Murderer, poisoner and cannibal. But also, from a different social class:

> One is struck, when reading Victorian memoirs, by the many obscure terrors that seem to have haunted the children of that period. (Was that because so many things were discussed before them in hushed voices, or because they were so constantly in the company of uneducated people?) Lady Sybil Lubbock, in spite of her happy surroundings, was no exception. She was terrified by the 'Eye of God' burglars, 'Penny for the Guy' urchins, the May Day 'Jack in the Green' and his capering chimney-sweep attendants, mad dogs and gipsy women. These only sprang to life at night, and were soon laid to rest by Nanny who came in with a shaded candle to soothe her. But even Nanny could not cope with the effect on her nervous system of 'Jack the Ripper' of whose nightmare exploits she had gathered something from the whispers of servants.
>
> Magdalen King-Hall

Most families lacked Nanny. The infant Keir Hardie shared a one-room cabin with his parents and nine siblings. Slum children, huddled together, could hide from some terrors, though perhaps develop others. Scores of children were reared in brothels, for abstruse sexual torments. In 1910, a twelve-year-old English boy got a birching and a seven-year sentence, ostensibly for stealing a fivepenny lump of coal. An eight-year-old girl was the oldest of a group working fourteen hours a day in the fenlands, under an old overseer 'carrying a long stick which he did not forget to use'. British ships carried world-wide power, their discipline not that of friendly discussion. Olivia Manning's father, born in 1859, recalled boys sent aloft to dress the ship overall for a royal visit and ordered to remain there throughout. Royalty lingered so long that two boys fainted from cold and crashed to their deaths.

Poverty still accused wealth, and sometimes threatened, in what was less a golden age than an age of gold: 63 per cent of those saved from the *Titanic* were from the First Class. Vita Sackville-West visited a Polish grandee and hereditary dwarfs passed the cigarettes.

Wealth alone, however, did not divide peoples. In India, in 1906, the future George V noted: 'I could not help being struck by the way in which all salutations by the Natives were disregarded by the persons to whom they were given. Evidently we are too much inclined to look upon them as a conquered and down-trodden race and the Native, who is becoming more and more educated, realizes this.'

Lord Curzon himself, who did much for India, nevertheless regarded 'the Natives' as 'crooked-minded and corrupt, unfit for administration'. The dangerous distinction between Them and Us was not monopolized by India. George V's biographer, Kenneth Rose, quotes an observer at Edward VII's lying-in-state. 'The Prime Minister was there with Miss Asquith leaning against one of the lamp standards and watching the people pass. I thought his attitude and general demeanour rather offensive. I fear he had dined well and he seemed to regard the occasion as a mere show.'

Everywhere were exciting, thrusting, eccentric and exotic personalities: in politics, sport, theatre, music hall, pot house . . . Offenbach, D'Annunzio, C. B. Fry – the only English cricket captain to be offered the throne of Albania – Bismarck, Diaghilev, Dan Leno – 'profound comedian, with streaks of insanity' and 'the eyes of a wounded animal or great tragedian', repeating the poetic query of the immemorial Fool: 'Ah, what is Man? Wherefore does he why? Whence did he whence? Whither is he whithering?' Yet philosophies were developing which held Man as victim of the predetermined – genetics, environment, class, the unconscious. A child could assert 'No one's the same, especially me!' and, for Ethel Smythe, at fifteen, 'I am the most interesting person I know and I don't care if no one else knows it.' Adults, however, were invited to rejoice with Bernard Shaw that life's true joy was in acknowledging yourself as 'being part of a mighty purpose, a force of nature, instead of a feverish, selfish little clod of ailments and grievances, complaining that the world will not devote itself to making you happy'. Less jauntily, refuting God, immortality, soul, free will, Ernst von Haeckel, *The Riddle of the Universe*, 1889, pontificated 'the great abstract law of mechanical causality now rules the entire universe, as it does the mind of man. It is the steady, immutable pole star, whose clear light falls on our path through the dark labyrinth of the countless separate phenomena.'

Actually, little was wholly predictable. In a single home, one died of diphtheria, another did not. Politicians might fear the extension of franchises, as likely to endanger property, but forgot that the poor do not despise property but merely want more of it for themselves. Louis Napoleon trusted the plebiscite, as if remembering Proudhon's complaint that universal suffrage is a vote for counter-revolution. British Liberals actually lost popular votes when, plausibly enough, they expected 'The Peers versus the People' to increase them. This gives some ballast to Chesterton's belief, reiterated in different, less friendly terms by Lenin, that the English were more interested in the inequality of horses than in the equality of man.

Henry James, in 1878, feared that a growing decadence which lay behind Britain's peace policies would one day deliver her to 'a supreme and unendurable affront' which would force her into a war, unsuccessful, but heroic in defeat, and lose her her status as a Great Power.

The British, like their neighbours, enjoyed the drama not only of royal and sporting occasions but of lurid murder cases, which were not invariably due to poverty, illiteracy, injustice. Henry Wainwright, author of *The Wit and Eccentricities of Sydney Smith*, shot his lover in 1875, cut her throat, then, having mistaken the dissolving effects of chloride of lime for those of quicklime, tried, vainly, to dispose of her in ten pieces. The public avidly followed the matter of Mary Anne Cotton, hanged in 1873, for poisoning twenty-five people; the still controversial Charles Bravo death; the exploits of Charles Peace, burglar, violinist, murderer, escapist; and the fate of M. Lubanski, stabbed thirty-four times on the Marseilles–Vienna train by a fellow-passenger after a dispute about a cushion.

Little of this detracted from a vigorous popular culture of handicrafts, bell ringing, gardening, dance, balladry, street shows, amateur music and dramatics. A more assorted human tableau probably then existed, in the ordinary day. From 1914, Sacheverell Sitwell remembers:

> a ragged man and two young girls with round, round faces whom I had seen upon a winter evening leading a bear by the school library as it was getting dark. The man had a thick stick in one hand and was leading the bear, a yellow bear upon a chain. I remember the cheap look of its fur and wondering whether they huddled against it for warmth at night. There was only a little moment to ask them who they were, and one of the young girls answered 'Bohémiens' to the young boy in top hat and tail coat who was myself, and certainly no less far-fetched and peculiar in her eyes.

I am anxious to entertain. Politics, what Aldous Huxley calls the science of averages and war, must share my pages with poetry, random anecdotes, private memories. I have a magpie mind and was delighted to learn that G. M. Trevelyan's housemaster at Harrow firmly believed in the advantages of useless knowledge. I enjoy knowing (from E. M. Forster) that T. E. Lawrence teased naval officers by continually referring to the bridge as the verandah, and that Cardinal Mazarin's cruel and prudish son-in-law liked to sit in sunlight and be watered, fancying himself to be a tulip. Charles Dickens had a teacher who wore onions in his ears.

A memorial in Brompton Cemetery celebrates one who 'suddenly fell asleep in Jesus at the Pinner Railway Station, while waiting for a train to return to London'. Rev. J. Radford would wander the countryside seeking a gypsy with whom to wrestle. Louis Napoleon, when young, was reputed expert in Blind Man's Buff and at making animal shadows on a wall, skills perhaps foreshadowing his later foreign policy. Karl Marx deplored Ramsgate for being full of Jews and fleas. W. G. Grace's grandfather drove from Bristol to London in a kite-drawn carriage of his own invention. In the Admiralty Islands, Rev. Elisha Fawcett had his wooden leg buried with him: allegedly, it took root and provided cricket bats. Wellington had his lawn mowed by an elephant in special boots. Charles Kingsley presented a set of his sermons to Mr Ackland, aged two. For his last thirteen years as a senior civil servant at the Colonial Office, Sir Henry Taylor never once visited the actual office. None of this is important but I do not regret knowing it. Here, I am trying to convey through swift details a sense of what Isaiah Berlin calls the complex crooked nature of men and institutions. Human behaviour shows drastic extremes without, despite war and revolution, suggesting any significant change in human nature. Genetics scarcely explain the transformation of Swiss and Scandinavians from warriors to peace-lovers. Mongols devastated Europe but, in China, accepted local cultural superiority. West Indians enjoy cricket, Africans do not.

People enact primeval rituals, whether in skins or morning coats. Current resentments are mostly antique: Hume considered that in habits more than reason was the governing principle of mankind. Changes are slow. As Belloc wrote of a General Election:

The accursed power which stands on Privilege
(And goes with Women, and Champagne and Bridge)
Broke – and Democracy resumed her reign:
(Which goes with Bridge, and Women and Champagne).

All history, Croce held, is contemporary history. Let readers fill in
the following gaps, and they may agree:

Every . . . offense, absence from . . . defamation of . . . praise
of . . . possessing unsuitable books . . . wearing the wrong kind
of clothes or wrong length of hair might involve examination
by . . . and punishment by . . . Informers were active . . . The
. . . had their self-criticism sessions, and this practise spread to the
Civil governing body.

Maurice Latey is not describing . . . or even . . . not even . . . but
sixteenth-century Calvinist Geneva.

 To what extent was the Great War a surprise? Today, the omens,
threats and diplomatic provocations seem to advance inexorably,
yet probably most Europeans were as bewildered as they were in
1870. My citations will prove nothing. A Russian proverb runs, 'He
lies like an eye-witness,' and Samuel Butler opined, 'If a man is not a
good, sound, honest, capable liar, there is no truth in him.'

 Leonard Woolf remembered:

It seemed that human beings might really be on the point of
becoming civilized . . . the forces of reaction and barbarism
were still there, but they were in retreat. They had suffered a
tremendous defeat in the Dreyfus Case. In the Zabern incident
and in the Denshawi incident a new note began to be heard in
what may be called world opinion. It seemed at last to be
generally agreed that for a German officer to beat up an Alsatian
cobbler was an outrage against law and order and decency and
civilization. When at Denshawi a British court passed savage
sentences upon Egyptian villagers for killing a British officer who
insisted on killing the villagers' pigeons, a cry went up, not against
the villagers but against the insolence of the officers and the
vindictiveness and savagery of the judges. For the first time in the
history of the world the rights of Jews, cobblers, coloured men,
not to be beaten, hanged or judicially murdered by officers,
junkers or white men was publicly admitted; and it looked for a

moment as if militarism, imperialism and anti-semitism were on the run.

Mary Moorman notes that 'at Gladstone's centenary in 1909, they had closed the schools in Bulgaria and held celebrations all over the country in his honour'.
Oskar Kokoshka was adult in 1914:

> The Hapsburg Empire, ruled by the old Emperor in the enlightened spirit of Joseph II, was not an ideal State; but before the First World War summary trials, witch hunts, torture, public executions, secret death-sentences, concentration camps, deportations and dispossessions were unknown there; so were slave labour – Austria had no colonies – and child labour.

In Tsarist Russia itself there was less capital punishment and slavery than exists today, and juries sometimes acquitted for political offences. There are more secret police and censorship in Prague than under Franz Josef.

Nevertheless, premonitions were felt. C. M. Bowra mentions Russian poems by Tyutchov, Ivanov, Bryusov, forecasting some purging catastrophe, with titles such as *The Coming Huns* and instances of Attila the cruel conqueror swooping to destroy books, and history itself.

A. J. P. Taylor considered, in 1951, that to accuse Germany of consciously planning the war of 1914 was 'to credit her with more direction than she possessed'. Probably, as in 1870, Great Powers were ready for a limited conflict which might well not occur, though in each ruling class were a few downright aggressive groups and individuals.

War solves few public problems but too many private ones. There was pronounced overlapping of old and new and the realization that the difference can be less than expected. A great scientist, Isaac Newton, was also a religious mystic: the Nazis, in Orwell's words, used science in the cause of superstition. Wagner's 'Music of the Future', within themes of self-transformation and transcendence, included values and images from the primitive and brutal. Tribal loyalties and fetishes persisted within modernist élites. Socialists everywhere forwent their much vaunted General Strike, in 1914. Almost alone of major writers, Heinrich Mann and Romain Rolland openly opposed the war. Kokoshka, in a war he had not applauded, after wounds almost fatal, for goals to which he was indifferent, refused to desert. 'Had I not sworn an oath to the Emperor? His uniform was a new skin concealing my emotional scars so that others could not see them.'

People are not all of a piece. After watching pre-war German manoeuvres, Churchill wrote, 'Much as war attracts me and fascinates my mind with its tremendous situations – I feel more deeply every year what vile and wicked folly and barbarism it all is.'

1870 and 1914 show that in war, all ages are one.

An ex-soldier once said to me: 'Funny things happen in war too, you know. For instance, off we went, five of us, to the nearest wood, to fetch some branches, when, suddenly, one of those devilish German shells crashed down on us. I was chucked into a hole, buried in earth and covered with stones. When I recovered I lay there and thought: "You're finished, Semion, my lad!" But not a bit of it! I recovered all right, rubbed my eyes and couldn't see anything of my pals. But up there were some trees, bare, leafless, and from the branches strings of innards were hanging. At this, I fairly burst out laughing! It was too funny to see the remains of my friends dangling on those branches. Naturally, a little later, I began feeling rather bad about it. After all, they were my comrades, chaps just like me. And now, suddenly – not a scrap left of them anymore – as if they'd not lived at all. But at first – I laughed.'

(Maxim Gorki)

Marx considered, with whatever accuracy, 'Certain periods of highest development of art stand in no direct connection with the general development of society nor with the material basis and skeleton structure of its organization.' Whether or not they confirm this, the poems I have chosen are at least reminders of lives and visions outside public events. The language of love and hate, private grief and loneliness, exaltation and despair, can outdistance even its occasions.

Another language inevitably accompanies this, like an evil imp, and within months after the close of this book Henry James was writing for the *New York Times*:

The War has used up words; they have weakened, they have deteriorated like motor car tires; they have, like millions of other things, been more overstrained and knocked about and voided of the happy semblance during the last six months than in all the long ages before, and we are now confronted with a depreciation of all our terms, or otherwise speaking with a loss of expression through increase of limpness, that may make us wonder what ghosts will be left to walk.

Essentially, I wish to convey some sense of life – tragic, comic, muddled, absurd, heaving, beneath the topical slogans, the 'telegrams and anger'.

Sinister in his watchtower,
Love waits in ambush, bending his fatal bow.
I know the weapons in his ancient arsenal:
Crime, horror and madness.

(Baudelaire)

To retain a personal flavour, I have largely quoted from books in my own possession, and have reluctantly confined myself to European events. Save in the *Prelude*, most extracts from outside the given period are italicized.

July 1983 P.V.

PRELUDE
1789–1869

I swear it exists . . . that tender impetuous and irresistible passion, torment and delight of magnanimous souls, that deep horror of tyranny, that compassionate zeal for the oppressed, that sacred love of one's country, that more sublime and sacred love of humanity without which a great revolution is merely one dazzling crime that destroys another; it exists, that generous ambition to establish on earth the first Republic in the world; that unselfishness of men not departed which finds its celestial joy in the calm of a pure conscience and the delightful vision of the public good. You feel it burning in your soul at this very instant. I feel it in you.

> Maximilien Robespierre

There must be one will and one will only.

> Maximilien Robespierre

The Revolutionary Government owes its opponents nothing but death.

> Maximilien Robespierre

To be safe we must kill everyone.

> Jacques-René Hébert

They made and recorded a sort of institute and digest of anarchy, called the Rights of Man.

> Edmund Burke

I seem to see a miserable wretch killed in order that he may be cured.

Louis-Antoine de Saint-Just

The words we have spoken will never be lost upon the earth.

Louis-Antoine de Saint-Just

Plots, massacres, assassinations, seem to some people a trivial price for obtaining a revolution. A cheap, bloodless reformation, a guiltless liberty, appear flat and vapid to their tastes. There must be a great change of scene, there must be a magnificent stage-effect; there must be a grand spectacle to rouse the imagination, grown torpid with the lazy enjoyment of sixty years' security, and the still unanimating repose of public prosperity.

Edmund Burke

Priests

In later life – usually at about fifty – the priests of the Duchy take either to drink, or else to religion – the latter normally consequent upon the death of one of their mistresses; and when *that* happens, they voluntarily take upon themselves the most fantastic penances, and find relief in an attempt to persecute their younger colleagues. The customary reward is a fine display of public contempt and hatred. In 1792, when the émigré priests from France began to flood into Italy, Italian priests throughout the land were profoundly shocked by the restraint and sobriety of their lives.

Stendhal

1830: Revolution in Paris

Society is dissolving, nothing of the past should exist any longer, and we have come to warn you that the people demand that the whole of life be made new.

Two young delegates of the clandestine *Les Amis du Peuple*, to King Louis-Philippe

National differences and antagonisms between peoples are steadily
vanishing.

> Communist Manifesto, 1848

Youth will explode like the boiler of a steam engine . . .The new
barbarians are the intellectuals.

> Honoré de Balzac

All those we love
Are cups of acid to be drunk, eyes closed;
And the heart, transfixed, drawn on by grief,
Dies, daily, blessing the arrow.

> Baudelaire

THE KRAKEN

Below the thunders of the upper deep;
Far far beneath in the abysmal sea,
His ancient, dreamless, uninvaded sleep
The Kraken sleepeth: faintest sunlights flee
About his shadowy sides: above him swell
Huge sponges of millennial growth and height;
And far away into the sickly light,
From many a wondrous grot and secret cell
Unnumber'd and enormous polypi
Winnow with giant fins the slumbering green.
There hath he lain for ages and will lie
Battening upon huge seaworms in his sleep,
Until the latter fire shall heat the deep;
Then once by men and angels to be seen,
In roaring he shall rise and on the surface die.

> Alfred Tennyson, 1842

1848: Revolution in Paris

The city is in confusion. The shops are closing. Women buy food in
haste, the streets empty, and all hearts are seized with the agonies of
disaster. Blood will soon flow in the streets. You come upon a
creature radiating bliss, he carries strange volumes of hieroglyphics.

'And what side are you on?' you demand. 'My dear sir, I have just uncovered some extremely unusual facts about the marriage of Isis and Osiris.' 'The Devil take you. May Isis and Osiris be blessed with many brats, but get the hell out of our lives!'

Baudelaire

We are living at a period of most wonderful transition which tends rapidly to accomplish that great end to which indeed all history points – the realization of the unity of mankind.

Prince Albert

Of the 1848 revolutions, Philip Guedalla wrote, in 1936, that they featured *'the sudden elevation of a number of embarrassed thinkers to political power, and in particular German politics suffered from a rush of professors to the head.'*

THE PRINCESS

For woman is not undevelop'd man,
But diverse: could we make her as the man,
Sweet love were slain: his dearest bond is this,
Not like to like, but like in difference.
Yet in the long years liker must they grow;
The man be more of woman, she of man;
He gain in sweetness and in moral height,
Not lose the wrestling thews that throw the world;
She mental breadth, nor fail in childward care,
Nor lose the childlike in the larger mind.

Alfred Tennyson

The key to the understanding of the character of the conscious life lies in the region of the unconscious.

K. G. Carus

From a Letter, 1849

We know where to find the enemies of the Revolution. They are in Russia and the Slav countries of Austria. No affirmation about the democratic future of these countries can prevent us from considering our enemies as such . . .

We need a pitiless fight to the death against Slavs, traitors to Revolution, a war of extermination, terror without scruple, not in the interests of Germany but in the cause of Revolution . . . The coming of World War will wipe out from the face of the earth not only reactionary classes and dynasties but reactionary peoples as a whole. That also forms a part of progress.

> Friedrich Engels

Pot Luck

M. Marcellus, the Christian nobleman, took communion at his château only with the consecrated wafers stamped with his coat of arms. One day the priest observed in horror that the supply of stamped wafers was finished. He ventured to offer the exalted, pious lips a common, plebeian wafer, the wafer of the vulgar herd, simultaneously tendering this truly admirable apology:

'Pot luck, Monsieur le Comte.'

> *The Goncourt Journal*

Diplomacy, 1858

Have you no boundary dispute with Austria, no old neighbourly quarrel which would yield a plausible pretext for a rupture?

> Napoleon III, to Count Cavour's private envoy, Count Constantine Nigra

1861

Hammer the Poles until they wish they were dead . . . if we want to exist we have no choice but to wipe them out: wolves are only what God made them, but we shoot them all the same when we can get at them.

> Otto von Bismarck

I have always found the word 'Europe' on the lips of those statesmen who want something from a foreign power which they would never dare ask for in their own name.

> Otto von Bismarck

To Napoleon III

To the Horses of the Sun, you hitch your *cab*.

    Victor Hugo

Statistics possess a certain eloquence, with which all false theories must clash.

    Napoleon III

On Napoleon III

At a distance he is something – close at hand, nothing . . . A Sphinx without a secret.

    Otto von Bismarck

That he is a very *extraordinary* man with great qualities, there can be *no* doubt. I might almost say a mysterious man. He is evidently possessed of *indomitable courage, unflinching firmness of purpose, self-reliance, perseverance* and *great secrecy*; and to this should be added a great reliance on what he calls his *Star*, and a belief in omens and incidents as connected with his future destiny which is almost romantic, and at the same time he is endowed with a wonderful *self-control*, great *calmness*, even *gentleness*, and with a *power of fascination*, the effect of which upon those who have become more intimately acquainted with him is *most sensibly* felt.

    Queen Victoria

The Emperor's head seems to have fallen on to his shoulders from a great height.

    The Goncourt Journal

1867

Let us put Germany in the saddle, so to speak – it already knows how to ride.

    Otto von Bismarck

I often think that a violent revolution is very much needed to give that general shake-up to the torpid mind which the French Revolution gave to Continental Europe. England has never had a general break-up of old associations, and hence the extreme difficulty of getting any ideas into its stupid head.

> John Stuart Mill

I have the impression that the Emperor Napoleon is a judicious and amiable man, but not so shrewd as the world considers him.

> Otto von Bismarck, to King Wilhelm of Prussia

On Napoleon III and the Empress Eugénie

I have seen two amusing women but no men.

> Otto von Bismarck

The Jews

The Jewish tribe has indeed a different blood than the Christian peoples of Europe, a different body, a different constitution, other affects and passions, and with his physical constitution is connected his alienness . . . he yearns for the domination of others, for their suppression and exploitation . . . If we add to these peculiarities the thick, white skin and the volatile, mostly disease-inclined blood, we see before us the Jew as white negro, but the robust nature and the capacity for physical work of the negro are missing and are replaced by a brain which by size and activity bring the Jew close to the Caucasians.

> Herman Wagener

The number of jobs in the gift of the government should be limited, for this has often turned a free people into a nation of toadies. That disastrous tendency should be avoided, which causes the State to do what individuals can do as well or better.

> Napoleon III

The Nation is a slave who must be convinced that he is seated on the throne.

> Napoleon III

Possibly the greatest danger of modern times is this false opinion
with which people have been indoctrinated, that a government can
do everything, and that any particular system must attend to all
needs and remedy all evils.

Napoleon III

The history of England says clearly to kings: March at the head of
the ideas of your century, and these ideas follow you and support
you. March behind them, and they drag you after them. March
against them, and they overthrow you.

Napoleon III

The Roman kings vanished because their mission was accomplished. There appears to exist a supreme law establishing a useful
period of life for institutions as well as for human beings. Until this
period is over, nothing can resist them; plots and revolts all fail
against the invulnerable power of what they struggle to demolish.
But when an institution, apparently invulnerable, ceases to assist
human progress, then neither traditions, nor courage, nor the
memories of a glorious history can postpone by a single day the
débâcle decreed by Fate.

Napoleon III, from *Life of Julius Caesar*

Prussia's military forces are far from formidable.

Adolphe Thiers, 1868

On the Second Empire

Instead of Liberty, Equality, Fraternity, it is Cavalry, Infantry,
Artillery.

Karl Marx

France made two mistakes: the first when she imagined that Napoleon III was a fool: the second, when she imagined him a genius.

Adolphe Thiers

On Children

There is not the slightest difficulty in disposing of any number of children, so that they may give no further trouble and never be heard of, at £10 a head.

British Medical Journal, 1868

The Wit of 'La Lanterne', Paris

France has twenty million subjects, not counting the subjects of discontent.

Henri Rochefort

Seventy-eight years ago, at this very hour, the People were plundering the Tuileries. Today sees the exact reverse.

Henri Rochefort

I am a Bonapartist to my very depths. But, allowed to choose my own dynastic hero, I am fully entitled to select Napoleon II. He is my ideal sovereign. Undeniably he once ruled, for his successor is Napoleon III. What a government, my friends, what a government! No taxes, no fruitless wars followed by increased taxation: no expeditions to distant lands costing 600 million francs: no all-devouring Civil Lists: no Ministers of State holding five or six posts at 100,000 francs each; that's the monarch I want. Yes, Napoleon II, I love and admire you above all. Who would now deny my Bonapartism?

Henri Rochefort

The Decay of Murder

The tyranny of the majority, of which we have so much, has entered into our souls as well as our lives, and is insidiously transforming us into a very dull, highly respectable, and intensely monotonous collection of insignificant units. If manners have grown softer we suffer from a stifling atmosphere of public opinion, in which any vigorous development of peculiar idiosyncrasies is fast becoming impossible . . . Originality is growing to be a term of abuse; and ridicule is becoming a more terrible instrument of oppression than

was ever wielded by oppressors in the old days of persecution with
fire and sword. We have ceased to grow forest trees, and are content
with a vast growth of carefully clipped and preserved garden shrubs.

Leslie Stephen

Politics

In a progressive country change is constant, and the great question
is not whether you should resist change which is inevitable, but
whether that change should be carried out in deference to the
manners, the customs, the laws, and the traditions of a people, or
whether it should be carried out in deference to abstract principles,
and arbitrary and general doctrines.

Benjamin Disraeli

A Royal Thought

Danger lies *not* in the power given to the Lower Orders, who are
becoming more well-informed and more intelligent, and who will
deservedly work themselves up to the top by their own merits,
labour and good conduct, but in the conduct of the *Higher Classes*
and of the *Aristocracy*.

Queen Victoria

1870–79

THE DISTURBANCES IN PARIS: THE BARRICADE AT BELLEVILLE.

The Terrible Year

The year 1870, I am sure, cannot but consolidate this general agreement, and tend to the increase of peace and civilization.

> Napoleon III

June–July 1870

I have never during my long experience known so great a lull in Foreign Affairs.

> The British Permanent Under-Secretary, to the Foreign Secretary

In whatever direction one looks, one sees no irritating question arising; at no time in history has the maintenance of peace in Europe been more certain.

> Émile Ollivier, Prime Minister of France

George Eliot at Oxford, May 1870

As we turned into the quadrangle of Lincoln – suddenly, at one of the upper windows of the Rector's lodgings . . . there appeared the head and shoulders of Mrs Pattison, as she looked out and beckoned smiling to Mrs Lewes. It was a brilliant apparition, as though a French portrait by Greuze or Perronneau had suddenly slipped into a vacant space in the old college wall. The pale, pretty head, blond-cendrée; the delicate smiling features and white throat; a touch of black, a touch of blue; a white dress; a general eighteenth-century impression as though of powder and patches: Mrs Lewes perceived it in a flash, and I saw her run eagerly to Mr Lewes and draw his attention to the window and its occupant. She took his arm, while she looked and waved. If she had lived longer, some day and somewhere in her books, that vision at the window, and that flower-laden garden would have reappeared. I seemed to see her consciously and deliberately committing them both to memory.

Mrs Humphry Ward, 1918

MAY 5, 1870

London

Commenced at Bow Street Police-court the examination into charges made against Ernest Boulton and Frederick William Park, of personating women and frequenting places of public resort in female apparel for improper purposes. In the early stages of the examination it did not appear that the prisoners had been guilty of any more heinous offence than indiscretion, but as the case proceeded, Mr Poland (instructed by the Solicitor to the Treasury) submitted evidence tending to show that the readiness and completeness with which the prisoners could personate female characters in private theatricals had gradually exceeded the bounds of propriety and given occasion for scandal against them of the gravest description. In the letters produced, reference was made to the fact that Boulton was 'living in drag'. This was explained to be a slang phrase for dressing in women's clothes.

Annals of our Time

Miss Sylvester

Mrs Nott told me that Louie of the Cloggau was staying in Presteign with her aunt Miss Sylvester, the woman frog. This extraordinary being is partly a woman and partly a frog. Her head and face, her eyes and mouth are those of a frog, and she has a frog's legs and feet. She cannot walk but she hops. She wears very long dresses to cover and conceal her feet which are shod with something like a cow's hoof. She never goes out except to the Primitive Methodist Chapel. Mrs Nott said she had seen this person's frog feet and had seen her in Presteign hopping to and from the Chapel exactly like a frog. She had never seen her hands. She is a very good person. The story about this unfortunate being is as follows. Shortly before she was born a woman came begging to her mother's door with two or three little children. Her mother was angry and ordered the woman away. 'Get away with your young frogs,' she said. And the child she was expecting was born partly in the form of a frog, as a punishment and a curse upon her.

Francis Kilvert

London

It was evening, and the restless Lothair walked forth without a purpose, and in a direction which he rarely visited. 'It is a wonderful place,' said he, 'this London; a nation, not a city; with a population greater than some kingdoms, and districts as different as if they were under different governments and spoke different languages. And what do I know of it? I have been living here six months, and my life has been passed in a park, two or three squares, and half a dozen streets!'

So he walked on and soon crossed Oxford Street, like the Rhine a natural boundary, and then got into Portland Place, and then found himself in the New Road, and then he hailed a cruising Hansom, which he had previously observed was well-horsed.

' 'Tis the gondola of London,' said Lothair as he sprang in. 'Drive on till I tell you to stop.'

And the Hansom drove on, through endless boulevards, some bustling, some dingy, some tawdry and flaring, some melancholy and mean; rows of garden gods, planted on the walls of yards full of vases and divinities of concrete, huge railway halls, monster hotels, dissenting chapels in the form of Gothic churches, quaint ancient almshouses that were once built in the fields, and tea-gardens and stingo houses and knackers' yards. They were in a district far beyond the experience of Lothair, which indeed had been exhausted when he had passed Eustonia, and from that he had been long separated. The way was broad but ill-lit, with houses of irregular size but generally of low elevation, and sometimes detached in smoke-dried gardens. The road was becoming a bridge which crossed a canal, with barges and wharves and timber yards, when their progress was arrested by a crowd. It seemed a sort of procession; there was a banner, and the lamp-light fell upon a

religious emblem. Lothair was interested, and desired the driver not
to endeavour to advance.

Benjamin Disraeli

MAY 23, 1870

A Discovery

Discovery of the murder of the Marshall family, at Denham,
Uxbridge. Suspicion being excited by the unusual stillness prevail-
ing for the last day or two around their humble roadside dwelling,
the door was forced open, and the shocking spectacle was revealed
of the murder of an entire family. The names of the victims were
Emmanuel Marshall, aged thirty-five; Charlotte, his wife, thirty-
three; Mary Anne Marshall, his sister, twenty-nine (to have been
married in a few days); Mary Marshall, grandmother, seventy-five;
and three children – Gertrude, four; Theresa, six; and Mary, eight.
The bodies lay for the most part huddled together in the front room
and back kitchen. Just inside the doors were found the bodies of Mrs
Marshall and Mary Anne Marshall, that of the younger woman
inclining towards the other. A gown was loosely thrown over Mrs
Marshall's nightdress, as though she had hurriedly put it on before
coming downstairs. Mary Anne Marshall had nothing but her
nightdress on. The heads of both were horribly disfigured, and there
was a pool of blood quite close to them; near this was a large smith's
hammer, with which they were supposed to have been murdered.
There was also a large blood stain on the wall near the door,
evidently caused by Mrs Marshall's head coming in contact with it.
In a little room between the front parlour and the back kitchen the
bodies of the two elder children were found. They were piled on one
another near the fireplace, and there was no doubt, from the
position in which they were, that their inhuman murderer brutally
flung them here after having smashed their heads with one of the
terrible weapons afterwards discovered. The bodies of the poor
children were partly uncovered. The body of old Mrs Marshall and
that of the youngest child were discovered in the back kitchen, and
the wounds visible on them were even worse than those which
caused the death of the others. The body of Marshall himself was
found in the smith's shop adjoining the house, in which he wrought,
partly covered by sacks, and giving evidence, in the nature and
number of the wounds, taken in connexion with the condition of the

apartment, of a violent struggle having preceded death. He was partly dressed in his Sunday clothes.

Annals of our Time

The Inimitable

One whom young and old, wherever the English language is spoken, have been accustomed to regard as a personal friend is suddenly taken away from among us. CHARLES DICKENS is no more. The loss of such a man is an event which makes ordinary expressions of regret seem cold and conventional. It will be felt by millions as nothing less than a personal bereavement. Statesmen, men of science, philanthropists, the acknowledged benefactors of their race might pass away, and yet not leave the void which will be caused by the death of DICKENS. They may have earned the esteem of mankind; their days may have been passed in power, honour, and prosperity; they may have been surrounded by troops of friends, but, however pre-eminent in station, ability, or public services, they will not have been, like our great and genial novelist, the intimate of every household. Indeed, such a position is attained not even by one man in an age. It needs an extraordinary combination of intellectual and moral qualities to gain the hearts of the public as DICKENS has gained them. Extraordinary and very original genius must be united with good sense, consummate skill, a well-balanced mind, and the proofs of a noble and affectionate disposition before the world will consent to enthrone a man as their unassailable and enduring favourite. This is the position which Mr DICKENS has occupied with the English and also with the American public for a third of the century. If we compare his reputation with that of the number of eminent men and women who have been his contemporaries, we have irresistible evidence of his surpassing merits. His is a department of literature in which ability in our time has been abundant to overflowing. As the genius of the Elizabethan age turned to the drama, so that of the reign of VICTORIA seeks expression in the novel.

The Times, JUNE 10, 1870

The Brickmaker

'I wants it done, and over. I wants a end of these liberties took with my place. I wants a end of being drawed like a badger. Now you're a-going to poll-pry and question according to custom – I know what you're a-going to be up to. Well! You haven't got no occasion to be up to it. I'll save you the trouble. Is my daughter a-washin? Yes, she is a-washin. Look at the water. Smell it! That's wot we drinks. How do you like it, and what do you think of gin instead! An't my place dirty? Yes, it is dirty – it's nat'rally dirty, and it's nat'rally onwhole-some; and we've had five dirty and onwholesome children, as is all dead infants, and so much the better for them, and for us besides. Have I read the little book wot you left? No, I an't read the little book wot you left. There an't nobody here as knows how to read it; and if there wos, it wouldn't be suitable to me. It's a book fit for a babby, and I'm not a babby. If you was to leave me a doll, I shouldn't nuss it. How have I been conducting of myself? Why, I've been drunk for three days; and I'd a been drunk four, if I'd a had the money. Don't I never mean for to go to church? No, I don't never mean for to go to church. I shouldn't be expected there, if I did; the beadle's too gen-teel for me. And how did my wife get that black eye? Why, I giv' it her, and if she says I didn't, she's a Lie!'

Charles Dickens

Mr Skimpole

'Enterprise and effort,' he would say to us (on his back), 'are delightful to me. I believe I am truly cosmopolitan. I have the deepest sympathy with them. I lie in a shady place like this, and think of adventurous spirits going to the North Pole, or penetrating to the heart of the Torrid Zone, with admiration. Mercenary creatures ask, "What is the use of a man's going to the North Pole! What good does it do?" I can't say; but, for anything I can say, he may go for the purpose – though he don't know it – of employing my thoughts as I lie here. Take an extreme case. Take the case of the Slaves on American plantations. I dare say they are worked hard, I dare say they don't altogether like it, I dare say theirs is an unpleasant experience on the whole; but they people the landscape for me, they give it a poetry for me, and perhaps that is one of the pleasanter objects of their existence. I am very sensible of it, if it be, and I shouldn't wonder if it were!'

Charles Dickens

Pain

'I think there's a pain somewhere in the room,' said Mrs Gradgrind,
'but I couldn't positively say that I have got it.'

    Charles Dickens

Miss Petowker

'There's something in his appearance, quite – dear, what's the word
again? – what do you call it when lords break off door-knockers and
beat policemen, and play at coaches with other people's money, and
all that sort of thing? – ah, aristocratic!'

    Charles Dickens

Mr Jingle's Story

'Terrible place – dangerous work – other day, five children –
mother – tall lady eating sandwiches – forgot the arch – crash –
knock – children look round – mother's head off – sandwich in her
hand – no mouth to put it in – shocking, shocking.'

    Charles Dickens

Two gazed into a pool, he gazed and she,
Not hand in hand, yet heart in heart, I think,
Pale and reluctant on the water's brink,
As on the brink of parting which must be.
Each eyed the other's aspect, she and he,
Each felt one hungering heart leap up and sink,
Each tasted bitterness which both must drink,
There on the brink of life's dividing sea.
Lilies upon the surface, deep below
Two wistful faces craving each for each,
Resolute and reluctant without speech:-
A sudden ripple made the faces flow,
One moment joined, to vanish out of reach:
So those hearts joined, and ah were parted so.

      Christina Rossetti

The Franco-Prussian War

The outbreak was as near-accidental and unnecessary as most wars, though more probable after the Prussian shock-victory over Austria in 1866. Prussia, since defeat by Napoleon I, had been methodically increasing her influence over the numerous German states. A minority of noblemen, generals and bureaucrats saw a federalized Germany under Prussian leadership not only as emotionally satisfying but as a vital defence against France, currently under a second Napoleon. Bismarck was to insist that, in the last two centuries, France had attacked the Germans thirty times.

Since 1864, France, despite outward brilliance, had lived nervously. Since Napoleon I, she had suffered two revolutions, the murderous street fighting, 1848, a coup d'état, 1851. Napoleon III (of whom the courtesan 'Skittles' said he had eyes as green as glass), thoughtful and intelligent, believed in the humane advantages of Nationalism, tempered by free trade and international congresses. He had helped promote Italian independence and applauded Prussian advance in Germany, confident that, were conflict to arise, he would find support from the Catholic, anti-Prussian South German States, and prepared his 1870 campaign on this assumption. Meanwhile, at least in public, he seemed content with the international drift.

'The transformations which have taken place in Italy and Germany are preparing the realization of this vast programme of the Union of the States of Europe in one single confederation.' (1866)

The Emperor had achieved impressive industrial and economic successes. More modern-minded than his uncle, he saw the future dominated by railways, canals, iron ships, planned sanitary towns. He pioneered the Common Market. Nevertheless, he lacked first-rate ministers, and his own nature, conspiratorial rather than managerial, made him difficult to serve. He lacked, not courage, but decisiveness. He believed that nations, political parties, labour unions and individuals are grateful for benefits received. He was wrong.

After 1862, his foreign policy faltered. He seems to have long regarded Bismarck more as a gifted trainee than as a likely menace. By 1865, Napoleon III, virtually a dictator since 1851, was overworked and suffered ailments he kept secret but which periodically impaired his judgment. His heir was still a child. His dynasty lacked roots, save in the affections of a populace notoriously fickle, itself resentful of Prussia and Napoleon's humiliating interference in

Mexico. Diplomatic failures and a less favourable economic situation revived urban republicanism. Genial and hedonistic, Napoleon had represented order, the answer to wild revolutions, the restorer of French glory after the disasters of Waterloo and Moscow. France still looked to him for solutions but a virulent opposition was set to exploit his setbacks and sabotage his plans for much-needed military reform, more on Prussian than traditional French lines. He had to grant concessions, from what seemed weakness rather than the magnanim-ity which had sometimes allowed him to declare himself a socialist, not altogether insincerely.

His personal charm had won over the republican, Émile Ollivier, to assist in the restoration of parliamentary powers, though, as Philip Guedalla put it, 'France has more generally regarded parliamentary institutions as a source of scandal than a form of government.' 1869 saw 'The Liberal Empire', an effort to appease the future through more representative government and larger political freedoms. It was more forward-looking than Bismarck's Second Reich. 'Had not the war intervened, Ollivier might well be remembered as the author of one of the most original political achievements of the century.' (Theodore Zeldin) A plebiscite, held in February 1870, confirmed it by an immense majority. Yet by September, the Empire had vanished for ever, with Napoleon III, the 'New Caesar', buried in the rubble, and Ollivier explaining himself in nineteen volumes.

A diplomatic crisis convulsed France in July 1870, when a Prussian prince accepted the Spanish throne. Napoleon was confronted by jingoistic newspapers and Parisians, and an opposition which seemed to be demanding war more as an attempt to dislodge the dynasty than to inconvenience the Prussians. He knew the haphazard state of his armies and his own incapacities, yet he was also a Bonaparte, inheritor of military legend. With an untried Premier and an inexperienced Foreign Minister, the Duc de Gramont, rated by Bismarck 'the stupidest man in Europe', he strove for peace and contrived an effective triumph when the Prussian candidate with-drew. Then, fatally, to soothe the streets and parliament, the Emper-or and several ministers, goaded by parliament and public opinion, with Ollivier not present, further insisted on a royal promise that the candidature would never be renewed. Feeling that he had done sufficient, King Wilhelm refused this to a tactless French ambassador, though in terms which Bismarck, by shortening the royal text for the public, made appear more peremptory than they actually were. He doubtless envisaged the hysteria which this would provoke, if not in France, at least in Paris; though in his memoirs he often claimed more foresight than perhaps he had. Whatever the truth, France declared war.

'It seems impossible to our judgement that the Prussians will be ready on time to take the initiative,' pronounced the London Standard.

Napoleon III had prospective allies and a reasonable battle plan, but all depended on swift mobilization, rapid movement, energetic command, solid morale and wholehearted loyalty.

I accept the responsibility for war with a light heart.

> Émile Ollivier, to the Deputies

Paris

How can I feel anything but concern on the eve of great events? Here is a great country like France, peaceable, prosperous, and now engaged in a conflict from which, even if all goes well, so much destruction, so much sorrow will come. France's honour is engaged: but what disaster if fortune betrays her! We have but a single card to play. If victory is not for us, France will not only be diminished and plundered, but engulfed in the most frightful revolution ever seen.

> Empress Eugénie

Berlin

All hope is now at an end, and we have the horrible prospect of the most terrible war Europe has yet known before us, bringing desolation and ruin, perhaps annihilation. We have been shamefully forced into this war, and the feeling of indignation against such an act of crying injustice has risen in two days here to such a pitch that you will hardly believe it; there is a universal cry 'To arms'! to resist an enemy who so wantonly assaults us.

> Crown Princess Victoria of Prussia, to her mother Queen Victoria

We have only to stretch out our hand to take Berlin.

> Émile Ollivier, to General Maxim de Camp

Berlin

The Confederate Governments and I myself, are acting in the full consciousness that victory and defeat are in the hands of Him who decides the fate of battles. With a clear gaze we have measured the responsibility which, before the judgment-seat of God and of mankind, must fall upon him who drags two great and peace-loving peoples of the heart of Europe into a devastating war. The German and French peoples, both equally enjoying and desiring the blessings of a Christian civilization and of an increasing prosperity, are called to a more wholesome rivalry than the sanguinary conflict of arms. Yet those who hold power in France have, by preconcerted misguidance, found means to work upon the legitimate but excitable national sentiment of our great neighbouring people for the furtherance of personal interests and the gratification of passions.

King Wilhelm of Prussia, to the North German Parliament

Paris

We have done all in our power to avert the war, and I may say that it is the whole nation which has, by its irresistible impulse, dictated our decisions. I confide to you the Empress, who will call you around her if circumstances should require it. She will know how to fulfil courageously the duty which her position imposes upon her. I take my son with me; in the midst of the army he will learn to serve his country. Resolved energetically to pursue the great mission which has been entrusted to me, I have faith in the success of our arms, for I know that behind me France has risen to her feet, and that God protects her.

Napoleon III, to the Corps Législatif

The Courtesan

Nana remained alone, her face looking up in the light from the candle. It was a charnel-house scene, a mass of tissue-fluids and blood, a shovelful of putrid flesh thrown there on a cushion. The pustules had invaded the entire face with the pocks touching each other; and, dissolving and subsiding with the greyish look of mud, there seemed to be already an earthy mouldiness on the shapeless mucosity, in which the features were no longer discernible. An eye, the left one, had completely subsided in a soft mass of purulence; the other, half-open, was sinking like a collapsing hole. The nose was still suppurating. A whole reddish crust was peeling off one cheek and invaded the mouth, distorting it into a loathsome grimace. And on that horrible and grotesque mask, the hair, that beautiful head of hair still preserving its blaze of sunlight, flowed down in a golden trickle. Venus was decomposing. It seemed as though the virus she had from the gutters and from the tacitly permitted carrion of humanity, that baneful ferment with which she had poisoned a people, had now risen to her face and putrefied it.

The room was empty. A great blast of desperation came up from the boulevard and swelled the curtain.

'To Berlin! To Berlin! To Berlin!'

> Émile Zola

We must be neutral *as long as* we can be, but no one here conceals their opinion as to the extreme *iniquity* of the war, and the unjustifiable conduct of the French.

> Queen Victoria, to her daughter, the Crown Princess Victoria of Prussia

Nothing will ever persuade me that the Prussians will withstand the French, and I would lay my last shilling upon Casquette against Pumpernickel.

> John Delane, Editor, *The Times*

Noble, patient, deep, pious and solid Germany . . . Vapouring, vainglorious, gesticulating, quarrelsome, restless and over-sensitive France.

> Thomas Carlyle

Our poverty, our dull towns, our plodding, hardworking *serious* life, has made us strong and determined; is wholesome for us.

> Crown Princess Victoria of Prussia, to Queen Victoria

The King embraced me with profoundest emotion. Both of us felt that we must prepare ourselves for a contest involving the most sacred rights and privileges, perhaps the Fatherland's very exist-

ence, a contest that must be fought out with streams of our People's
noblest blood.

Crown Prince Frederick of Prussia

Force is all that matters. War is sacred.
Hanging is excellent. We don't need too much knowledge.
Build more prisons and fewer schools.

Victor Hugo

The Question

Partings are at all times painful, but it would be difficult to conceive
any farewell more tinged with sadness than that of the Emperor and
the Empress on his departure from Paris. There are no two people
in Europe who have played so prominent a part in history during the
last twenty years as the royal couple whose fate hangs upon the
result of the present war. When they meet again, if, indeed, they
ever do meet, what an eventful story will have been told, and each
line written in letters of blood! To France, though the issues are
great, the war is but one chapter in her history; but to the Emperor
and the Empress it may be the last chapter in the records of their
career. For him at least there is no future but in success; in drawing
the sword he has thrown away the scabbard, he has burned his ships.
That gay and glorious city which as with an enchanter's wand he has
remodelled and rebuilt, will either close her gates to the fugitive or
welcome the return of a victorious leader. Bold as the Emperor may
be to beard Bismarck in his power, it will require more boldness still
to reappear at home without his army.

Pall Mall Gazette

From Another Country

The mere fact that at a moment when official France and Germany
are plunging headlong into fratricidal war, the workers of France
and Germany are exchanging messages of peace and goodwill, this
great fact, unparalleled in past history, opens up the perspective of a
better future. It proves that in the face of the old society with its
economic misery and political furies a new society is arising, a law
whose international relations will be *peace* because its national
legislator will be everywhere the same, *Labour*.

Karl Marx, to the London branch of the International

War for empire or dynasty can be regarded by the workers as simply a criminal absurdity.

Paris section of the International

An English View

The real cause of war, the vote of fifty thousand soldiers against the Empire is, of course, not mentioned, but Paris has gone mad with patriotic pride, the French army is moving on the Rhine, and Europe must pass through a year, perhaps years, of misery, in order that one single man may secure the career and the position of one single child. This war has no cause, no motive, no justification save the fear of Napoleon Bonaparte that without it his boy's succession would not be clear.

Spectator

Telegrams

Our troops are in full retreat. Nothing must be thought of now beyond the defence of the Capital.

Napoleon III, to Empress Eugénie

Courage then: with energy we will master the situation. I will answer for Paris.

Empress Eugénie, to Napoleon III

Proclamation from the Tuileries

Frenchmen! The opening of the war has not been in our favour. Our arms have suffered a check. Let us be firm under this reverse and let us hasten to repair. Let there be but one party among you, that of France; one single flag, that of national honour. I am here in your midst. Faithful to my mission and to my duty, you will see me in the forefront of danger to defend the flag of France.

Empress Eugénie

At Châlons: Greetings to the Supreme Commander

THE OFFICER: Vive l'Empereur.
THE TROOPS: Un! Deux! Trois! *Merde!*

Crown Prince Frederick of Prussia's Victory at Froeschwiller

Wonderful News.

Queen Victoria

I confess to you, that were I a German, I should feel it my duty to send my last son, my last shilling, and after all, my own self to the war, to get that done which must be done, so that it will never need doing again. I trust that I should be able to put vengeance out of my heart, to forget all that Germany has suffered for two hundred years past, from that vain, greedy, restless nation.

Charles Kingsley, to Sir Charles Bunbury

An Apparition

They all sprang to their feet. Between the poplars lining the white high road there appeared a platoon of Cent-Gardes still correctly dressed in their luxurious, resplendent uniforms, with large golden suns glittering upon their breastplates. In the open space behind them came the Emperor on horseback, escorted by his staff, which was followed by a second detachment of Cent-Gardes. Everyone uncovered, and a few acclamations were heard; and the Emperor raised his head as he passed by, so that one could clearly see his face, drawn and very pale, with dim wavering eyes which appeared full of water. He seemed as if he were waking out of a doze, smiled faintly at the sight of the sunlit tavern, and then saluted.

Meantime, Bouroche had darted at Napoleon the quick glance of an experienced practitioner, and Jean and Maurice, who were standing in front of the surgeon, distinctly heard him growl: 'There's a nasty stone there, and no mistake.' And then he completed his diagnosis in two words, '*Done for.*'

Émile Zola

A Medical Orderly

Telegram from the king today about the decisive victory under his leadership. We just chloroformed a Frenchman for a plaster-of-Paris dressing (the hand is shattered; under the anaesthetic he called out 'Mon Dieu, Mon Dieu I am coming'). Before that a girl of eleven, to save her leg from amputation. A few days earlier in a house, a boy with a big head-wound chloroformed; great trouble. Yesterday a Prussian died in hospital, shot in the lung, today a second. A Prussian, Liebig, in a good state; healthy appetite, but little hope, arm-bone splintered, impossible to dress with plaster-of-Paris.

            Friedrich Nietzsche

The Foot

Gilberte had just turned round, Delaherche having told her that it was finished, and that she could look. However she caught sight of the captain's foot as the attendant carried it off into the garden. The charnel-place was now becoming more and more crowded; two more corpses were lying there, one with the mouth wide open and black, looking as though it were still howling; the other shrunk by an abominable agony, reduced to the size of a puny, deformed child. The annoyance was that the pile of remnants was now stretching into the path near by. The attendant hesitated for a moment as to where he might fitly deposit the captain's foot, but at the last he made up his mind to throw it on the heap.

            Émile Zola

A Zouave, who, with his intestines escaping from a ghastly wound, was raising a continuous roar, like a dying wild beast. Farther on, there was another one – on fire; his blue sash was burning, the flame was rising and singeing his beard, whilst he shed big tears, unable to move because his spine was broken. Then there was a captain whose left arm was torn off, and whose right side was laid open to the thigh, and who, stretched on his stomach, dragged himself along upon an elbow, begging all those who passed, in a shrill, horribly supplicating voice, to have the compassion to despatch him. And there were others and others still, all suffering abominably, strewing the grassy paths in such numbers that it was necessary to be careful lest one should tread upon them in passing. The dead, the wounded, no longer counted, however. The comrade who fell was abandoned, forgotten. Nearby, another man, shot through the forehead, remained standing, held upright by two young birches.

Émile Zola

Two bodies had rolled under the sink – a Zouave, a well-built man with a black beard, and a brawny Prussian with red hair. They were locked together in a savage embrace; the Frenchman's teeth had bitten into the German's cheek, and their stiffened arms had in no degree relaxed their grasp, but were still bending and cracking each other's broken spine, uniting them both in such an intricate knot of everlasting fury, that they must needs be buried together.

Émile Zola

The Carts

Now they were drawn up on the roadside, waiting to discharge their loads into the public rubbish tip. Feet stuck out, pointing up to the sky, and a head could be seen, hanging down almost severed from its body. And as the three carts moved off again, jolting through the puddles, a livid hand, dangling over the side, began rubbing the wheel, gradually wearing away the skin and exposing the bone.

Émile Zola

Sedan

Your Majesty has no need to worry. In the morning I'll have thrown the foe into the Meuse.

General de Wimpffen

The Disaster at Sedan

My dear Eugénie, I cannot tell you what I have suffered and am still suffering. We made a march contrary to the rules and to common sense; it was fated to produce disaster, total disaster. I would have preferred death than to witness a surrender so catastrophic, and yet, things being what they are, it was the only way to avoid the slaughter of 60,000 men. And again, if only all my agonies concentrated here!

I think of you, of our own son, of our unhappy country. May God protect you! What will happen in Paris?

> Napoleon III

Tell General de Wimpffen that I will not be involved in the sacrifice of several thousand lives so as to secure my own escape.

> Napoleon III

Sir, my Brother. Having failed to meet death in the midst of my troops, nothing more remains for me but to surrender my sword into Your Majesty's hands. I am Your Majesty's good brother.

> Napoleon III, to the King of Prussia

The Wife

Why didn't he get himself killed? Why isn't he buried under the walls of Sedan? Had he no feeling that he was disgracing himself? What a name to leave his son!

> Empress Eugénie

The News

What a spectacle, Paris tonight, with the news of MacMahon's defeat and the Emperor's capture spreading from one group to another! Who can describe the dismay on each face, the sound of aimless and random footsteps on pavements, the worried talk of shopkeepers and concierges on doorsteps, the siege for newspapers, triple lines of readers around every gas-jet, and at the back of the shops the seated, wretched women whom one senses are alone, robbed of their menfolk?

Then there is the menacing roar of the mob, replacing stupefaction with fury. Next come immense crowds moving along the boulevards, preceded by flags and yells: 'Down with the Empire' . . .

Finally, the wild, stormy sight of a nation resolved on death, or salvation by a stupendous effort, by one of those impossible deeds from the days of the Revolution.

> *The Goncourt Journal*

The Third Republic

This is the third awakening, and it is beautiful beyond imagination.
      George Sand

Here is the scene outside the Chamber at about four o'clock. Against the grey exterior, from which sunlight has faded, around the columns and all over its steps, a crowd, a vast multitude of men, their smocks making blue and white smudges amid the black coats. Many holding branches, with green leaves in their hats. A few soldiers with twigs tied to rifles.

Above the crowd a hand chalked the names of the Provisional Government in big red letters, on a column. On another, someone had already scrawled: *The Republic has been proclaimed.* Shouts, cheers, hats thrown aloft: people clambering on to pedestals, crowding together under Minerva; a smocked fellow calmly smoking a pipe on the knees of the Chancellor de l'Hopital; groups of women hanging on the railing opposite the Pont de la Concorde.

All around, people fervently greeting each other: 'It's happened!' And at the summit of the Chamber, a man stripped the blue and white stripes from the tricolour, leaving only the red waving. On the terrace above the Quai d'Orsay, infantrymen were tearing apart shrubs and giving green shoots over the ledge to women struggling for them.

At the Tuileries gate, near the great pool, the gilt 'N's were hidden beneath old newspapers, and wreaths of immortelles hung instead of the vanished eagles.
      The Goncourt Journal

Another Proclamation

It is in Paris that one feels the beating of Europe's heart. Paris, city of cities. Paris, city of men. There has been an Athens, a Rome, and there is a Paris. Is the nineteenth century to witness this atrocious phenomenon? A nation fallen from an organised state to mere barbarism, wiping out the capital of nations; Germans extinguishing Paris. Can you present this to the world? Can you, Germans, revert to vandals, impersonate barbarism beheading civilization . . .

Let the streets devour the foe, let windows burst open with

fury . . . Despotism has assaulted Liberty, Germany is assailing France . . .

We ask not for help. If Europe is scared, let her remain so. We shall still do her service.

Victor Hugo

The Advertisement

Notice for the benefit of English gentlemen wishing to attend the Siege of Paris. Comfortable apartments, completely shell-proof; rooms in the basement, for impressionable persons.

An Interested Party

However the war may end, it has yielded the French proletariat practice in arms, and that is the best guarantee of the future.

Karl Marx, to Dr Kugelmann

After Surrender

The Emperor lingered about in the garden of the weaver's cottage; he seems to have desired fresh air after his unpleasant talk with the Chancellor. Mr Moritz Busch, who had hurried to the spot, has left a characteristic description of the Emperor. He saw there 'a little thick-set man,' wearing jauntily a red cap with a gold border, a black paletôt lined with red, red trousers, and white kid gloves, 'The look in his light grey eyes was somewhat soft and dreamy, like that of people who have lived hard. His whole appearance,' says the irreverent Busch, 'was a little unsoldierlike. The man looked too soft, I might say too shabby, for the uniform he wore,' – phrases which suggest a lack of sympathy with adversity, and severe physical as well as mental suffering. But imagination can realize a picture of the fallen potentate, whose dynasty, crashing down, drew so much with it, as he was seen by the cynical German, talking to his officers, or to the burly Chancellor, or walking alone up and down a potato field in flower, with his white-gloved hands behind his back, smoking a cigarette; 'betrayed by fortune' or fate, as he believed, but pursued, as others might say, by the natural consequences of his marvellous adventures, and of a strange neglect of the one source of strength on which he relied, the Army. He had failed in the business upon the conduct of which he prided himself; he was a bankrupt Emperor.

George Hooper

Aftermath

And there, on that tragic, corpse-strewn plateau of Illy, occurred the legendary meeting – the wretched Emperor, no longer able to endure the motion of the vehicle, sinking down under the violence of some spasm, maybe mechanically smoking his everlasting cigarette, whilst a flock of haggard, blood-and-dust-covered prisoners, whom their captors were escorting from Fleigneux to Sedan, ranged themselves at the edge of the road to allow the carriage to pass; the first ones silent, the next ones growling, and the others, beyond, growing more and more exasperated until they burst into jeers and brandished their fists with gestures of insult and malediction. And after that there was yet the interminable journey across other portions of the battlefield, a league of broken-up roads, past ruins, and the corpses with widely-opened, threatening eyes; and then came a bare stretch of country with vast, silent woods, and the frontier atop of an incline; and beyond it the end of everything – a dip into a narrow valley where the road was edged with pines . . .

All the train of the Imperial household, the cumbersome accursed baggage vans, had remained at Sedan, in distress behind the sub-prefect's lilac bushes. Those in charge were at a loss how to spirit them away, how to remove them safely from the sight of the poor folks dying of misery, so intolerable indeed became the aggressive insolence which they had assumed, the frightful irony with which the defeat had imbued them. A very dark night had to be waited for, and then the horses, the carriages, and the vans, with their silver saucepans, their spits, and their baskets of fine wines, went forth from Sedan with great mystery, and in their turn betook themselves to Belgium, journeying with muffled tread and roll along the dark roads amid an uneasy shivering, such as attends a theft.

Émile Zola

The Horses at Sedan

Each time that the bugles sounded, the abandoned French horses, at large on the other side of the canal, galloped up and leaped into the water, as excited by those well-known flourishes as by the prick of the spur. Exhausted by hunger, however, they were mostly carried off by the current, few of them managing to reach the bank of the peninsula. They could be seen struggling lamentably, and so large a number of them was drowned that at last their floating, inflated carcasses obstructed the canal. As for those that managed to land, they were seized with madness, as it were, and galloped away across the waste fields . . .

The thousands of horses which had been led into captivity with the army, and could not be fed, proved a source of daily increasing danger. They had first eaten the bark of the trees, then they had attacked the trelliswork, the fences, all the planks they came upon, and now they were becoming cannibals. They could be seen throwing themselves upon one another and tearing off the hair of each other's tails, chewing it furiously with foaming jaws. But it was especially at night time that they became terrible, as though the darkness oppressed them with a nightmare. They gathered together in bands and rushed upon the few tents that had been pitched, attracted by the straw there. In vain had the men lighted large fires to keep them away; these fires only seemed to excite them more. Their neighing was so dolorous, so frightful at times that it seemed like the roaring of wild beasts. Driven away, they returned yet more numerous and more ferocious. And at every moment there sped through the darkness the long cry of agony of some soldier gone astray whom they had knocked over and crushed in their wild gallop.

Émile Zola

The Loser

For some time past England has had to admire him as the enlight-- ened ruler who could recognize progress and appreciate the demands of the 19th Century. England has also watched with tender interest the grand experiment of constitutional institutions. It seemed the EMPEROR's ambition to be a man of the age, and the foremost man of it. His peaceful displays, his splendid Exhibitions, all savoured of the present rather than the past. Thus, he has been ever drifting away from the old moorings of French Royalty. It is his disaster and downfall that save him. He is found to be like other men and other Kings. Men will now pity him, and perhaps think they discover in him the stuff Kings are made of. NAPOLEON has flung away his power, his fortune, his people, and his destiny. He has filled his country with fire, blood, and tears. He had challenged a great and chivalrous race to mortal combat without ascertaining his own strength, without proving his armour, and without even the defence of a good cause. He has exhibited the extremes of material magnificence and personal humiliation. He has been at once the strongest and the weakest of men. He has laboured hard for neighbours who requite his services as they would those of a fool or a traitor. He has played a dark and mysterious part on a brilliant and conspicuous stage. Lastly, he has gone beside himself that his people may pay the penalty. All this is kingly . . . Mankind abuse Kings in order that they may sympathize with them, and assure themselves that Kings are men, and men Kings. What a change in a day! We find ourselves pitying NAPOLEON III, and even paying due honours to his right royalty. So long as he reigned and commanded we could criticize coldly. In this war it has been rather angrily debated whether we gave him his due, or whether we did not give him more than his due. There is not a civil word for us anywhere on the Continent. There never has been, indeed, as far as human memory reaches. That is all over, we will hope at least. The Emperor and France appeal to that pity which is, or should be, the common instinct of all men. Would that Germany may feel it, too! She is new to such enormous victories. It is with her the revival of a time long ago, and the succession to a long lost or long denied inheritance. Can Germany feel that mercy becometh the strong? Does she know that it is the best preservative of political strength?

The Times

A Woman's View

The beautiful Empress, disguised, had fled in the carriage of her American dentist, for it was not even a Frenchman but a foreigner who was brave enough to protect the unfortunate lady. And the gentle Utopian Emperor had vainly sought death on the battlefield.

Two horses had been killed under him, without him getting even a scratch. After this, he had surrendered his sword. At home we all wept with anger, shame, grief at this surrender. Yet what courage must have been needed for so brave a man to have acted in such a way! He had wanted to save a hundred thousand lives, to reassure a hundred thousand mothers. Our poor, beloved Emperor! History will one day do justice to him, for he was good, humane, and confiding. Alas, alas! he was too confiding!

> Sarah Bernhardt

Like you, I am proud of having lost the throne without having placed any money abroad.

> Napoleon III, to Empress Eugénie

THE CHRIST OF AMMERGAU

They made the old Pope God –
Which God, if He will, may pardon –
And Christ stepped down from the cross,
Christ stepped out of the garden.

They made the old Pope God
While God was rolling His thunder,
And Christ came out from Ammergau
To massacre, burn and plunder.

Christ came out from the Play –
Children, love one another! –
In bitter earnest he came
To mash the skull of his brother.

Went to slay and be slain,
Arm'd with his gun and his sabre,
To show the world he loved himself
No better than his neighbour.

'Lebe der König!' 'Vive la guerre!'
Let the brother mangle the brother,
For, O little children, we see by this

What love ye bear one another.

> Alfred Tennyson, 1870

His Majesty the King of Bavaria accompanied his troops only on the piano.

> French Newspaper

Partisan Warfare

Experience has established that the most effective way of dealing with this situation is to destroy the buildings concerned – or, where participation has been on a larger scale, the whole village.

> General Helmuth von Moltke

All the French should be shot and stabbed to death, down to the little babies.

> Princess von Bismarck

A Nurse's Experience of the Siege: the Odéon Théâtre had become a Hospital

It was no longer 'The Country in Danger' that kept me so on edge, but the sufferings of the country's children. There were all those still away fighting, and brought in to us; the noble working-class women queuing for hours and hours for the vital rations of bread, meat, and milk for the poor infants at home. Ah, those poor women! I could see them from the theatre windows, jammed close together, blue with cold, stamping their feet to prevent them from freezing – for that winter was the cruellest for twenty years. Often one of those wretched, silent heroines was taken in to me either fainting from weariness or suddenly felled by the cold. On December 20, three of these unfortunates were brought in. One had her feet frozen, and she lost the big toe of her right foot. The second was enormously fat, suckling her baby, her poor breasts harder than wood. She simply howled with pain. The youngest was between sixteen and eighteen. She died of cold, on the trestle on which I sent her home. December 24 had fifteen degrees of frost. I often sent Guillaume, our orderly, out with a little brandy to warm those desolate women. Oh, the agonies they must have felt – those broken-hearted mothers, those sisters and betrothed girls – in their terrible fears! How excusable their rebellion seems during the Commune, even their blood-lust!

Sarah Bernhardt

The Coward

I was then very young, only twenty-four, but could nevertheless see the cowardice of some, the heroism of many others. A young Savoyard, of eighteen, had had his forefinger shot off. Baron Larrey was certain he had done it himself with his own gun, but I did not believe it. Nevertheless, I did notice that, despite our nursing and care the wound remained open. I bound it up in a different way, and next day realised that the bandage had been altered. I mentioned this to Madame Lambquin . . . The next day, on my arrival, she told me that she had caught him scraping the wound with his knife. I called him, and said that I should have to report this. He began to weep, promising that he would never do it again, and in five days he had recovered. I signed his discharge, and he was despatched to the Army of National Defence.

Sarah Bernhardt

The Menu, Paris, January 1871

Two francs for a small shrivelled cabbage, 1 franc for a leek, 45 francs for a rabbit (which might be taken for granted as cat), 25 francs for a pigeon, 22 francs for a 2 lb chub, 14 francs a pound for butter, cheese 25 francs a pound when procurable. Meat other than horseflesh absolutely not to be procured. I was assured that if I offered £50 down in bright shining gold for veritable beefsteak, I should have no claimant for the money! The last cow that changed hands – for an ambulance – fetched £80.

Daily News

The Solution

It would be most appropriate to employ Prussic Acid in killing Prussians, by using small india-rubber thimbles tipped with a small pointed tube filled with this. Should a lustful Prussian approach a pretty Parisian lady, she need only prick him with her finger, and he would at once fall dead. No matter how many of the enemy assault her, she will simply prick them one after the other and we will see her standing, still pure and holy, in a circle of corpses.

> Jules Allix

If you don't behave better I won't take you to see the bombardment.

> French Mother

The Victors

Bismarck has made us great and powerful, but he has robbed us of our friends, the world's sympathies, and – our conscience.

> Crown Prince Frederick of Prussia

Birth of the Future Kaiser Wilhelm II

May he grow up a good, upright, true and trusty man, one who delights in all that is good and beautiful, a thorough German who will one day learn to advance further in the paths laid down by his grandfather.

> Crown Prince Frederick of Prussia

On the Future Wilhelm II

Bring him up simply, plainly, not with that terrible Prussian pride and ambition which grieved dear Papa so much and which he always said would stand in the way of Prussia taking that lead in Germany which he ever wished her to do. Pride and ambition are not only so very wrong in themselves but they alienate affection and are in every way unworthy for great Princes – and great nations.

> Queen Victoria, to Crown Princess Victoria of Prussia

Siege of Paris

From curiosity I entered Roos's, the English butcher's shop on Boulevard Haussmann, where I observed varieties of weird remains. Hanging in the place of honour was the skinned trunk of young Pollux, the zoo elephant; and in the centre of nameless joints and peculiar horns, a boy offered camel's kidneys. The master-butcher was flourishing his words to a group of ladies. 'It's forty francs a pound for fillet and trunk . . . yes, forty . . . Expensive? But I do tell you I don't see how to make a sou out of it. I was expecting three thousand pounds of flesh and the brute's yielded only two thousand. The feet? You want the price of the feet? Twenty francs! For other bits, anything from eight to forty. But let me recommend black pudding. As you know, elephant's blood is unsurpassed in richness. His heart weighed twenty-five pounds. And, ladies, in my black pudding you'll find onion.'

I put up with two larks, which I took away for tomorrow's lunch.

> *The Goncourt Journal*

The shells have begun dropping in the Rue Boileau and the Rue La Fontaine. Doubtless tomorrow they will be dropping here; and even if I survive, they will destroy all I still love in life, my house, my little objects, my books.

The sufferings of Paris under siege? A joke for two months. In the third month the joke went sour. No one now finds it amusing any more, we are swiftly approaching starvation, or, at least for the moment, a gastritis epidemic. Half a pound of horsemeat, including the bones, rations for a couple, for three days, is lunch for a normal appetite.

> *The Goncourt Journal*

As the rats are imprisoned in a large cage, one has to choose the animal one wants from the medley. Using a small stick the vendor forces it into a smaller cage where it is alone, and then a bulldog is introduced, the little cage is shaken, and the rat escapes; but it is at once grabbed by the dog's powerful teeth. The dog breaks its back and drops it delicately at the customer's feet.

> *Paris Journal*

Sewer rats are considered far more a delicacy than young chickens.

> Charles Joseph Bonaparte

I do have feelings of guilt when I devour the friend of man, a dog. The other day I had a slice of spaniel, but it made me feel a cannibal.

Dog epicures inform me that poodle is easily the best, and they recommend me not to eat bulldog, which is coarse and lacks all taste.

Henry Labouchere

The Victor at Table

There is always one dish too many. I have already decided to ruin my stomach with goose and olives, and here is Reinfeld ham, of which I can't help taking too much . . . and, in addition, behold, Varzin wild boar.

Otto von Bismarck, at Château de Fersières.

WORDS DURING THE TIME OF TRIBULATION

We arrive on the margin of the fearful passage;
The abyss is there, shrouded, black, gloomy, filled with horror;
Facing us, the ordeal; we go
With no glance behind,
Pallid, we reach the sublime escarpment,
And kick the plank into the empty air.

Victor Hugo

A Promised Break-out from Paris

As for me, I have made a decision, and I swear before you and the entire country; I shall only return to Paris as a corpse, or in triumph. You may see me fall, but you will never see me give ground. So do not drag your feet, but exact vengeance for me. Forward, then! Advance! God protect us!

General Ducrot

He fought bravely, lost 12,000 men, and returned to Paris.

A New Empire Instead of the Old

In a newspaper annoucing the Capitulation, I read the news of King Wilhelm's enthronement as Emperor of Germany, at Versailles, under the nose of the stone Louis XIV in the courtyard outside. That really marks the extinction of France's greatness.

The Goncourt Journal

This is the doom of Germany.

> Jakob Burkhardt

The Prophet

I am certain that we are going to have a new war with you at a future date, and we desire to fight it under every advantage.

> Otto von Bismarck, to Jules Favre, insisting on France's surrender of Alsace-Lorraine to the new Germany

On the Signing of the Peace Treaty

The Hour will sound – I can feel already the coming of that immense revenge . . . Oh! then France will be a power to reckon with. We will see her, at a single stroke, resume possession of Alsace; resume possession of Lorraine! Is that all? No, we shall see her, at a single stroke, resume possession – mark well my words – of Trèves, Mayence, Cologne, Coblence . . . of all the left bank of the Rhine as well.

> Victor Hugo, to the National Assembly, Bordeaux

German Triumphant March Into Paris

Out rings the clarion of the trumpets, clash goes the silver music of the kettledrums, tempered by the sweet notes of the ophicleide. The horses, ever lovers of sweet sounds, arch their necks, champ the bits, and toss flecks of foam on the polished leathers of the riders. They are as proud as if they realised the meaning and glory of the day.

> Archibald Forbes, *Daily News*

There was an ugly moment when Bismarck found himself surrounded by a glaring crowd on the Place de la Concorde, but with superb aplomb he took out a cigar and asked the most hostile-looking spectator for a light.

> Alistair Horne, 1971

So It's All Over

Well! So it's all over. The shame is swallowed but not digested! I thought so much of you on Wednesday, and how I have suffered! The entire day I imagined I could see the Prussian arms shining in the sunlight, down the Champs-Élysées, and imagined that I could hear their military bands, their hateful bands ringing out under the Arc de Triomphe. The man who sleeps in the Invalides must turn in his grave with fury.

Gustave Flaubert, to Princess Mathilde Bonaparte

I passed through the most aristocratic and the most plebeian quarters, for the moment both are uninhabitable. The scum are everywhere. Excitement, anger, vice, laziness, drunkenness, rancour . . . ignorance and incompetence underneath, impotence at the top. The vulgar herd, with all its habitual passions, is spreading over all and covering the city like tainted oil . . . Nothing can convey a picture of this scum rising from the lowest depths of society.

Alexandre Dumas (fils), to Princess Mathilde Bonaparte

The Manifesto of the Paris Commune was issued – a challenge both to the Third Republic and to the German occupying armies. The French government was now at Versailles.

The Manifesto

The Communal Revolution, begun by Popular Initiative, March 18, establishes a New Political Era, experimental, positive, scientific. It marks the End of the old governmental and clerical world, of Militarism, of monopoly of privileges to which the Proletariat owes its slavery, the Nation its miseries and catastrophes. . .

Proclamation

Whereas the Versailles Government has ordered and begun the civil war, attacked Paris, killed and wounded National Guards, soldiers of the line, women and children; whereas this crime has been committed with premeditation and treachery against all right and without provocation, the Commune decrees . . .

The Witness

I have seen many organisations and many revolts during my life; but never did I witness anything to compare with the anarchy of the National Guard in 1871. Of its kind, perfect, and Proudhon would have been satisfied with the fruits which the tree he planted in 1848 bore in 1871.

Gustave Paul Cluseret

Pierre Joseph Proudhon, in 1840, had written 'Property is Theft'.

Enough of Militarism. Make Way for the People, the warriors, the bare arms! The hour of Revolutionary Warfare has struck.

Charles Delescluze

Revolutionary Dialogue

THE COMMUNE'S PUBLIC PROSECUTOR, RAOUL RIGAULT: What is your
    profession?
THE JESUIT: Servant of God.
RIGAULT: What is your employer's address?
JESUIT: He exists everywhere.
RIGAULT: Take this down. The accused, claiming to be servant of one
    God, vagrant.

The Demolition of the Vendôme Column, as demanded by Gustave Courbet, formerly a Commune official

The square is the centre of fantastic confusion and an assortment of astonishing uniforms. Some extraordinary National Guards are visible, one like a Velasquez dwarf, in a military overcoat with his twisted feet poking out beneath. I hear that Louvre employees are critically anxious. The Venus de Milo is concealed – guess where – at Police Headquarters. She is actually hidden very deep, and under another hiding-place stuffed with dossiers and other documents likely to halt any investigators. Still, it is imagined that Courbet is in her pursuit and the silly officials fear the worst if the crazy modernist grabs the Classical masterpiece.

The Goncourt Journal

The Column fell, crashing into three gigantic segments, and Courbet was subsequently presented with a bill of 250,000 francs for restoration, which he did not pay.

Two Versailles Generals Murdered

The mob which packed the courtyard broke into the street seized with a sort of frenzy. There were chasseurs, line soldiers, National Guards, women and children. All were shrieking like wild beasts without knowing what they were doing. I observed that pathological phenomenon which could be called blood-lust. A breath of madness seemed to have flitted over this mob. Men were dancing about, jostling each other in a kind of savage fury. Here was one of those extraordinary nervous outbreaks so common in the Middle Ages, which to this day happen amongst human masses in the stress of some primitive emotion.

Dr Georges Clemenceau, Mayor of Montmartre

I want sexual promiscuity. Prostitution is a social dogma.

Raoul Rigault

To Delegates from Paris to the Versailles Government

Do you come in the name of the Commune? If so I shall not listen to you. I refuse to recognize war-makers. I will accept no conditions, I have none to offer. The supremacy of law will be restored absolutely. State authority will be imposed upon Paris as it would be on any hamlet of a hundred souls.

Adolphe Thiers, Head of Government

A Death Sentence

RIGAULT: Was it you who from the Hotel de Ville demanded that troops should clear the Square? (thrice repeated)

GUSTAVE CHAUDEY: I was doing my duty. (thrice answered)

RIGAULT: So it was your duty to kill women and children! You killed Sapia, my friend! My duty is to inform you that you have three minutes to live.

CHAUDEY: But I am a Republican . . .

RIGAULT: Like your Versailles pals who will be murdering us tomorrow . . . Come along now. March!
CHAUDEY: But Rigault. I have a wife and child.
RIGAULT: The Commune will care for them better than you. Come
   along. March!

Paris Burns

On the left, the Tuileries was burning. The Communards had fired
both ends of the palace, the Pavillon de Flore and the Pavillon de
Marsan, at nightfall; and the flames were now rapidly gaining the
central Pavillon de l'Horloge, where a formidable mine had been
prepared, barrels upon barrels of gunpowder being piled up in the
Hall of the Marshals. At this moment the intervening buildings were
belching from their shattered windows great whirling coils of ruddy
smoke, through which darted blue flakes of fire. The roofs were
kindling, riddled with fiery crevices, and opening like volcanic soil
as the brazier within assailed them. No other portion of the palace,
however, burnt like the Pavillon de Flore where the torch had been
first applied, and which was flaring away, with a formidable roar,
from its ground floor to its lofty roof. The petroleum with which the
floorings and the hangings had been soaked imparted such intensity
to the flames that the iron work of the massive balconies could be
seen writhing and twisting, whilst the monumental chimneys, with
their great sculptured suns, became red hot and burst asunder.
   Then, on the right bank, came first of all the palace of the Legion
of Honour, set on fire at five o'clock in the evening. It had now been
alight for nearly seven hours, and was being consumed by a great
blaze, like some huge pile of wood, every log of which is kindled,
and fast burning to ashes. Next came the palace of the Council of
State, the most enormous, the most frightful of those immense
conflagrations, the whole gigantic parallelogram of stone, with its
two colonnaded storeys, vomiting flame upon flame of lurid fire.
The four blocks of building encompassing the spacious interior
courtyard had been ignited at one and the same moment, and the
petroleum poured by the cask-full upon the four staircases at the
four corners had streamed down them, rolling perfect torrents of
hell-fire from the highest to the lowest step. On the façade overlook-
ing the river, the sharp line of the attic storey stood out blackly
above the red tongues of flame which were licking its base; whilst

the colonnades, the entablatures, the friezes, all the sculptured ornaments acquired startling vividness amid the blind furnace-like glow beneath. Here especially there was such a rage, such a strength of fire, that the colossal monument was as though upheaved, and quaked and rumbled on its foundations; only the carcass of its massive walls being able to withstand this eruptive violence, which hurled the zinc of the roofs towards the sky. Then, near at hand, was the Orsay barracks, a whole side of which was burning in a lofty white column like a tower of light. And in the rear there were yet other conflagrations, seven houses in the Rue du Bac, two-and-twenty houses in the Rue de Lille, all setting the horizon aglow, with flames rising up in relief against other flames, in a sanguinary, endless sea of fire.

Émile Zola

An Eye-Witness

I felt that the Commune, about to sink, was firing its final distress rockets. Every minute I could see the wreck heave up, its breach widen, and then from inside I could distinguish men in the Hôtel de Ville clinging to their raft and continuing to sign decrees, decrees within all the din of wind and storm. Then one last surge of the ocean and the immense vessel foundered, drowning red banners, golden sashes, delegates in judges' robes and generals' panoply, its gaitered and feathered female warriors, its circus troops arrayed in Spanish képis and Garibaldi caps, Polish lancers and fantastic Turkish Guards, mad drunk, singing and whistling.

Alphonse Daudet

Fair Comment

The Laws of War! They are mild and Christian compared with the inhuman laws of revenge under which the Versailles troops have been shooting, bayoneting, ripping up prisoners, women and children during the last six days. So far as we can recollect there has been nothing like it in history.

The Times

The Commune

On the 20th May the Versailles army was close to the walls of Paris, and on the 21st the troops entered the city, without serious opposition, by the gate of St Cloud. There was afterwards sharp fighting round the Tuileries and at Montmartre, but the victory rested with the Government. It is impossible to ascertain with accuracy the various motives and doctrines which animated the different parties to the insurrection. The rank and file of the mutinous National Guards were perhaps chiefly influenced by the fear of losing the daily pay on which they had subsisted in unaccustomed idleness and comparative comfort during the siege. Many of the insurgents, who had learnt from the teaching of LOUIS BLANC, of VICTOR HUGO, and of other popular writers, to deify ROBESPIERRE and his murderous associates, hoped to take their part in a mimic Reign of Terror; and the great mass of the workmen was deeply imbued with the Communist theory and with bitter hostility to the middle classes. A few dreamers may have accepted in earnest the absurd pretext of Municipal Independence, but of all revolutionary movements which have disorganized France, the Paris insurrection was the most anarchical. In the judicial proceedings which followed, nearly all the accused persons disclaimed responsibility, and attempted to prove that they had acted under compulsion. Of the chief criminals the greater number either perished in the final struggle or contrived to effect their escape. The necessity of defence had, fortunately, occupied the attention of the leaders, and prevented them, during their short possession of power, from exemplifying their doctrines in practice; but at an early period of the struggle they gave an earnest of their modes of action by seizing the Archbishop of PARIS, the PRESIDENT of the COURT of CASSATION, and a large number of priests and respectable laymen, as hostages for the security of themselves and their accomplices. When the chance of resistance was at an end, the doctrines of the Commune and the passions of the rabble were at last relieved from temporary restraint. While the troops were entering Paris, the insurgents avenged themselves by burning the Tuileries, the Hôtel de Ville, and other buildings of less historical and architectural value. The Louvre, with its inestimable treasures, was with difficulty saved; but even the incendiary fires were for the moment almost forgotten in the contemplation of a more atrocious crime. Monseigneur DARBOY, Archbishop of PARIS, a prelate of blameless character and tolerant disposition; the Curé of the Madeleine, the Chief Judge of the Supreme Court of France, and between fifty and sixty of their helpless companions, were murdered in cold blood by order of the Commune.

The Times

The Prisoner

A large fellow, true southerner, sweating, panting, found it hard to keep up. Two cavalrymen came up, tethered his arms, and trunk, and galloped away. The man tries to run, but falls; he is dragged, a mass of oozing flesh that utters cries; the crowd murmurs in pity: 'shoot him and have done'. One soldier reins his horse, comes and fires into the moaning, kicking package of meat.

Alphonse Daudet

Human nature shrinks in horror from the deeds that have been done in Paris. The crimes of the Insurgents have surpassed the most gloomy forebodings of what would be accomplished under the Red Flag. The burning of Paris was diabolical; the shooting of the hostages 'a deed without a name'. But it seems as if we were destined to forget the work of these maddened savages in the spectacle of the vengeance wreaked upon them. The wholesale executions inflicted by the Versailles soldiery, the triumph, the glee, the ribaldry of the 'Party of Order' sicken the soul.

The Times

Retribution

I was walking today by the railway line near Passy station when I saw various men and women encircled by soldiers. I pushed through a gap in the fence and found myself at the edge of the road down which the captives were awaiting escort to Versailles. There were a large number of prisoners, for I heard an officer declare to the Colonel, as he passed him a paper: 'Four hundred and seven, with sixty-six women.'

They came from all social classes: hardfaced workmen, bourgeois wearing middle-class hats, National Guards who had lacked time to discard their uniforms, and two infantrymen pale as ghosts – the stupid, fierce, indifferent.

The same variety existed among the women. Women in kerchiefs stood alongside those in silk gowns. I saw housewives, working-girls, and prostitutes, one of them clad as a National Guard. Prominent in their midst was the bestial head of a creature whose face was half blotted out by a huge bruise. None displayed the apathetic resignation of the men. Anger and scorn lit their faces, many eyes showed a gleam of madness. Among them was one of supreme beauty, the implacable beauty of a young Goddess of Fate. A girl with dark, curled hair, steel eyes, and cheekbones scarlet from dried tears. She stood frozen as if from defiance, hurling insults at officers and men from throat and lips so contracted by fury that she was incoherent. Her mouth, mute and distorted, chewing imprecations that she could not actually spit out. 'She's just like the girl who stabbed Barbier!' said a young officer to a friend . . .

Driving in a cab along the Champs-Élysées I saw, in the distance, legs running towards the Grand Avenue. I leaned from the window. The whole Avenue was filled with an immense crowd between two files of soldiery. I descended and joined those running to discover what this crowd was. It was the prisoners, just captured at the Buttes-Chaumont, passing in fives, several women amongst them. 'Six thousand of these,' a soldier in the escort said to me. 'Five hundred were shot on the spot.' Leading this haggard multitude, a man of ninety was moving with trembling legs.

    The Goncourt Journal

Vengeance

Two courts-martial had been sitting since the Wednesday, one at the Luxembourg palace, the other at the Chatelet theatre. The men condemned by the former tribunal were executed in the palace gardens, whilst those sentenced by the latter were dragged to the Lobau barracks, where firing parties, kept under arms throughout the day, shot them down almost at point-blank range, in the inner courtyard. And here especially did the butchery prove frightful: men, mere boys, condemned to death on the flimsiest evidence -- because their hands were black with powder, or simply because they were wearing regulation shoes; innocent men, too, falsely de-nounced, victims of private malice shouting out explanations to which their military judges would not listen; droves of prisoners huddled together pell-mell in front of the gun-barrels, so many poor wretches brought in for execution at the same time, that the men of the firing-party had not bullets enough for all of them, and despatched those whom their discharge had merely wounded with the butt-ends of their guns. From morning till evening blood streamed and tumbrils carried away the corpses. And then, too, here and there throughout the conquered city, amid the frequent outburst of vengeful fury, there were other executions in front of the barricades, against the blank walls of deserted streets, and on the steps of the public buildings.

Émile Zola

The Hôtel de Ville, for over a Century the Headquarters of Political Dissent

It is a splendid, a magnificent ruin. All pink and ash-green and the tints of white-hot steel, or transformed to glittering agate where the stone has been scorched by paraffin, it resembles a wrecked Italian palace, touched by the sunlight of several centuries or, more accurately, the desolation of a palace of enchantment, swamped in the theatrical glow of electric light. With empty niches, shattered or lopped statues, smashed clock, tall window-frames and chimneys still aloft in mid-air by some miracle of balance, and its jagged silhouette lined against blue sky, it is a picturesque marvel that ought to be preserved if only the country were not irrevocably condemned to the restorations of M. Viollet-le-Duc. The irony of chance! In the utter ruin of the entire edifice there gleams, on a marble slab intact in fresh gilt frame, the lying inscription:

Liberty, Equality, Fraternity

The Goncourt Journal

A Communard Speaks from the Dock

I do not wish to defend myself. I do not wish to be defended. I belong absolutely to the Social Revolution, and I say that I accept the responsibility of all my actions, I accept it without reservation.

You accuse me of having taken part in the execution of the generals. To that I reply: they intended to have the people shot and I should not have hesitated to have those who gave such orders shot.

As to the arson at Paris, yes, I took part in it. I wanted to place a

barrier of flames in the way of the invaders from Versailles. I have
no accomplices. I acted of my own accord . . .

What I ask of you who call yourselves a council of war, who
regard yourselves as my judges, and who do not conceal yourselves
as a 'Commission of Grace', is the field of Sartory where my
brothers have already fallen. You must remove me from society:
they have told you to do so. Very well: the commissar of the
Republic is right. Since it appears that every heart which beats for
liberty has only the right to a bit of lead, I claim my piece. If you let
me live I shall not cease to cry for vengeance and I shall claim the
assassins of the commission of grace for the vengeance of my
brothers . . .

THE PRESIDENT: I cannot allow you to speak.

LOUISE MICHEL: I have finished. If you are not cowards, kill me.

> Louise Michel

The smell of dead bodies nauseates me less than the stench of
egotism breathed from all mouths. The view of wrecked buildings is
nothing compared to the utter imbecility of the people of Paris.
With few exceptions everyone seems to me raving mad. Half the
population yearns to strangle the other half, which shares the same
longing.

> Gustave Flaubert

Communards Speak before Sentence

I was despatched to the Commune by fellow-citizens; I suffered for
it; I was on the barricades and regret not meeting death there; I
should not then be enduring the sad sight of my associates who
shared in the activities now refusing to share the responsibilities. I
am a rebel and don't mind admitting it.

> Trinquet, cobbler of Belleville
> *Penal Servitude for Life*

I am a member of the Commune. I am in the hands of its conquerors. They want my head. Let them have it! I will never save
myself by playing the coward. I have lived a free man; I intend to die
one. I have one more word: Fate is capricious; I leave Posterity to

look after my memory and my revenge.

> Theophile Ferré
> *Shot*

The Prophet

Working-men's Paris, with its Commune, will be for ever celebrated as the glorious harbinger of a new society. Its martyrs are enshrined in the great heart of the working class. Its exterminators History has already nailed to that eternal pillory from which all the prayers of their priests will not avail to redeem them.

> Karl Marx

Actually, as in the French Revolution, there were few genuine members of the working class in the Commune, which was both Jacobin and anarchist rather than communist.

The highest point of humiliation and national infamy.

> Ex-Emperor Napoleon III, on the Commune

The Last Letter of a Communard

I do not wish, and am unable, to act as victim and toy of victorious reaction. Forgive me for leaving life before you, you who have given up your life for me. But I no longer feel myself brave enough to submit to yet another defeat, after so many others. I give you a thousand embraces, with all my love. Your memory will be the last that will enter my thoughts before going to rest.

> Charles Delescluze, to his sister

Never have we had such a chance of curing Paris of the moral gangrene that has been gnawing her for the last twenty years. The people of Paris must submit to the laws of war, however dire. Mercy now is madness.

> *Le Figaro*

The proletariat halted in mid-course; instead of going on to 'expropriate the expropriators', it surrendered to visions of establishing supreme justice throughout the land . . . The second mistake was the

needless generosity of the workers; instead of wiping out the enemy,
they tried to reduce the importance of pure militarism in a civil war.
> Lenin, 1908

THE SLEEPER IN THE VALLEY

In a green hollow where a river sings,
Circling the grasses with specks of silver-white,
From his proud steeps the sun ascendant flings
Splendour. The valley scintillates with light.
Open-mouthed, capless, a young soldier lies
Where the fresh blue cresses cool his bare head;
Pale in the light raining down from the skies
He sleeps, stretched at length on his green mossy bed.

His feet bruise the iris where he takes his nap
Smiling like a sick child on its mother's lap;
He is cold. Earth, warm him! Cradle him to rest!
He heeds not the scents that ride about his head;
In the sun he dozes, hand on quiet breast.
In his right side two bullet holes have bled.
> Arthur Rimbaud

DANCING GIRL

Is she a dancing girl? In dawn's blue hour
She will destroy herself as dies a flower . . .
Before the open splendour where is heard
The thriving city's bosom hugely stirred!

Beauty too great, too great! But needed yet
For the Corsair's song, the Fisherwoman's net,
And the belief the last masks still confessed
In midnight revels on pure ocean's breast!
> Arthur Rimbaud

Vowels

A black, E white, I red, U green, O blue – one day
Vowels, I shall disclose your occult springs:
A – the black velvet stomacher of wings
Where flies swarm round a stench of foul decay.

Black-shadowed pit; E – pure as steam, white kings
Tents, glacier's fang or blossom's trembling spray;
I – purple-red – spilt blood or smiles that play
On pretty lips in drink or quarrellings.

U – aeons, stirring of the sea's green wonder,
Peace of the pastured herds, the wrinkled grandeur
Alchemy graves on foreheads of the wise;
O – the great Clarion, harsh with chords unproved,
The silences where worlds and angels moved;
O – Omega, blue lightnings of Her Eyes!
                    Arthur Rimbaud

The Gypsy Poet

Fists probing my torn pockets, off I'd wander,
My overcoat more holes than cloth and I
Poetry's bondslave under the open sky;
Oh lord, what splendid dreams of love I'd squander!
Torn were my only trousers at the knees;
As inn-sign in the sky, the Great Bear shone
And stars, like twinkling silk, smiled down upon
Tom Thumb, the dreamer, shelling rhymes like peas.

I'd listen from the roadside on those fine
September nights while dew-drops' heady wine
Moistened my brow; fantastic shadows pressed
About me as in search of rhymes I'd tug
The laces of my worn-out boots and hug
One foot just like a lyre against my chest.
                    Arthur Rimbaud

CLAIR DE LUNE

Your soul is a sealed garden, and there go
With masque and bergamasque fair companies
Playing on lutes and dancing and as though
Sad under their fantastic fripperies.

Though they in minor keys go carolling
Of love the conqueror and of life the boon
They seem to doubt the happiness they sing
And the song melts into the light of the moon,

The sad light of the moon, so lovely fair
That all the birds dream in the leafy shade
And the slim fountains sob into the air
Among the marble statues in the glade.

       Paul Verlaine

LOVE LIES BLEEDING

Love, that is dead and buried, yesterday
Out of his grave rose up before my face;
No recognition in his look, no trace
Of memory in his eyes dust-dimmed and grey;
While I, remembering, found no word to say,
But felt my quickened heart leap in its place;
Caught afterglow thrown back from long-set days,
Caught echoes of all music passed away.
Was this indeed to meet? – I mind me yet
In youth we met when hope and love were quick,
We parted with hope dead but love alive:
I mind me how we parted then heart-sick,
Remembering, loving, hopeless, weak to strive:-
Was this to meet? Not so, we have not met.

       Christina Rossetti

On the Peace of 1871

The ceding of Alsace-Lorraine is war eternal disguised as peace.

       Edgar Quinet

Despite herself, in twenty or thirty years' time, Prussia will be forced to become aggressive. Then Europe will overwhelm her.

Ex-Emperor Napoleon III

Henceforward Europe has two nations which will be formidable: one because it is victorious, the other because it is beaten.

Victor Hugo

Lasting Peace

Lasting peace, rather than war, tends to harden and bestialize humanity, to generate cruelty and cowardice, and, first and foremost, intellectual stagnation.

F. M. Dostoevsky

The Professional

War is a holy thing and of divine institution. It is war that preserves for man all the great and noble sentiments such as honour, disinterestedness, virtue, courage. In a word, it is war that prevents man from relapsing into the most hideous materialism.

Field Marshal Count von Moltke

The Post-War World

What a world we live in . . . the bourgeoisie is so confused that it has lost even the instinct of self-preservation, and the newcomers will be worse. I'm filled with a melancholy like that of Fourth Century Roman patricians, as I sense an irresistible tide of barbarism emerging from the depths . . . Never have intellectual matters been more disregarded, the contempt for Beauty, the curses against literature, been more obvious.

Gustave Flaubert

Winston Churchill's Mother Revisits Paris

Ruins everywhere: the sight of the Tuileries and the Hôtel de Ville made me cry. St Cloud, the scene of many pleasant expeditions, was a thing of the past, the lovely château razed to the ground. And if material in Paris was damaged, the social fabric was even more so. In vain we tried to pick up the threads. Some of our friends were killed, others ruined or in mourning, and all broken-hearted and miserable, hiding in their houses and refusing to be comforted.

The statues at the Place de la Concorde, representing the most important towns of France – Strasbourg, Lille, Nancy, Orleans – swathed in crepe, . . . reminded one daily, if one needed it, of the trials and tribulations France had just gone through. Only the embassies and a few foreigners, principally Americans, received or entertained . . . A few opened their houses, but the French on the whole were shy of going out at all, and if Paris had any gaiety left in those days, it was owing to her cosmopolitan character.

> Jennie Jerome

The Exiles

No, Eugénie, I will not defend myself. Some catastrophes are so grievous for a nation that it is right to place all the blame, however unjustly, on its ruler. A monarch, especially an Emperor, would demean himself, by pleading his cause against his own subjects; he has no excuses, no extenuating circumstances. His highest prerogative is to accept for himself alone all the responsibilities incurred by those who have served him – or betrayed him.

> Ex-Emperor Napoleon III

The French have great and brilliant qualities but they have few convictions and they lack constancy. Their minds are supple but their characters are fickle. They love glory and all that is brilliant and showy, but they do not know how to endure the strokes of misfortune. For them, right is confused with success . . .

There is no land on earth where so little distance exists between the sublime and the absurd. And how history repeats itself! For a hundred years every French regime has ended in revolution and flight. Only the other day some people were expressing fear that a new defeat might cause the fall of the Empire. I told them that I would never leave the Tuileries in a cab, like Louis-Philippe. And that is exactly what I have done.

> Ex-Empress Eugénie

The pearly-grey English sky is like a dish cooked without salt. One needs great hunger to appreciate it.

> Ex-Empress Eugénie

Dictatorship can only be a temporary regime, and yet a parliamentary system destroys the government that establishes it. So then what do you do?

> Ex-Emperor Napoleon III

Napoleon III dies at Chislehurst

Conneau, it's true, isn't it . . . We weren't cowards were we, at Sedan?

> *Last Words*

The dog is dead.

> Algernon Charles Swinburne

On his Wife

I trust that my memory will be dear to her, and that after my death she will forgive the griefs I may have caused her.

> Ex-Emperor Napoleon III, from his Will

His quiet and calm dignity and absence of all nervousness and irritability were the grandest examples of human moral courage that the severest stoic could have imagined.

> Lord Malmesbury, former Foreign Secretary

The dismal platitude that called itself a reign.

> Henry Labouchere, 1870

Perhaps the most reflective and *in*sighted, not far-sighted, of the modern statesmen of France.

> Walter Bagehot

It is only in recent years that Napoleon III has come to be seen as a precursor of the Common Market. His intentions were partly political – he wished to strengthen his alliance with England – but mainly economic, to stimulate agriculture and industry in France by competition and to benefit the masses by lower prices.

Theodore Zeldin, 1974

He had a strange charm for those with whom he came into contact. He could flatter without seeming hypocritical; he was generous, he was a good listener. But there was always something opaque about him, so that it was no easy matter following his lead. His silent meditations and his mystical communion with public opinion made him – when he was successful – a kind of wizard.

Theodore Zeldin, 1974

He did more for the French working classes than any other French government before or since.

A. J. P. Taylor, 1951

He did one bad action as a means, and then meant to do good ones.

George Eliot

It has been a life of marvellous vicissitudes and the most wonderful romance since that of Charles Edward.

Francis Kilvert

The Dynasty

But man does not know the measure of time nor the content of time; a wise dispensation for the Emperor's wife and still better for the mother of the boy whose name was also Louis Napoleon; the mother made her son's destiny a thing to marvel at, a thing wellnigh superhuman, whereas time was to make the boy's future as puny and pitiable as could be. Only six years more, and he would be twenty-three. The model boy at the military training school will soon be at the end of his studies, he will become one of the handsomest of lieutenants, since he has inherited his mother's good looks. But his voice is sweetly modulated like his father's and he speaks slowly, too. He is warm-hearted; his boldness comes from the maternal side, and his courage from both parents; for his father was undoubtedly courageous, though this courage was not of the showy kind. Sonnie is rather fed up with Mother, with her demonstrations of affection; she seems too precise in her love, as also in the matter of pocket-money. After so much love and schooling he longed for a taste of war – which would mean freedom. He became an unimaginably handsome little English officer in the colonial service, and was sent out to punish the Zulus who were in revolt against British suzerainty. A rebel assegai sent him to kingdom-come; indeed, so many spear-thrusts riddled the poor lad's body that, after it had been brought back in great pomp to England, it could only be recognised by the stopped teeth.

Ten o'clock till noon; 1872 to 1879; such measures of time are naught to Eugénie. For the wife, the mother, the elderly woman, the granddam, who was always dressed in black, a millionaire in the quantities of time at her disposal; a haunting horror grew up around her; life shuddered at its own sorely-tried forbearance; she herself applied the nickname of 'old bat' to the creature which looked at her from the mirror like an ancient owl; and she lived on and on, till one day from her house in Farnborough she heard bells ringing, the Farnborough bells joining in the mighty chorus of bells which sounded from Scotland to Sicily proclaiming the end of the Great War forty-eight years after Sedan.

Alfred Neumann, 1936

She was to condemn the allied policy of Reparations against Germany 1919, regularly visited Paris and was once rebuked by an official for plucking a rose in the gardens of the vanished Tuileries.

I am tired; it is time for me to go away.

Ex-Empress Eugénie, 1920

The Sibyl George Eliot at Cambridge, 1873

Taking as her text the three words which have been used so often as the inspiring trumpet-calls of men, – the words *God*, *Immortality*, *Duty*, – pronounced with terrible earnestness, how inconceivable was the *first*, how unbelievable the *second*, and yet how peremptory and absolute the *third*. Never, perhaps, have sterner assents affirmed the sovereignty of impersonal and unrecompensing law. I listened, and night fell; her grave, majestic countenance turned towards me like a sibyl's in the gloom, it was as though she withdrew from my grasp, one by one, the two scrolls of promise, and left me the third scroll only, awful with inevitable fates. And when we stood at length and parted, amid that columnar circuit of the forest-trees, beneath the last twilight of starless skies, I seemed to be gazing, like Titus at Jerusalem, on vacant seats and empty halls, – on a sanctuary with no Presence to hallow it, and heaven left lonely of a God.

F. W. H. Myers

Ireland

'And so Phineas is to be Secretary for Ireland . . . That is promotion and I am so glad! Poor Phineas! I hope they won't murder him, or anything of that kind. They do murder people, you know, sometimes.'

'He's an Irishman himself.'

'That's just the reason why they should. He must put up with that, of course.'

Anthony Trollope

A Victorian Marriage

The horror which the bride expressed was, as Mrs Carbuncle well knew, no mock feeling, no pretence of antipathy. She tried to think of it, and to realise what might in truth be the girl's action and ultimate fate when she should find herself in the power of this man whom she so hated. But had not other girls done the same thing, and lived through it all, and become fat, indifferent, and fond of the world? It's only the first step that signifies.

Anthony Trollope

He and my mother had been victims of an arranged marriage. She was seventeen, still in the schoolroom and, I was told, had met my father twice at luncheon. They can never, I take it, have been alone together for more than a few minutes before marriage.

Sacheverell Sitwell, 1973

The Adversary

The irritation continued growing worse, and on examination I found the prepuce swollen, and on turning it down, I found the whole of the inside salmon-coloured, as you called it, only little spots as though the skin had been eaten away so as to show the flesh and it almost looked as though it was bleeding. I applied a little of the subtilissimus, but the end continues to be irritated. The prepuce is a little hard as well; and there was a drop or two of yellow matter near the red spots.

I don't know what an ulcer should look like. Are these anything like the symptoms of soft chancre? Or is it like your inflammation? Or do you think it is only balanitis?

Please answer by return – I hope this will find you – and excuse me thrusting this frightful communication on you in a time of felicity. But answer instanter, for I tremblingly await my doom! . . .

Yours, non hilariter

J.G.B.

Quoth the raven, 'Never more'.

Should the subtilissimus go a bright green after being applied?

John George Black, to George Gissing, 1876

A Girl at Church

My back still aches in memory of those long services. Nothing was spared us – the whole of the 'Dearly beloved', never an omission of the Litany, always the full ante-Communion Service, involving a sermon of unbelievable length. The seats and kneeling-boards were constructed for grown-ups (and not too comfortable for them), and a child had the greatest difficulty in keeping an upright kneeling position all through the long intoned Litany. We found some alleviations even here. How would the officiating priest take the fence in intoning 'uncharitableness'? Canon Milman was our delight over this, because he used to quaver forth ' –table–' all by itself and leave a long pause of suspense before he could reach the high note of ' –ness–'. After this we looked forward to beating down Satan under our feet, partly because it seemed a nice final thing to do, and partly because it was the half-way mark. Some energetic clergymen put in extra prayers at the end, even the thanksgiving – always associated with my blackest thoughts.

Like all children I put some kind of workable meaning into the strange Prayer Book phrases. 'The Scripture moveth us in sundry places' must mean that it pokes us in various parts of our body – a spiritual dig in the ribs: 'Come now, own up.'

'Deal not with us after our sins' was surely a foolish request. Mother's indignant refusal to 'deal with' the butcher was her last word of annoyance, and why should we go out of our way to pray for such treatment? Still more idiotic did it seem to pray, 'Neither reward us after our iniquities'. If God was so generously inclined, why prevent him? As for asking him to rule the Church in the right way, that was mere impertinence. Surely he could be trusted to do it rightly!

M. V. Hughes

From Belgium

When I was in England, I applied for a position as evangelist among the coal miners, but they put me off, saying I had to be at least twenty-five years old. You know how one of the roots or foundations, not only of the Gospels, but of the whole Bible is 'Light that rises in the darkness', *from darkness to light*. Well, who needs this most, who will be receptive to it? Experience has shown that the people who walk in the darkness, in the centre of the earth, like the miners in the black coal mines, for instance, are very much impressed by the words of the Gospel, and believe them, too. Now in the south of Belgium, in Hainaut, near Mons, up to the French frontier – aye, even far across it – there is a district called the Borinage, which has a unique population of labourers who work in the numerous coal mines . . .

If I could work quietly in such a district for about three years, always learning and observing, then I should not come back without having something to say that was really worth hearing. I say this in all humility and yet with confidence. If God wills, and if He spares my life, I would be ready by about my thirtieth year – beginning with my own unique training and experience, mastering my work better and being riper for it than now.

Vincent Van Gogh

Russian Spring

Spring had set in late. During the first weeks of Lent the weather had been clear and frosty. It thawed in the sunshine by day, but at night the thermometer went down to sixteen degrees Fahrenheit. The snow was covered with a crust of ice so thick that carts could pass even where there were no roads. Easter found snow still on the ground; but on Easter Monday a warm wind began to blow, the clouds gathered, and for three days and nights warm stormy rain poured down. On the Thursday the wind fell and a thick grey mist rose as if to hide the secret of the changes nature was carrying on. Beneath the mist the snow-waters rushed down, the ice on the river cracked and moved, and the turbid, foaming torrents flowed quicker, till on the first Sunday after Easter toward evening the mist dissolved, the clouds broke into fleecy cloudlets and dispersed, the sky cleared, and real spring was there. In the morning the bright rising sun quickly melted the thin ice on the water and the warm air all around vibrated with the vapour given off by the awakening earth. Last year's grass grew green again and new blades came up like needle-points, buds swelled on the guelder rose and current bushes and on the sticky, pungent birch trees, and among the golden catkins and on the willow branches the bees began to hum. The unseen larks burst into song above the velvety fresh green and the frozen stubble, the peewits began to cry above the water brought down by the storm and still flooding the low-lying places and marshes, and high up the cranes and geese flew, uttering their spring call. The cattle, who were just beginning to lose their winter coats, began to low in the meadows; the crooked-legged lambs began to play round their bleating mothers, who were losing their wool; swift-footed children began to run along the quickly-drying paths marked with imprints of bare feet, the merry voices of women who were bleaching their linen began to chatter by the ponds, and the axes of peasants, getting ready their wooden ploughs and harrows, sounded in the yards.

The real spring had come.

Leo Tolstoy

Summer in Russia

Now, in the hottest part of the day, the work did not seem so hard to him. The perspiration in which he was bathed was cooling, and the sun which burnt his back, his head and his arms – bare to the elbow – added to his strength and perseverance in his task, and those unconscious intervals when it became possible not to think of what he was doing recurred more and more often. The scythe seemed to mow of itself. Those were happy moments. Yet more joyous were the moments when, reaching the river at the lower end of the swaths, the old man would wipe his scythe with the wet grass, rinse its blade in the clear water, and dipping his whetstone-box in the stream, would offer it to Levin.

'A little of my *kvas*? It's good!' said he, with a wink.

And really Levin thought he had never tasted any nicer drink than this lukewarm water with green stuff floating in it and a flavour of the rusty tin box. And then came the ecstasy of a slow walk, one hand resting on the scythe, when there was leisure to wipe away the streams of perspiration, to breathe deep, to watch the line of mowers, and to see what was going on around in the forest and field.

The longer Levin went on mowing, the oftener he experienced those moments of oblivion when his arms no longer seemed to swing the scythe, but the scythe itself his whole body, so conscious and full of life; and as if by magic, regularly and definitely without a thought being given to it, the work accomplished itself of its own accord. These were blessed moments . . .

Levin did not notice how time passed. Had he been asked how long he had been mowing, he would have answered 'half an hour', although it was nearly noon. As they were about to begin another swath the old man drew Levin's attention to the little boys and girls approaching from all sides along the road and through the long grass, hardly visible above it, carrying jugs of *kvas* stoppered with rags, and bundles of bread which strained their little arms.

'Look at the midges crawling along!' he said, pointing to the children and glancing at the sun from under his lifted hand. They completed two more swaths and then the old man stopped.

'Come, master! It's dinner-time,' said he with decision. All the mowers on reaching the river went across the swaths to where their coats lay, and where the children who had brought their dinners sat waiting for them. The men who had driven from a distance gathered in the shadow of their carts; those who lived nearer sheltered under the willow growth, on which they hung grass.

Levin sat down beside them; he did not want to go away.

All the peasants' restraint in the presence of the master had vanished. The men began preparing for dinner. Some had a wash. The young lads bathed in the river; others arranged places for their after-dinner rest, unfastened their bags of bread and unstoppered their jugs of *kvas*. The old man broke some rye bread into a bowl, mashed it with a spoon handle, poured over it some water from his tin, broke more bread into it and salted it, and then, turning to the East, said grace.

'Come, master, have some of my dinner,' said he, kneeling in front of his bowl.

The bread and water was so nice that Levin gave up all intention of going home to lunch. He shared the old man's meal and got into conversation with him about his domestic affairs, taking a lively interest in them and telling him about his own, giving him all the particulars which would interest the old peasant. When the old man got up and, having said grace, lay down beneath the willows with an armful of grass under his head, Levin did the same, regardless of the flies, importunate and persistent in the sunshine, and of the crawling insects that tickled his perspiring face and body. He at once fell asleep, waking only when the sun touched the opposite side of the willows and reached him. The old man had already been long awake and sat whetting the scythes for the young men.

Leo Tolstoy

The Russian Woman

When she poured out her usual dose of opium and thought that she need only drink the whole phial in order to die, it seemed to her so easy and simple that she again began thinking with pleasure of how he would suffer, repent, and love her memory when it was too late. She lay in bed with open eyes, looking at the stucco cornice under the ceiling by the light of a single burnt-down candle, and at the shadow of the screen which fell on it, and she vividly imagined what he would feel when she was no more, when she was for him nothing but a memory. 'How could I say those cruel words to her?' he would say. 'How could I leave the room without saying anything? But now she is no more! She has gone from us for ever! She is there . . . ' Suddenly the shadow of the screen began to move and spread over the whole of the cornice, the whole ceiling. Other shadows rushed toward it from another side; for an instant they rushed together, but then again they spread with renewed swiftness, flickered, and all was darkness. 'Death!' she thought. And such terror came upon her that it was long before she could realise where she was and with trembling hand could find the matches to light another candle in the place of the one that had burnt down and out. 'No – anything, only to live! Why, I love him! and he loves me! All this has been, but will pass,' she said, feeling that tears of joy at this return to life were running down her cheeks. And, to escape from her fears, she hastily went to him in his study.

He was sleeping in the study and was sound asleep. She came up, and holding the light above him looked at him long. Now, when he was asleep, she loved him so that she could not restrain tears of tenderness while looking at him; but she knew that if he were to wake he would look at her with a cold expression, conscious of his own integrity, and that before telling him of her love she must prove to him that he was to blame toward her. Without waking him she returned to her room, and after a second dose of opium toward morning she fell into a heavy but troubled sleep, without ever ceasing to be conscious of herself.

In the morning a terrible nightmare, which had come to her several times even before her union with Vronsky, repeated itself and woke her. An old man with a tangled beard was leaning over some iron and doing something, while muttering senseless words in French; and as always in that nightmare (this was what made it terrible) she felt that this peasant was paying no attention to her but was doing something dreadful to her with the iron. And she awoke in a cold perspiration.

Leo Tolstoy

Disbelief in Progress

It is so clear and understandable as to be obvious that evil is concealed in mankind deeper than the physician-socialists suppose; that in no social organization will evil be evaded; that the human soul will remain unchanged; that abnormality and sin derive from it; and finally, that the laws of the soul are so unknown to science, so uncertain and so mysterious, that there are and can be no doctors nor even ultimate judges except He who says 'Vengeance is Mine, I will Repay'.

F. M. Dostoevsky, reviewing *Anna Karenina*

Tears in my Heart

Rain falling on the City. Stories without Words.

> Paul Verlaine

Experience of Life

I think you listen too much to the soldiers. No lesson seems to be so deeply inculcated by the experience as that you should never trust experts. If you believe the doctors, nothing is wholesome; if you believe the theologians, nothing is innocent; if you believe the soldier, nothing is safe. They all require to have their strong wine diluted by a very large admixture of common sense.

> Lord Salisbury, to Lord Lytton

From this window I look down upon the Wilhelmstrasse and see many a cripple look up and think that if that man up there had not made that wicked war I should be at home healthy and strong.

> Otto von Bismarck

The Germans want to be masters and slaves simultaneously, and Anarchism accepts neither.

> Mikhail Bakunin

For Children

Satan is glad – when I am bad,
And hopes that I – with him shall lie
In fire and chains – in dreadful pains.

> *The Peep of Day: Prize Book for Children*

On the Education of Princes

Will a nautical education not engender and encourage national prejudices and make them think that their own Country is superior to any other? With the greatest love for and pride in one's own Country, a Prince, and especially one who is some day to be its Ruler, should not be involved with the prejudices and peculiarities of his own Country, as George III and Wilhelm III were.

> Queen Victoria, to Rev. John Neale Dalton

Manners

Manners were attended to with special care. When the young ladies were invited out to tea they were set down to a meal of thick bread and butter before starting, in order that their appetites should appear elegant. They were commanded to leave something on their plate, however pleasing the dish.

M. V. Hughes

Miracle at School

In school 'time was all withdrawn'. This was brought home to me by a curious experience one dreary morning. I was seated with my school-fellows at a long table, copying again and again 'Alfred Tennyson is a poet', my writing getting steadily worse as the hated statement was repeated. Doubt began – perhaps people had denied that he was a poet? Glancing up at the school clock to see how far off it still was to the lunch-interval at a quarter to eleven, I beheld a miracle. As I looked, the big hand slipped from ten past ten to twenty past! If the sun had done a similar turn in the sky I could not have been more astonished. And it was not an answer to a prayer like Joshua's, though it might well have been. I watched to see what would happen next: the clock resumed its usual duty at twenty past, and nobody noticed anything.

M. V. Hughes

The division of classes is *the one thing* which is most dangerous and reprehensible, never intended by the law of nature, and which the queen is always labouring to alter.

Queen Victoria

'An I thowt 'twur the will o' the Lord,
But Miss Annie she said it wur draains.'

Alfred Tennyson

The Prophet

In a socialist society the 'fragmented' man would be replaced by the 'completely developed', he for whom different social functions are but alternative forms of activity. People would fish, hunt, or engage in literary criticism without being professional fishermen, huntsmen or critics.

Karl Marx

If we had a keen vision of all that is ordinary in human life, it would be like hearing the grass grow or the squirrel's heart beat, and we should die of that roar which is the other side of silence.

George Eliot

Etiquette

Any pretty fancy ring may be worn as an engagement ring. Pearls or diamonds are considered the proper gems. The engagement ring is not considered after marriage to answer the purpose of a keeper. A keeper should be a chased gold ring without stones in it. It is worn on the same finger as the wedding ring. And 'opals', on account of their signification being 'sorrow' are not fashionable for engagement rings.

The Young Ladies' Journal

The Host

I came home across America from San Francisco to New York, visiting Utah and Brigham Young on the way. I did not achieve great intimacy with the great polygamist of the Salt Lake City. I called upon him, sending to him my card, apologising for doing so without an introduction, and excusing myself by saying that I did not like to pass through the territory without seeing a man of whom I had heard so much. He received me in his doorway, not asking me to enter, and inquired whether I were not a miner. When I told him that I was not a miner, he asked me whether I earned my bread. I told him that I did. 'I guess you're a miner,' said he. I again assured him that I was not. 'Then how do you earn your bread?' I told him that I did so by writing books. 'I'm sure you're a miner,' said he. Then he turned upon his heel, went back into the house, and closed the door. I was properly punished, as I had been vain enough to conceive that he would have heard my name.

Anthony Trollope

On His Father

He could not endure stupidity . . . He resembled almost all Englishmen in being ashamed of the signs of feeling, and by the absence of demonstration, starving the feelings themselves.

> John Stuart Mill

An Advertisement

Boarding schools wanted, in London, for a boy, nine years, and two boys, six and seven years old, requiring firm discipline, having become wild and unruly, through neglect occasioned by family misfortune. No holiday could be given, as holidays destroy any good affected at school. The father, quite a gentleman, can only pay 20 guineas each. This advertisement is only intended for schools of pre-eminent efficiency for such cases, and prosperous enough to be able and willing to accept such terms and undertake the needful taste of reformation for the sake of the schools' additional credit of success.

> *Punch*

British Egypt

People are dying by the roadside, great tracts of country are uncultivated, because of the fiscal burdens, and the farmers have sold their cattle and the women their finery, and usurers are filling the mortgage offices with their suits of foreclosure.

> *The Times*, March 31, 1879

The Family Doctor

So few were our demands on the doctor that he used to pay mother unofficial calls, in the middle of his morning rounds. To cheer himself up, I fancy. These visits were glory for me because they broke into my morning's work and gave me a chance to hear juicier bits than the ordinary visitor provided. The mysterious undertone would excite me and impress my memory far more than a matter-of-fact style.

'You have no idea, Mrs Thomas, how many ladies I attend whose only malady is secret bottles.'

'But how do they manage to get the stuff?'

'The grocer supplies it, and puts it down as sugar on the bills.'

'How did you find that out?'

'From a grocer patient.'

'How do you treat them?'

'Well, you see, I have my living to make, and dare not be frank with them. They would be offended and call in someone else.'

　　　M. V. Hughes

On the Need for an Indian Factory Act

On what principle, or what theory, is India to be exempted from the duties and obligations of civilised society? Creed and colour, latitude and longitude, make no difference in the essential nature of man. No climate can enable infants to do the work of adults, or turn suffering women into mere steam-engines . . . But what say you, my lords, to a continuity of toil, in a standing posture, in a poisonous atmosphere, during thirteen hours, with fifteen minutes to rest? Why, the stoutest man in England, were he made, in such a condition of things, to do nothing during the whole of that time but be erect on his feet and stick pins in a pincushion, would sink under the burden. What say you, then, of children – children of the tenderest years? Why, they become stunted, crippled, deformed, useless. I speak what I know; I state what I have seen . . .

In Bradford, in 1838, I asked for a collection of cripples and deformities. In a short time more than eighty were gathered in a large courtyard. They were mere samples of the entire mass. I assert without exaggeration that no power of language could describe the varieties, and I may say the cruelties, in all those degradations of the human form. They stood or squatted before me in the shapes of the letters of the alphabet. This was the effect of prolonged toil on the tender frames of children at early ages. When I visited Bradford under the limitation of hours, some years afterwards, I called for a similar exhibition of cripples; but, God be praised, there was not one to be found in that vast city . . .

Forty-six years ago I addressed the House of Commons in a kindred appeal and they heard me; I now turn to your Lordships, and I implore you in the same spirit, for God's sake and in His name, to have mercy on the children of India.

> Anthony Ashley Cooper, Seventh Earl of Shaftesbury, to the House of Lords

Measures were subsequently passed, but failed to be enforced.

AN ADMONITION

'Tis proper, Sophy, to be sure,
To pity and relieve the poor:
But do not waste your pity here,
Work is not hard to her, my dear,
It makes her healthy, strong and gay,
And is as pleasant as your play.

> Anon

The Revolutionary's Catechism, St Petersburg

To reach his aim of merciless destruction the revolutionary is forced to live in society pretending to be completely different from what he really is, for he must penetrate everywhere: into all the higher and middle-class circles, into the business world, the great houses, the bureaucracy, the military and the literary world, yes, into the Third Department and even into the Winter Palace of the Tsar.

This whole evil society is to be divided into certain categories. The first category consists of men condemned to immediate death. When the lists are being drawn up, it is not a man's hatefulness or his wickedness which should decide his place on them. His very iniquity, and the hatred it arouses, can even be useful in so far as it incites people to revolt. The first to be eliminated will therefore be those who are particularly dangerous to the revolutionary organization or those whose sudden violent death may plunge the Government into confusion and alarm by being robbed of its cleverest and most energetic supporters. The second category consists of persons whose lives will be spared for the time being as they drive people to revolt by their misdeeds. The third category comprises the majority of high-ranking persons who do not excel either by particular cleverness or energy but who enjoy power and importance thanks to their position, their wealth or their connections. They must be inveigled into positions where they become embroiled in dirty affairs. Then they can be harnessed to our cause, and their power, influence and capital will become an inexhaustible treasure-house for all our undertakings. The fourth category consists of ambitious statesmen and liberals of all shades. The revolutionary must join them and pretend to collaborate with them in their programmes until he gets hold of all their secrets and they are completely in our hands. The fifth category comprises revolutionary doctrinaires and conspirators who cut a great figure on paper and in their cliques. They must be constantly driven on and led to make dangerous declarations; that will cost most of them their heads, but a minority will become real revolutionaries.

We are convinced that the toiling masses can achieve complete freedom and happiness only through an all-embracing destructive popular revolution, and therefore we will work with all our power and all our means to foster the spread of oppression and evil, until they break the patience of the people and force them into a general revolt.

By a revolution we understand not an orderly movement on the western pattern which has always stopped short of attacking the rights of property and the traditional moral code of this so-called civilization. If the revolution is to bring salvation to the Russian people it must eradicate the whole traditional order together with its class structure . . . We must join hands with the wild bandit and the highway-robber, the only true revolutionaries in Russia. To weld their divided efforts into one single unconquerable and all-destructive force, that is the whole task of our organization and conspiracy.

Ascribed to Sergei Nechaev

Italian Anti-Austrian Nationalism: a letter from Trieste, still part of the Austro-Hungarian Empire

For me the finest thing would be if this pen were suddenly to become a rifle and make holes instead of letters; I wish that I might be there and not here; I wish for lots of other nice things too and it grieves me when I think that they haven't happened yet.

Patience! Actually we can have more than enough of that if we want it. Meanwhile, so that we don't fill our stomachs too full with it, we absolutely must work because inactivity is the father of all vices.

We want to do something really worthwhile here and I hope that at your end you'll do likewise. When the time comes I'll tell you something a little more precise . . .

Those who are quick to understand don't need many words! In view of the fact that many friends felt bored to death here, we thought of founding a Music and Drama Society in the meantime with the intention of enacting drama more than any other productions, and tragedies too if needs be. Let's hope that it will be done well and will prove to be an infallible method of killing the boredom and ridding ourselves of apathy.

Otherwise I have no news in my bag. I think you already know very well what sort of an anniversary is at hand and further words are unnecessary.

No news at all from Trieste. It seems odd that those stupid ruffians of agitators keep their hands in their pockets. Are they doing that for some secret purpose? Because they are preparing something new? The fools! What can they do to oppose the right of power? For them too the moment will come, the day of reckoning, and we shall see them dangling from some gallows, carrion in death as much as they were in life – and may it be so.

> Wilhelm Oberdank, to Marco Stefani, January 10, 1879

Youth

He then proceeded to declare that the day had arrived for them to do something practical, and all at once became heated, though no one had contradicted. He bit his lips, and hoarsely, vehemently, started castigating the enormities now occurring, maintaining that all was now ready for them to start, that only cowards would hold back, that a certain amount of violence was just as essential as the prick of a lancet to the abscess, however ripe it might be. The lancet simile was not original, but one he had somewhere overheard. He appeared to enjoy it, and used it whenever possible.

> Ivan Turgenev

The Anarchist

We are the natural enemies of such revolutionaries – future dictators, makers of regulations, brow-beaters who, even before the revolution are planning how to end it and gag the people; who would again condemn the masses to discipline, passivity, death, by handing them over to slavery and exploitation by a new pseudo-revolutionary aristocracy . . .

The Revolution, as we understand it, must utterly destroy the State and all its institutions from the very first day.

Mikhail Bakunin

I do not want to be I, I want to be We.

Mikhail Bakunin

The smallest and most inoffensive State is still criminal in its dreams.

Mikhail Bakunin

On Revolution

Beginning with limitless Liberty, it will arrive at limitless Despotism.

F. M. Dostoevsky

Ladies should cultivate an expression of languid uselessness.

Alexandra Magazine

'Mr Plantagenet Palliser'

There is no error so vulgar – that is to say, common or erroneous – as that by which men have been taught to say that mercenary tendencies are bad. A desire for wealth is the source of all progress. Civilization comes from what men call greed. Let your mercenary tendencies be combined with honesty and they cannot take you astray.

Anthony Trollope

Fashionable Life, London

For the fashionable beauty, life is an endless carnival, and dress a round of disguises. She does everything and the wings of Mercury might be attached to her tiny bottines, so rapid are her changes of scene and character. She is a sportswoman, an athlete, a ballroom divinity. She is alternatively a horsewoman, a huntress, a bold and skilful swimmer; she drives a pair of horses like a charioteer, mounts the roof of a four-in-hand, plays lawn tennis, is at home on a race course or the deck of a fast yacht. She is aware of the refinements of dining and has a pretty taste in vintages. She is a power at the theatre or the Opera; and none is more brilliant at a supper party. Of the modern young lady *à la mode*, who wields alike the fiddle-bow, the billiard-cue and the etching-needle, who climbs mountains and knows the gymnasium, none but herself can be the prototype.

>   *Graphic Magazine*

On Madame Grévy, Wife of the French President

I don't want the Princess to be seen with that cook.

>   Edward, Prince of Wales

A Nineteenth-Century Aunt

Aunt Stella eloped when she was sixteen with a well-known Bavarian artist, Alexander Svoboda. My grandfather would not tolerate this love affair, and he must, I think, have locked her into a room, for we were told she escaped by climbing up the wide chimney of a Moorish house, her sisters helping her to drag up a box by a rope. I take it she was successfully helped down into the street, where Svoboda was waiting for her . . .

The marriage was not happy; Svoboda was intensely jealous. Aunt Stella had a bird, which used to feed from her lips. One day this infuriated Svoboda . . . in a fit of jealousy, wrung the bird's neck before her eyes . . .

My Aunt Stella died at twenty-nine, leaving behind her just this little sequence: her beauty, her young love, her escape up the chimney, her bird killed to spite her, and her early death.

>   Mrs Patrick Campbell

Destiny

There is a destiny now possible for us, the highest ever set before a nation to be accepted or refused. We are still undegenerate in race; a race mingled with the best northern blood . . . Will you youths of England make your country again a royal throne of kings, a sceptred isle, for all the world a source of delight; mistress of learning and the arts, faithful guardian of the honoured principles! This is what England must do or perish, she must found colonies as fast as she is able, formed of her most energetic and worthiest men, seizing every piece of fruitful ground she can set foot on and there teaching her colonists that their first aim is to advance the power of England by land and sea.

John Ruskin

The British

I believe in this race, the greatest governing race, so proud, so tenacious, self-confident and determined, this race which neither climate nor change can degenerate, which will infallibly be the predominating force of future heritage and universal civilization.

Joseph Chamberlain

The noblest men methinks are bred
Of ours the Saxon-Norman race.

Alfred Tennyson

No man will treat with indifference the principle of race. It is the key to history.

Benjamin Disraeli

Religious Decline

Of this I am sure as of the motion of the earth. My belief is that Faith has gone from society as such; morals are going and politics will end with the paralysis of the governing power. The end of this must be anarchy or despotism. How soon I do not know . . . My belief is that society without Christianity is like the Commune.

Archbishop Manning, to W. E. Gladstone

Scepticism

It appears that the Caribs, who know little of theology, regard thieving as a practice peculiarly connected with Christian tenets, and probably they could allege experiential grounds for this.

George Eliot

THE TAY BRIDGE

Beautiful Railway Bridge of the Silvery Tay!
I hope that God will protect all passengers
By night and by day,
And that no accident will befall them while crossing
The Bridge of the Silvery Tay,
For that would be the most awful to be seen
Near by Dundee and the Magdalen Green.

The failing North British Railway, in an attempt to outbid the rival Caledonian Railway, had decided, in 1870, to span the Tay River, assisted by the Dundee Provost and Council, themselves in commercial conflict with Perth and needing to outflank competitors by a swifter route. Completed by 1877, the Bridge, nearly two miles long, was hailed as the greatest in the world, the masterpiece of Victorian civil engineering.

Beautiful Railway Bridge of the Silvery Tay!
Which will cause great rejoicing on the opening day,
And hundreds of people will come from far away,
Also the Queen, most gorgeous to be seen,
Near by Dundee and the Magdalen Green.

Beautiful Railway Bridge of the Silvery Tay!
And prosperity to Provost Cox, who has given
Thirty thousand pounds and upwards away
In helping to erect the Bridge of the Tay,
Most handsome to be seen,
Near by Dundee and the Magdalen Green.

Doubts followed. The central arches swayed ominously in high winds. Painters discovered fallen bolts, seven foot rents, undue rust. Preachers denounced the use of the bridge on the Sabbath, perceptively enough, for on Sunday December 28, 1879, the Great Storm tossed away the central span, hurling an entire train into the torrents a hundred feet below. Weeks later, North British Railway were still paying £5 for each body hooked out of the water. The Inquiry at Westminster Hall revealed an unqualified Inspector, shoddy foundry work, faulty design, criminal irresponsibility in maintenance – holes repaired with beeswax coated with iron dust – parts of the structure built not on rock but on gravel.

Oh! Ill-fated Bridge of the Silvery Tay,
I must now conclude my lay
By telling the world fearlessly without the least dismay
That your central girders would not have given way,
At least many sensible men do say,
Had they been supported on each side with buttresses,
At least many sensible men confesses,
For the stronger we our houses do build,
The less chance we have of being killed.

      The Great McGonagall

Hints of the Tay and its bridge may possibly exist in T. S. Eliot's 'Four Quartets'.

From *The Brothers Karamazov*

She grew up under the roof of a general's widow, a wealthy old lady of good position, who was simultaneously benefactress and tormentor. I am ignorant of details, but have only heard that the orphan girl, meek and gentle, was once cut down from a halter in which she was dangling from a nail in the loft, so terrible were her sufferings from the whims and unending nagging of this crone, apparently not naturally vicious but rendered an impossible tyrant through idleness.

      F. M. Dostoevsky

'There are moments when people love crime,' said Alyosha thoughtfully.

'Yes, yes. You have uttered my thought, they love crime, they always love it, not merely at "certain moments". You know, it's as if people had agreed to tell lies about it, and have done so ever since. They all imagine they hate evil, but secretly they all adore it.'

      F. M. Dostoevsky

There is a soundless and long-suffering sorrow encountered amongst peasants. It withdraws into itself and is still. But a grief exists, breaking out and releasing itself in wailing. This is particularly common amongst the women. But it is no lighter a grief than the silent. Lamentations comfort only by tearing the heart still more. Such grief does not want consolation. It actually feeds on the sense of its hopelessness. Lamentations rise only from the constant craving to re-open the wound.

> F. M. Dostoevsky

If you and I were truly righteous, no third person would become a criminal.

> F. M. Dostoevsky

Lisa and Alyosha

'Alyosha, is it true that at Easter the Jews steal a child and kill it?'

'I don't know.'

'There's a book here in which I read about the trial of a Jew, who took a child four years old and cut off the fingers from both hands, and then crucified him on the wall, hammered nails into him and crucified him, and afterwards, when on trial, said that the child died soon, within four hours. That was meant by "soon". He said the child moaned, kept on moaning, and he stood there admiring it! How lovely!'

'Lovely?'

'Lovely! Sometimes I imagine that it was I who'd done the crucifying. He'd hang there doing his moans and I'd sit there in front of him eating pineapple compote. I'm terribly fond of pineapple compote. Do you enjoy it?'

Silently, Alyosha regarded her. Her face, pale, sallow, suddenly contorted: her eyes burned.

'You know, when I read about that Jew I shook with sobs all night long. I kept fancying how the little chap cried and moaned . . . and always the thought of pineapple compote haunted me.' ·

> F. M. Dostoevsky

Man is seeking not so much God as the miraculous.

> F. M. Dostoevsky

My father has been murdered, and they pretend they are horrified. They keep up the sham with each other. Liars! They all desire the death of their fathers.

F. M. Dostoevsky

The arch-noxious Dostoevsky.

Lenin, 1913

Lord Ernest Hamilton's Childhood

With his brothers Ernest had watched tray-loads of gold and silver ornaments being polished prior to being carried up to the great dining-room. The most interesting to him were the four massive deer-stalking groups modelled by Landseer which were to occupy the centre of the table. These were flanked by squadrons of figures in silver offering salt, and overhead a colossal silver chandelier weighing nearly half a ton hung menacingly from the ceiling, while the sideboard glistened under the weight of huge embossed salvers adroitly poised on their edges, and all the dishes used during the first six courses were of solid silver. How irritating for the little boys to hear that the sideboards at Dudley House were 'piled up to the ceiling with gold plate'. Knowing the servants intimately, they could see that the house steward was anxious. 'The entire responsibility for success or failure rested on his well-set, massive shoulders and only too well did he know that of the imposing platoon of six-foot servitors on whom the diners were dependent, he himself was the only one who was strictly sober . . . '

He, and the 'Groom of the Chambers' my father's valet – usually a sober and virtuous man who on these occasions, always got drunk and got into everyone's way like the clown at the circus – were in the conventional dress of the family butler. Temporarily resplendent in pink and silver, the under-butler and three footmen stood majestically in the background, their equilibrium, which was certain to be slightly impaired before the close of the evening, being so far irreproachable . . . Behind the scenes, so to speak, but open to our view if not to that of the diners, was a little army of shirt-sleeved underlings hurrying up the innumerable courses from the kitchen and rushing off with piles of dirty silver plates to be washed and polished up for the next course but one. This last, of course, was a stage secret not disclosed to the public.

Prepared by the Italian chef there would be soup, fish, two consecutive entrées, joint, game, sweet and savouries, followed, quaintly enough, by bread and cheese and mustard and cress – supposed I believe to clean the palate for the serious business of after-dinner drinking.

Anita Leslie

1880–89

THE GENERAL ELECTION: A SCRUTINEER AT THE ELBOW OF MARY'S AGENT—(SEE PAGE 30.)

A Story

In the year of 1879, just after I had left Oxford, I met at a reception at the house of one of the Foreign Ministers a woman of very curious exotic beauty. We became great friends, and were constantly together. And yet what interested me most in her was not her beauty, but her character, her entire vagueness of character. She seemed to have no personality at all, but simply the possibility of many types. Sometimes she would give herself up entirely to art, turn her drawing-room into a studio, and spend two or three days a week at picture galleries or museums. Then she would take to attending race-meetings, wear the most horsey clothes, and talk about nothing but betting. She abandoned religion for mesmerism, mesmerism for politics, and politics for the melodramatic excitements of philanthropy. In fact, she was a kind of Proteus, and as much a failure in all her transformations as was that wondrous sea-god when Odysseus laid hold of him. One day a serial began in one of the French magazines. At that time I used to read serial stories, and I well remember the shock of surprise I felt when I came to the description of the heroine. She was so like my friend that I brought her the magazine, and she recognized herself in it immediately, and seemed fascinated by the resemblance. I should tell you, by the way, that the story was translated from some dead Russian writer, so that the author had not taken his type from my friend. Well, to put the matter briefly, some months afterwards I was in Venice, and finding the magazine in the reading-room of the hotel, I took it up casually to see what had become of the heroine. It was a most piteous tale, as the girl had ended by running away with a man absolutely inferior to her, not merely in social station, but in character and intellect also. I wrote to my friend that evening about my views on John Bellini, and the admirable ices at Florian's, and the artistic value of gondolas, but added a postscript to the effect that her double in the story had behaved in a very silly manner. I don't know why I added that, but I remember I had a sort of dread over me that she might do the same thing. Before my letter had reached her, she had run away with a man who deserted her in six months. I saw her in 1884 in Paris, where she was living with her mother, and I asked her whether the story had had anything to do with her action. She told me that she had felt an absolutely irresistible impulse to follow the heroine step by step in her strange and fatal progress, and that it was with a feeling of real terror that she had looked forward to the last few chapters of the story. When they appeared, it seemed to her that she was compelled to reproduce them in life, and she did so. It was a most clear example of this imitative instinct of which I was speaking, and an extremely tragic one.

> Oscar Wilde

Indian Empire

After a long course of happy rule, we may surrender India to natives, grown into a capability of self-government. Our posterity may then see an experiment of the glorious spectacle we now witness when India shall be added to the roll of free and independent Powers that wait on the Mother Country, and daily rise up and call her blessed. But to attain this end we must train them to British sentiments, infuse into them British principles, imbue them with British feeling, and rising from the vulgar notion of an Emperor, teach them that the deepest thought and the noblest expression of a genuine Briton is to fear God and honour the King.

> Lord Salisbury

Existence is conflict with fiends
That swarm in the brain and heart;
To write is to summon one's self
And to act the judge's part.

> Henrik Ibsen

A gentleman cannot do better than to marry a lady. And though it is much to be a nobleman, it is more to be a gentleman.

> Anthony Trollope

Paris

It is in the Rue de la Paix where the veritable Temple of Fashion is situate and the *Sanctum Sanctorum* of feminine frivolity, over the more than Eleusinian mysteries of which the great Worth presides in person. The masculine eye has no more chance of penetrating its arcana than those of the Bona Dea; yet reports have from time to time reached me that the hierophant combines the suavity of a Grenville, the diplomatic address of a Metternich, the firmness of a Wellington, and the prompt *coup d'oeil* of a Napoleon: and that before him princesses discrown themselves, duchesses tremble, countesses bow their aristocratic heads in mute acquiescence, and citizenesses of the Transatlantic Republic humbly abnegate that self-assertiveness which is one of their most prominent characteristics.

> George Augustus Sala

Afternoon Tea

Under certain circumstances there are few hours in life more agreeable than the hour dedicated to the ceremony known as afternoon tea. There are circumstances in which, whether you partake of the tea or not – some people of course never do – the situation is in itself delightful. Those that I have in mind in beginning to unfold this simple history offered an admirable setting to an innocent pastime. The implements of the little feast had been disposed upon the lawn of an old English country house in what I should call the perfect middle of a splendid summer afternoon. Part of the afternoon had waned, but much of it was left, and what was left was of the finest and rarest quality. Real dusk would not arrive for many hours; but the flood of summer light had begun to ebb, the air had grown mellow, the shadows were long upon the smooth, dense turf. They lengthened slowly, however, and the scene expressed that sense of leisure still to come which is perhaps the chief source of one's enjoyment of such a scene at such an hour. From five o'clock to eight is on certain occasions a little eternity; but on such an occasion as this the interval could be only an eternity of pleasure. The persons concerned in it were taking their pleasure quietly, and they were not of the sex which is supposed to furnish the regular votaries of the ceremony I have mentioned. The shadows on the perfect lawn were straight and angular; they were the shadows of an old man sitting in a deep wicker-chair near the low table on which the tea had been served, and of two younger men strolling to and fro, in desultory talk, in front of him. The old man had his cup in his hand; it was an unusually large cup, of a different pattern from the rest of the set and painted in brilliant colours.

> Henry James

It has always been the uneasy, spiritless and exhausted ages which have played with the idea of perpetual peace. Condemnation of war is absurd and immoral.

> Heinrich von Treitschke

War is a moral medicine used by Nature when she has no other ways of restoring people to the right path.

> Otto von Bismarck

A Nihilist, before Trial and Condemnation for Assisting in the Murder of Tsar Alexander II

MY DEAR, ADORED MAMMA,
The thought of you oppresses and torments me always. My darling, I implore you to be calm, and not to grieve for me; for my fate does not afflict me in the least, and I shall meet it with complete tranquillity, for I have long expected it, and have known that sooner or later it must come. And I assure you, dear mamma, that my fate is not such a very mournful one. I have lived as my convictions dictated, and it would have been impossible for me to have acted otherwise. I await my fate, therefore, with a tranquil conscience, whatever it may be. The only thing which oppresses me is the thought of your grief, oh, my adored mother! It is that which rends my heart; and what I would not give to be able to alleviate it? My dear, dear mother, remember that you have still a large family, so many grown-up, and so many little ones, all of whom have need of

you, have need of your great moral strength. The thought that I
have been unable to raise myself to your great moral height has
always grieved me to the heart. Whenever, however, I felt myself
wavering, it was always the thought of you which sustained me. I
will not speak to you of my devotion to you; you know that from my
infancy you were always the object of my deepest and fondest love.
Anxiety for you was the greatest of my sufferings. I hope that you
will be calm, that you will pardon me the grief I have caused you,
and not blame me too much; your reproof is the only one that would
grieve my heart.

In fancy I kiss your hands again and again, and on my knees I
implore you not to be angry with me.

Remember me most affectionately to all my relatives.

And I have a little commission for you, my dear mamma. Buy me
some cuffs and collars; the collars rather narrow, and the cuffs with
buttons, for studs are not allowed to be worn here. Before appear-
ing at the trial, I must mend my dress a little, for it has become much
worn here. Good-bye till we meet again, my dear mother. Once
more, I implore you not to grieve, and not to afflict yourself for me.
My fate is not such a sad one after all, and you must not grieve about
it.

Sophia Perovskaya

Trieste

I respectfully report that at seven o'clock today, in the small
courtyard of the main barracks, the execution took place of the
deserter of the 22nd Infantry Regiment, Wilhelm Oberdank.

Since the day before yesterday, when the sentence was
announced to him, he has behaved not only with resolution but with
outright insolence. He rejected the spiritual solace offered by the
curate, the Reverend Huth, stating in the brusquest possible manner that he was a complete atheist. When this morning, at the foot of
the gallows, Major Judge-Advocate Fongarolli read out the death
sentence once more to him, he repeatedly nodded his head in
agreement. After this reading, and while the hangman Willen-
bacher and his helpers put the shackles on him and the other
preparations for the execution took place, he continually shouted,
'Long live Italy! Long live free Trieste! Out with the strangers!'

These shouts could be heard above the rolling of the drums until they drowned in his death rattle.

> Senior Police Inspector Zempirek, to the Director of Police, Trieste

If one could judge a man's importance by the number of streets named after him, Oberdank would rank close to Dante or Verdi.

> Alfred Alexander, 1977

There is not a spot upon the whole map, where you can lay your finger and say, there Austria did good.

> W. E. Gladstone

The New Man

Become hard. Your greatest gentleness must become your greatest hardness. Those who are consistently protective towards themselves will thereby make themselves sickly . . . To see *much*, one must learn to look away from oneself – every mountaineer must learn to climb over himself and look above himself . . . I have not reached my peak until I can look down on myself and on my stars.

> Friedrich Nietzsche

I advise you that not work but war, war and bravery, have done more glorious deeds than love for one's kin.

> Friedrich Nietzsche

Paris

Turgenev's funeral brought out of Paris homes a swarm of creatures with gigantic bodies, squashed features and God the Father beards; a little Russia whose existence in the capital none of us has ever suspected.

> *The Goncourt Journal*

London, 1882

It is difficult to speak adequately, or justly, of London. It is not a pleasant place; it is not agreeable, or easy, or exempt from reproach. It is only magnificent.

Henry James

Education

You go to a great school not so much for knowledge as for arts and habits. For the habit of attention, for the art of expression. For the art of entering quickly into another person's thoughts. For the art of indicating assent or dissent in graduated terms. For the art of working out what is possible in a given time. For taste, for discrimination, for mental courage and mental soberness.

William Cory

Education: a Girl's View

I amused myself by studying the teacher's mannerisms in voice, movement of jaw, roving of eye, or nervous fidgeting with her brooch. Choice bits of careful English were also treasured, such as 'Commence at the commencement'. With imitations of these I regaled my fellows during the scanty times when we were allowed to talk. The girl who usually sat next to me would laugh on the slightest provocation, and it was my cue to upset her by moving my hand sideways in an impressive manner whenever the teacher said something more than usually fatuous. There was no rule against this gesture, though we amused ourselves by framing one that would meet the case: 'No girl must move her hand sideways in class'.

Marks were the life-blood of the school. No work whatever was done without them, so that a large proportion of time was consumed in assigning them, counting them, entering them in huge books, adding them, and checking them. Great precautions were taken against cheating, as if this were the natural thing to expect. Tests done in class were marked by one's neighbour. Each desk was provided with a board that could be fixed into iron sockets at the edge and form a screen, so that the next girl couldn't see what one was writing. After every test done in class there would follow a cascade of questions as to whether some answer might 'count' or not. Thus:

'Please will it count if 1488 is put instead of 1588 for the Armada?'

'Well, dear, give it a half-mark.' . . .

The study of a play of Shakespeare's was simplicity itself. We had to learn the footnotes given in our texts. These consisted mainly of foolish paraphrases of any lines supposed to be obscure, and it was in these notes, believe me, and not in the text, that we had to be word-perfect.

M. V. Hughes

Words

Ah, but I love to draw beautiful words, like trumpets of light . . . I adore you, words who are sensitive to our sufferings, words in red and lemon yellow, words in the steel-blue colour of certain insects, words with the scent of vibrant silks, subtle words of fragrant roses and sea-weed, prickly words of sky-blue wasps, words with powerful snouts, words of spotless ermine, words spat out by the sands of the sea, words greener than the Cyrene fleece, discreet words whispered by fishes in the pink ears of shells, bitter words, words of fleur-de-lis and Flemish corn-flowers, sweet words with a pictorial ring, plaintive words of horses being beaten, evil words, festive words, tornado and storm-tossed words, windy words, reedy words, the wise words of children, rainy, tearful words, words without rhyme or reason, I love you! I love you!

James Ensor

Women's Burden, Their Bodies

They begin to shape us to our cursed end . . . when we are tiny things in shoes and socks. We sit with our little feet drawn up under us in the window, and look out at the boys in their happy play. We want to go. Then a loving hand is laid on us: 'Little one, you cannot go,' they say; 'your little face will burn and your nice white dress be spoiled.' We feel it must be for our good, it is so lovingly said; but we cannot understand; and we kneel still with one little cheek wistfully pressed against the pane. Afterwards we go and string blue beads, and make a string for our neck; and we go and stand before the glass. We see the complexion we are not to spoil, and the white frock, and we begin to look into our own great eyes. Then the curse begins to act on us. It finishes its work when we are grown women, who no more look out wistfully at a more healthy life; we are contented.

Olive Schreiner

POOR BUT HONEST

She was poor, but she was honest,
  Victim of the squire's whim:
First he loved her, then he left her,
  And she lost her honest name.

Then she ran away to London,
  For to hide her grief and shame;
There she met another squire,
  And she lost her name again.

See her riding in her carriage,
  In the Park and all so gay:
All the nibs and nobby persons
  Come to pass the time of day.

See the little old-world village
  Where her aged parents live,
Drinking the champagne she sends them;
  But they never can forgive.

In the rich man's arms she flutters,
  Like a bird with broken wings:
First he loved her, then he left her,
  And she hasn't got a ring.

See him in the splendid mansion,
  Entertaining with the best,
While the girl that he has ruined,
  Entertains a sordid guest.

See him in the House of Commons,
  Making laws to put down crime,

While the victim of his passions
    Trails her way through mud and slime.

Standing on the bridge at midnight,
    She says: 'Farewell, blighted Love.'
There's a scream, a splash – Good Heavens!
    What is she a-doing of?

Then they drag her from the river,
    Water from her clothes they wrang,
For they thought that she was drownded;
    But the corpse got up and sang:

'It's the same the whole world over,
    It's the poor that gets the blame,
It's the rich that gets the pleasure.
    Isn't it a blooming shame?'
                    Anon

EXPULSION

As for me I'll hand you the truth,
Princes – they're capitalists,
The Worker's exploited,
Behold, the death of the socialist.

Together with princes, down with the aristocrats,
Out with police, throw away generals,
Wipe out the disgusting rich in their mansions
Drunk on the Worker's sweat.

At last, when everyone's downed,
There'll only be anarchists around.
                    Maurice MacNab (Paris Cabaret Song)

On Prayer

Our view is that a special form of prayer for the cholera is not a sign

of gratitude or confidence in the Almighty, and is signally and
distinctly undesirable.

> Queen Victoria, to the Archbishop of Canterbury

London Poor

Before going to the lower depths, where our investigations were
principally carried on, we find in the neighbourhood of Old Ford, in
147 consecutive houses, inhabited for the most part by the respectable working class, 212 families, 118 of which never, under any
circumstances, attend a place of worship. Out of 2,290 persons
living in consecutive houses at Bow Common, only 88 adults and 47
children ever attend, and as 64 of these are connected with one
Mission Hall, only 24 out of the entire number worship elsewhere.
One street off Leicester Square contains 246 families, and only 12 of
these are ever represented at the house of God. In another street in
Pentonville, out of 100 families only 12 persons attend any sanctuary, whilst the number of attendants in one district of St George's-
in-the-East is 39 persons out of 4,235. Often the numbers given of
those who do attend include such as only go once or twice a year, at
some charity distribution, so that our figures are more favourable
than the actual facts. Constantly we come across persons who have
never been to church or chapel for 20 years, 28 years, more than 30
years; and some persons as old as 64 never remember having been in
a place of worship at all. Indeed, with the exception of a very small
proportion, the idea of going has never dawned upon these people.

> Andrew Mearns

Consolation

The poor have the Gospel preached to them still, and many a cup of
pure bright pleasure does it lift to their lips . . . they went back to
their poor hovels, their cabbage, their crust, and their dull monotonous work, feeling that life was not all a bare dry desert.

> J. Baldwin Brown

The World, 1883

The World is too much occupied . . . with the reciprocal cannonading and chopping, with cutting of throats and burning of homes, with murder of infants and mutilation of mothers, with warding off of famine and civil war, with lamenting the failure of its sources, the dullness of trade, the emptiness of its pocket.

Henry James

On his Landlady's Daughter

She's an English character. She's what they call in England 'a person'. She isn't a lady and she isn't a woman; she's a person.

Henry James

Progress

My father used to say that the world had only improved in three respects in his lifetime. Anaesthetics had been discovered, antiseptics had been introduced and torture was no longer used in any civilized country.

Anthony Eden, 1976

The Materialist

There are two deadly sins. Vanity and meanness – shun these more than adultery, murder or parricide. Make your brain and body a cunning instrument in the hand of your will, and dissociate your mind from sympathy with the weapon. Disabuse your mind of the illusion of identity, associate yourself with the great humanity of making, teaching, conquering the dead world. Be an enthusiast devoid of sentiment, a dumb prophet like Moses, a materialist in earnest. This is

the true gospel of
faithfully your friend,
H. G. Wells, to A. T. Simmons

Richard Wagner dies, 1883

It may be he was mistaken in supposing that the modern world could ever recapture the attitude of ancient Greece to the religious aspect of musical aroma, but he certainly induced it to take music, and especially opera, far more seriously than it had ever done before.

Edward J. Dent, 1940

You want only to understand,
Always, what you have always known,
My own mind reaches out towards
Things that have never occurred.

Richard Wagner

My passion of the Wagnerian enchantment has been with me ever since I was first aware of it and began to make it my own and infuse it with my understanding. All that I owe to him, of enjoyment and enlightenment, I can never forget: hours of profound and unalloyed radiance within crowded theatres, hours of nervous and intellectual transcendence and joy, perceptions of great and moving significance, such as given only by this art.

Thomas Mann, 1933

The most boring German *canaille*, notwithstanding all his fame.

F. M. Dostoevsky

In the growth of civilization, so destructive to man, we can at least anticipate this happy conclusion: the burdens and fetters it piles on nature assume such huge proportions that finally it creates in crushed but indestructible Nature the pressure essential to shed them with a single violent gesture.

Richard Wagner

Here is a musician who is a greater master than all others in discovering tones peculiar to souls suffering, oppressed, tortured, who can articulate even dumb misery. None can touch him in rendering the colours of late autumn, in the indescribably affecting delight of a last, a very last, and all too brief gladness; he knows a chord expressing the soul's secret and weird midnight hours, when cause and effect seem to have fallen asunder.

Friedrich Nietzsche

None of his heroines bears children.

> Friedrich Nietzsche

Wagner has done undeniable good in humbling the singers.

> Max Beerbohm

I do not understand all this fuss about Wagner: after all, the fellow was only a simple conductor.

> Kaiser Wilhelm II

Table Manners

On one occasion Wagner became so upset to discover himself not leading the conversation, and, in fact, to observe his guests quietly chatting among themselves that, to regain their attention, he simply opened his mouth and screamed.

> Robert Gutman, 1979

A pretentious bag of tricks.

> Leo Tolstoy

A Girl Student at Cambridge, 1885

To go steadily on in the path one has chosen, in spite of trouble, disappointment and even pain – how hard it is! How dark everything looks sometimes – all evil so possible, all good so unlikely. How one longs to give in – to struggle no more – but the will is still there, and reason knows that when the cloud has cleared away, the path will look as clear and right as before – and in spite of the weakness and weariness of the body – these two, will and reason, will not let us despair nor turn back from the plough. On the rack we cry for mercy, but with cessation of pain comes renewed strength of purpose and fresh determination to endure.

> Winnie Seebohm

Karl Marx's Daughter 'Tussy'

My Olive, I wonder if I bore you with my stupid letters – as I wonder if, one of these days you will get horribly tired of me altogether. This is no figure of speech. I really *do* wonder, or rather fear. I have such a terror of losing your love . . . I keep wanting to hear you say you love me just a little. You do not know, Oh, how my whole nature craves for love. And since my parents died I have had so little *real* – i.e. pure, unselfish love. If you had ever been in our home, if you had ever seen my father and mother, known what *he* was to me, you would understand better both my yearning for love, given and received, and my intense need for sympathy . . . Edward is dining with Quilter and went off in the highest of spirits because several ladies are to be there (and it just occurs to me, that you may be one! How odd that would be!) and I am alone, and while in some sense relieved to be alone, it is also terrible . . . I would give anything just now to be near you . . . How natures like Ed's (i.e. pure Irish and French) are to be envied, who in an hour completely forget anything . . . With all the pain and sorrow (and not even you, my Olive, know quite how unhappy I am), it is better to have these stronger feelings than to have practically no feelings at all. It is too bad of me to go on scribbling like this. But you would forgive me if you knew the help it is to me. Writing to you I see your dear face before me and that gives me courage and strength. Write me a line. Just one line – say you love me. That will be such a joy, it will help me get through the long miserable days, and longer, more miserable nights, with less heavy a heart. There is so little in me to like or interest people. That *you* care for me is one of those mysteries that remain for ever inexplicable. Good night, little girl . . .

      Eleanor Marx, to Olive Schreiner

Victorian Country Life

'For my part I don't see why men who have got wives, and don't want 'em, shouldn't get rid of 'em as those gipsy fellows do their old horses,' said the man in the tent. 'Why shouldn't they put 'em up and sell 'em by auction to men who are in want of such articles? Hey? Why, begad, I'd sell mine this minute if anybody would buy her!'

    'There's them that would do that,' some of the guests replied, looking at the woman, who was by no means ill-favoured.

'True,' said a smoking gentleman, whose coat had the fine polish about the collar, elbows, seams, and shoulder-blades that long-continued friction with grimy surfaces will produce, and which is usually more desired in furniture than on clothes. From his appearance he had possibly been in former times groom or coachman to some neighbouring county family. 'I've had my breedings in as good circles, I may say, as any man,' he added, 'and I know true cultivation, or nobody do; and I can declare she's got it – in the bone, mind ye, I say – as much as any female in the fair – though it may want a little bringing out.' Then, crossing his legs, he resumed his pipe with a nicely-adjusted gaze at a point in the air.

The fuddled young husband stared for a few seconds at this unexpected praise of his wife, half in doubt of the wisdom of his own attitude towards the possessor of such qualities. But he speedily lapsed into his former conviction, and said harshly:

'Well, then, now is your chance; I am open to an offer for this gem o' creation.'

She turned to her husband and murmured, 'Michael, you have talked this nonsense in public places before. A joke is a joke, but you may make it once too often, mind!'

'I know I've said it before; I meant it. All I want is a buyer.'

Thomas Hardy

Captain Sholto

Sholto was a curious and not particularly edifying English type, as the Princess further described him; one of those odd figures produced by old societies that have run to seed, corrupt and exhausted civilizations. He was a cumberer of the earth – purely selfish for all his devoted disinterested airs. He was nothing whatever in himself and had no character or merit save by tradition, reflection, imitation, superstition. He had a longish pedigree – he came of some musty mouldy 'county family', people with a local reputation and an immense lack of general importance; he had taken the greatest care of his little fortune. He had travelled all over the globe several times, 'for the shooting', in that murdering ravaging way of the English, the destruction, the extirpation of creatures more beautiful, more soaring and more nimble than themselves. He had a little taste, a little cleverness, a little reading, a little good furniture, a little French and Italian (he exaggerated these latter quantities), an immense deal of assurance and unmitigated leisure. That, at bottom, was all he represented – idle, trifling, luxurious, yet at the same time pretentious leisure, the sort of thing that led people to invent false humbugging duties because they had no real ones. Sholto's great idea of himself, after his profession of being her slave, was that he was a cosmopolite and exempt from every prejudice. About the prejudices the Princess couldn't say and didn't care; but she had seen him in foreign countries, she had seen him in Italy, and she was bound to say he understood nothing of those people.

Henry James

Paris

He passed down the Rue Royale, where comparative stillness reigned; and when he reached the Place de la Concorde, to cross the bridge which faces the Corps Législatif, he found himself almost isolated. He had left the human swarm and the obstructed pavements behind, and the wide spaces of the splendid square lay quiet under the summer stars. The plash of the great fountains was audible and he could almost hear the wind-stirred murmur of the little wood of the Tuileries on one side and of the vague expanse of the Champs Élysées on the other. The place itself – the Place Louis Quinze, the Place de la Révolution – had given him a sensible emotion from the day of his arrival; he had recognized so quickly its tremendous historic character. He had seen in a rapid vision the guillotine in the middle, on the site of the inscrutable obelisk, and the tumbrils, with waiting victims, were stationed around the circle now made majestic by the monuments of the cities of France. The great legend of the French Revolution, a sunrise out of a sea of blood, was more real to him here than anywhere else; and, strangely, what was most present was not its turpitude and horror, but its magnificent energy, the spirit of creation that had been in it, not the spirit of destruction. That shadow was effaced by the modern fairness of fountain and statue, the stately perspective and composition; and as he lingered before crossing the Seine a sudden sense overtook him, making his heart falter to anguish – a sense of everything that might hold one to the world, of the sweetness of not dying, the fascination of great cities, the charm of travel and discovery, the generosity of admiration.

Henry James

The City of Light: Paris, 1886

The neighbours of an establishment famous for its excellent bread, pastry, and similar products of luxury, complained again and again of the disgusting smells which prevailed therein and which penetrated into their dwellings. The appearance of cholera finally lent force to those complaints, and the sanitary inspectors who were sent to investigate the matter found that there was a connection between the water-closets of these dwellings and the reservoir containing the water used in the preparation of the bread. This connection was cut off at once, but the immediate result thereof was a perceptible deterioration of the quality of the bread. Chemists had no difficulty in demonstrating that water impregnated with 'extract of water-closet' has the peculiar property of causing dough to rise particularly fine, thereby imparting to bread the nice appearance and pleasant flavour which is the principal quality of luxurious bread.

The General Homeopathic Journal

A Letter from Berlin, 1888

A storekeeper in Berlin was punished some years ago for having used the urine of young girls with a view to make his cheese richer and more piquant. Notwithstanding, people went, bought and ate his cheese with delight.

Dr Gustav Jaeger, to J. G. Bourke

Russia: The Convict Settlement

The women, bent under bundles and knapsacks, trudge along the road: apathetic, still affected by sea-sickness, followed like buskers at a fair by crowds of peasants, urchins and hangers-on of government offices. It is like the herring swarming in the river Aniva, pursued by regiments of whales, seals and dolphins lusting for a dainty morsel of roe.

Anton Chekhov

We have let millions of men rot in prisons, let them rot barbarously, without reason; we have driven men in manacles for tens of thousands of miles, we have infected them with syphilis, we have corrupted them morally, we have multiplied the numbers of prisons and blamed it all on red-nosed prison officials.

> Anton Chekhov

I am neither liberal nor conservative, nor monk, nor a neutralist. I would like to be a free artist and no more, and regret that God has not allowed me strength to be one. Pharisaism, stupidity, tyranny, do not only reign in merchants' houses and police stations. I see them in science and literature among the younger men. I regard tags and labels as prejudices. My holy of holies is the human body, health, intelligence, talent, inspiration, and the most absolute freedom imaginable: freedom from violence and lies . . .

> Anton Chekhov

The English always remember that countries taken under Russian protection have all ended by losing their independence.

> Tsar Alexander II

On his socialist rival, Ferdinand Lassalle

The Jewish nigger.

> Karl Marx

All the good in the world has been done either by priests or prigs.

> Beatrice Webb

'Mr Sherlock Holmes'

His ignorance was as remarkable as his knowledge. Of contemporary literature, philosophy and politics he appeared to know next to nothing. Upon my quoting Thomas Carlyle, he inquired in the naïvest way who he might be and what he had done. My surprise reached a climax, however, when I found incidentally that he was ignorant of the Copernican Theory and of the composition of the Solar System. That any civilized human being in this nineteenth century should not be aware that the earth travelled round the sun appeared to be to me such an extraordinary fact that I could hardly realize it.

'You appear to be astonished,' he said smiling at my expression of surprise. 'Now that I do know it I shall do my best to forget it.'

'To forget it!'

'You see,' he explained, 'I consider that a man's brain originally is like a little empty attic, and you have to stock it with such furniture as you choose. A fool takes in all the lumber of every sort that he comes across, so that the knowledge which might be useful to him gets crowded out, or at best is jumbled up with a lot of other things, so that he has a difficulty in laying his hands upon it. Now the skilled workman is very careful indeed as to what he takes into his brain-attic. He will have nothing but the tools which may help him in doing his work, but of these he has a large assortment, and all in the most perfect order. It is a mistake to think that that little room has elastic walls and can distend to any extent. Depend upon it there comes a time when for every addition of knowledge you forget something that you knew before. It is of the highest importance, therefore, not to have useless facts elbowing out the useful ones.'

'But the Solar System!' I protested.

'What the deuce is it to me?' he interrupted impatiently: 'you say that we go round the sun. If we went round the moon it would not make a pennyworth of difference to me or to my work.'

> Sir Arthur Conan Doyle

You mention your name as if I should recognize it, but beyond the obvious facts that you are a bachelor, a scholar, a Freemason and an asthmatic, I know nothing whatever about you.

> Sir Arthur Conan Doyle

The Celebrated Headmistress, Miss Buss

Nowhere could I find a room labelled 'Upper Fourth', although there were several other species of Fourth. Presently I caught sight of a little white-haired old woman, cap on head, and dressed in black rather the worse for wear. Some caretaker or cleaner or something, I thought, but she may possibly have noticed the name of the classrooms; I can but try. So I hailed her in a manner I thought appropriate.

'I say, am I going right for the Upper Fourth, do you happen to know?'

Glaring at me she exclaimed, 'Do you know who I am?'

'I haven't the faintest idea; I've only just come.'

'I am Miss Buss!' and standing back a pace she drew herself up to mark the effect on me. It was not at all what she had expected, for I cheered up and said.

'Oh, then *you* are sure to know the way to the Upper Fourth, and I do so want to get there.'

At this suddenly her face changed, and with a little gay laugh she said, 'That way, child, down the stairs, the first door you come to at the foot. Run along with you.'

M. V. Hughes

A Future Prime Minister at Eight

WINSTON CHURCHILL: Sir, why does *Mensa* mean 'A Table, and O Table'?

THE MASTER: O Table? You would use that in addressing a table, in involving a table. You would use it in speaking to a table.

WINSTON CHURCHILL: But I never do.

THE MASTER: If you are impertinent you will be punished, let me tell you, very severely.

Winston Churchill

Indications of Scholarship

I wrote my name at the top of the page. I wrote down the number of the question, 'I'. After much reflection I put a bracket round it thus, '(I)'. But thereafter I could not think of anything connected with it that was either relevant or true. Incidentally, there arrived from nowhere in particular a blot and several smudges. I gazed for two whole hours at this sad spectacle; and then merciful ushers carried it up to the Headmaster's table. It was from these slender indications of scholarship that Mr Welldon drew the conclusion that I was worthy to pass into Harrow.

Winston Churchill

LOVERS OF LIGHT

Whatever you are, be brave, boys:
The liar's a coward and slave, boys:
Though clever at ruses
And sharp at excuses,
He's a sneaking and pitiful knave, boys.

Whatever you are, be frank, boys:
'tis better than money and rank, boys:
Still cleave to the right,
Be lovers of light,
Be open, above board, and frank, boys.

> *Boy's Own Paper*

Cavalry Charge

You are for the time being lifted up from and out of all petty thoughts of self and for the moment your whole existence, soul and body, seems to revel in a true sense of glory.

> Field Marshal Viscount Wolseley

My first was a cornet
in a regiment of dragoons;
I gave him what he didn't like,
and stole his silver spoons.

> Music Hall Song

In the 1880s

The nocturnal atmosphere had begun to thicken. All sorts of things were happening at night, things incomprehensible and alarming. My parents were sleeping apart. I slept in my father's room. From the door to my mother's room came frightening influences. At night mother was strange and mysterious. One night I saw coming from her door a faintly luminous, indefinite figure whose head detached itself from the neck and floated along in front of me, in the air, like a little moon. Immediately another head was produced and again detached itself. This process was repeated six or seven times. I had anxiety dreams of things that were now small, now large. For instance, I saw a tiny ball at a great distance; gradually it approached, growing steadily into a monstrous and suffocating object. Or I saw telegraph poles with birds sitting on them, and the wires grew thicker and thicker until the terror awoke me.

           C. J. Jung, 1963

To my immense confusion, it occurred to me that I was actually two different persons. One of them was the schoolboy who could not grasp Algebra and was far from sure of himself; the other was important, a high authority, a man not to be trifled with . . . This 'other' was an old man who lived in the eighteenth century, wore buckled shoes and a white wig and went driving in a fly with high, concave rear wheels between which the box was suspended on springs and leather straps.

           C. J. Jung, 1963

'Bloody Sunday'
Trafalgar Square, November 13, 1887

A huge radical and socialist demonstration, for free speech and popular rights, led to a violent confrontation with the police, in which one man was killed and mob-anger smashed windows in Pall Mall. An interested, scarcely heroic, onlooker was George Bernard Shaw.

We asked them for a life of toilsome earning,
They bade us bide their leisure for our bread;
We craved to speak to tell our woeful learning:
We come back speechless, bearing back our dead.
Not one, not one nor thousands must they slay,
But one and all if they would dusk the day.

They will not learn; they have no ears to hearken.
They turn their faces from the eyes of fate:
Their gay-lit halls shut out the skies that darken.
But lo! this dead man knocking at the gate.
Not one, not one nor thousands must they slay,
But one and all if they would dusk the day.

      William Morris

The Growth of a Myth

As regards the future form of the moral consciousness, we may
safely predict that it will be in a sense a return on a higher level to the
ethics of the older society, with the difference that the limitation of
scope to the kinship society in its narrower sense, which was one of
the elements of the dissolution of ancient society, will disappear,
and the identification of individual with social interests will be so
complete that any divorce between the two will be inconceivable to
the average man.

We may say in conclusion that this new ethic is no longer a mere
theoretic speculation, but that many thousands of lives are already
under its inspiration. Its first great popular manifestation was given
in the heroic devotion of the working classes of Paris in the
Commune of 1871 to the idea of true and universal freedom, which
was carried on by no less complete devotion of the little band of
Russian revolutionists who made so little account of their individual
lives in their engrossing passion for the general life of humanity.

William Morris and E. Belfort Bax

Colours

My house here is painted the yellow colour of fresh butter on the
outside with glaringly green shutters; it stands in the full sunlight in a
square which has a green garden with plane trees, oleanders and
acacias. And it is completely whitewashed inside, and the floor is
made of red bricks. And over it there is the intensely blue sky. In
this I can live and breathe, meditate and paint. And it seems to me
that I might go still farther into the South, rather than go up to the
North again, seeing that I am greatly in need of a strong heat, so that
my blood can circulate normally. Here I feel much better than I did
in Paris.

You see, I can hardly doubt that you on your part would also like
the South enormously. The fact is that the sun has never penetrated
us people of the North. It is already a few days since I started writing
this letter, and now I will continue it. In point of fact I was
interrupted these days by my toiling on a new picture representing
the outside of a night café. On the terrace there are the tiny figures
of people drinking. An enormous yellow lantern sheds its light on
the terrace, the house front and the sidewalk, and even casts a
certain brightness on the pavement of the street, which takes a

pinkish violet tone. The gable-topped fronts of the houses in a street stretching away under a blue sky spangled with stars are dark blue or violet and there is a green tree. Here you have a night picture without any black in it, done with nothing but beautiful blue and violet and green, and in these surroundings the lighted square acquires a pale sulphur and greenish citron-yellow colour. It amuses me enormously to paint the night right on the spot. They used to draw and paint the picture in the daytime after the rough sketch. But I find satisfaction in painting things immediately.

Vincent Van Gogh, to his sister Willemion

The Hearth Rug

It was a large room, with deep bay-windows, and the first thing I noticed was that the sofas and chairs were tightly upholstered in the gay Stuart tartan – a proof that to be Queen of Scotland involves painful aesthetic concessions.

On a large hearthrug – tartan, too, I think – in front of the grate, in which I rather fancy a few logs burned (though, given Her Majesty's hardy habits it seems improbable), stood the Queen, conversing with the Empress Eugénie in a lively manner that contrasted with the somewhat halting intercourse at Birkhall. Evidently, I said to myself, the animating effects of a good dinner may be counted on even at the less frivolous European Courts.

Leading up to the two august ladies was an avenue composed of Royal personages, ranged, as I afterwards found out, in order of precedence, the highest in rank being closest to the hearthrug, which avenue, broadening towards its base, gradually became mere ladies and gentlemen of the Court, and finally petered out in a group of Maids of Honour, huddled ingloriously in the bay-window.

What I ought to have done, I believe, was to stand rigid and silent among these last, endeavouring to catch the eye of the Queen and the Princesses, curtsy profoundly when successful, and await events. Will it be believed that what I did was to advance unconcernedly up the avenue, with a polite intention to say 'How do you do' to the Queen? . . .

If a young dog strays up the aisle during church no one says anything, no one does anything, but, none the less, he soon becomes aware that something is wrong. Even so, as the distance between myself and the hearthrug diminished, did I become aware that something was very wrong indeed; my cheerful confidence waned and my step faltered. I saw the Queen slightly turn her head, look at me for a second as if I were some strange insect, and resume her conversation with the Empress. If I had been a Brobdingnagian spider as big as a retriever she would not have acted differently. Someone would remove the creature; that was enough. I did not catch the Empress's eye, but I now know that since she could not shriek, 'Mon Dieu, n'avancez pas!' she must have wished the earth would open and swallow her up. At this moment dear, human Princess Christian, who had come more in contact with low life than the Queen, stepped forward and shook hands with me – and somehow or other, I know not how, I backed away into the obscurity from which I should never have emerged.

Ethel Smythe

Pollution

Cut forests, when it is a matter of urgency, you may, but it is time to stop destroying them. Every Russian forest is cracking under the axe, millions of trees are perishing, the abodes of beasts and birds are being ravaged, rivers are becoming shallow and drying up, wonderful landscapes are disappearing without leaving a trace; and all this because lazy man has not got the sense to stoop to pick up fuel from the ground. One must be a barbarian to burn that beauty in the fireplace, to destroy what we cannot create. Understanding and creative power have been granted to man to multiply what has been given him, but hitherto he has not created, he has only destroyed. The forests grow less and less, the rivers dry up, wild birds disappear, the climate is spoilt, and every day the earth grows poorer and uglier. You look at me ironically, and all I am saying seems to you antiquated and not serious, but when I pass by woods belonging to the peasants, woods which I have saved from being cut down, or when I hear the rustling of the young forest, which I have planted with my own hands, I realize that the climate is to a certain extent also in my power; and if a thousand years hence man is to be happy, I too shall have had a share in it. When I plant a little birch tree and then see how it is growing green and shaking in the wind, my soul is filled with pride from the realization that, thanks to me, there is one more life added on earth.

Anton Chekhov

For Children

Ah little one, with us 'tis so,
We know that soon we all must go;
And so we wonder, whispering low,
  'Whose turn next?'

Out of Town: a Child's Picture Book

From the Raj

To the Almighty God, care of the Rt Hon. Mountstuart E. Grant-
Duff . . .

Indian Petition

Empire

I contend that we are the first race in the world, and the more of the
world we inhabit, the better it is for the human race. I contend that
every acre added to our territory provides for the birth of more of
the English race who otherwise would not be brought into existence. Added to which the absorption of the greater portion of the
world under our rule simply means the end of all wars.

Cecil Rhodes

India

Year by year England sends out fresh drafts for the first fighting-
line, which is officially called the Indian Civil Service. These die, or
kill themselves by overwork, or are worried to death, or broken in
health and hope in order that the land may be protected from death
and sickness, famine and war, and may eventually become capable
of standing alone. It will never stand alone, but the idea is a pretty
one, and men are willing to die for it, and yearly the work of pushing
and coaxing and scolding and petting the country into good living
goes forward. If an advance is made, all credit is given to the native,
while the Englishmen stand back and mop their foreheads. If a
failure occurs the Englishmen step forward and take the blame.

Rudyard Kipling

And so, gentlemen, I say that while we are opposed to imperialism, we are devoted to the Empire.

W. E. Gladstone

The Revolutionary

He would cut up the ceiling of the Veronese into strips, so that everyone might have a little piece.

Henry James

On Queen Victoria

That was a woman! One could do business with her.

Otto von Bismarck

German Naval Power at Hamburg

It is a new world, a new age.

Otto von Bismarck

DANNY DEEVER

'What are the bugles blowin' for?' said Files-on-Parade.
'To turn you out, to turn you out,' the Colour-Sergeant said.
'What makes you look so white, so white?' said Files-on-Parade.
'I'm dreadin' what I've got to watch,' the Colour-Sergeant said.
    For they're hangin' Danny Deever, you can hear the Dead March
        play,
    The Regiment's in 'ollow square – they're hangin' him to-day;
    They've taken of his buttons off an' cut his stripes away,
    An' they're hangin' Danny Deever in the mornin'.

'What makes the rear-rank breathe so 'ard?' said Files-on-Parade.
'It's bitter cold, it's bitter cold,' the Colour-Sergeant said.
'What makes that front-rank man fall down?' said Files-on-Parade.
'A touch o' sun, a touch o' sun,' the Colour-Sergeant said.
    They are hangin' Danny Deever, they are marchin' of 'im round,
    They 'ave 'alted Danny Deever by 'is coffin on the ground;
    An' 'e'll swing in 'arf a minute for a sneakin' shootin' hound –
    O they're hangin' Danny Deever in the mornin'!

'Is cot was right-' and cot to mine,' said Files-on-Parade.
' 'E's sleepin' out an' far to-night,' the Colour-Sergeant said.
'I've drunk 'is beer a score o' times,' said Files-on-Parade.
'E's drinkin' bitter beer alone,' the Colour-Sergeant said.
   They are hangin' Danny Deever, you must mark 'im to 'is place,
   For 'e shot a comrade sleepin' – you must look 'im in the face;
   Nine 'undred of 'is county an' the Regiment's disgrace,
   While they're hangin' Danny Deever in the mornin'.

'What's that so black again the sun?' said Files-on-Parade.
'It's Danny fightin' 'ard for life,' the Colour-Sergeant said.
'What's that that whimpers over'ead?' said Files-on-Parade.
'It's Danny's soul that's passin' now,' the Colour-Sergeant said.
   For they've done with Danny Deever, you can 'ear the quickstep
     play,
   The Regiment's in column, an' they're marchin' us away;
   Ho! the young recruits are shakin', an' they'll want their beer
     to-day,
   After hangin' Danny Deever in the mornin'!
     Rudyard Kipling

All my streaming tears
Flow towards you!
And the last flame in my heart
Is flaring up for *you*!
Oh come back,
My unknown God! My torture! My ultimate happiness.
     Friedrich Nietzsche

Psychologically this talk of feeding the starving is nothing but an impression of the saccharine-sweet sentimentality as characteristic of our intelligentsia.
     Lenin

True goodwill could consist in the shedding of blood. Democracy could not be resisted by legal, but only by military methods.
     Otto von Bismarck

So long as the English are devoted to racing, socialism has no chance
with you.

>   Otto von Bismarck, to Disraeli

FROM FINLAND

Sad is the sea-gull
When swimming in wintry waters
Sadder still the homeless
Wandering in the wide world
Unhappy the heart of the dove
When in picking a foreign pittance
Throbbing the throat of the sparrow
When drinking icy droplets
Colder am I and wretched
Colder still than that.

>   Larin Paraska

IN THE OLD THEATRE, FIESOLE

I traced the Circus whose grey stones incline
Where Rome and dim Etruria interjoin,
Till came a child who showed an ancient coin
That bore the image of a Constantine.

She lightly passed; nor did she once opine
How, better than all books, she had raised for me
In swift perspective Europe's history
Through the vast years of Caesar's sceptred line.

For in my distant plot of English loam
'Twas but to delve, and straightway there to find
Coins of like impress. As with one half blind
Whom common simples cure, her act flashed home
In that mute moment to my opened mind
The power, the pride, the reach of perished Rome.

>   Thomas Hardy

The Universe

It limits us in and it knits us out. It has knitted time, space, death, corruption, despair and all the illusions – and nothing matters. I'll admit, however, that to look at the remorseless is sometimes amusing.

Joseph Conrad, to R. B. Cunningham Grahame

Women

Women spend their lives inactively, dreaming and waiting for something unknown that will give their lives meaning. Their emotional lives are unhealthy as a result, and they become victims of disillusion.

Henrik Ibsen

All the earth is full of tales to him who listens, and does not drive away the poor from his door. The poor are the best of tale-tellers, for they must lay their ear to the ground every night.

Rudyard Kipling

An Ex-Empress in Paris

They come to see me like a Fifth Act.

Eugénie

At Cap Martin

The face was the same. It had kept its delicate oval shape. The eyes had kept their heavenly blue, but the gaze had become diluted. An expanse of blue water inspected you. The blue, and the black eye shadow which underlined it, recalled the tattooed eyes of young sailors who are released from prison when they are old. In those old men you find to your surprise the indelible signs of angry beauty.

The Empress stopped: the blue water looked me up and down. Lucien Daudet introduced me. 'I can no longer decorate poets,' she said, 'here you are, I can give you this' – and with a rapid movement she tore off a white bunch of daphne, offered it to me, watched me put it in my buttonhole and went on with her walk. I walked beside her. She questioned me about dancing – Isadora Duncan and the *Ballet Russe*. She stopped and sometimes burst out laughing. That voice and that laughter – where had I heard it before? It is a memory of the bullring, the laughter and chatter of the young Eugénie de Montijo which were to frighten and fascinate the shy Napoleon III.

Jean Cocteau

A Vulgar Wish

I have been haunted . . . by the vulgar wish to write a novel. There is intense attractiveness in the comparative ease of descriptive writing. Compare it with work in which movements of commodities, percentages, depreciations, averages, and all the ugly horrors of commercial facts are in the dominant place, and must remain so if the work is to remain worthful . . .

What have the whole lot of novels accomplished . . . in the advancement of society on the one and only basis that can bring with it virtue and happiness – scientific method?

Beatrice Webb

From a Novel

Existence seemed hollow and uninteresting. We thought of the happy days of childhood, and sighed. We brightened up a bit, however, over the apple-tart, and, when George drew out a tin of pine-apple from the bottom of the hamper, and rolled it in to the middle of the boat we felt that life was worth living after all.

We are very fond of pine-apple, all three of us. We looked at the picture on the tin; we thought of the juice. We smiled at one another, and Harris got a spoon ready.

Then we looked for the knife to open the tin with. We turned out everything in the hamper. We turned out the bags. We pulled up the boards at the bottom of the boat. We took everything out on to the bank and shook it. There was no tin-opener to be found.

Then Harris tried to open the tin with a pocket-knife, and broke the knife and cut himself badly; and George tried a pair of scissors, and the scissors flew up, and nearly put his eye out. While they were dressing their wounds, I tried to make a hole in the thing with the spiky end of the hitcher, and the hitcher slipped and jerked me out between the boat and the bank into two feet of muddy water, and the tin rolled over, uninjured, and broke a teacup.

Then we all got mad. We took that tin out on the bank, and Harris went up into a field and got a big sharp stone, and I went back into the boat and brought out the mast, and George held the tin and Harris held the sharp end of the stone against the top of it, and I took the mast and poised it high up in the air, and gathered up all my strength and brought it down.

It was George's straw hat that saved his life that day. He keeps that hat now (what is left of it), and, of a winter's evening, when the pipes are lit and the boys are telling stretchers about the dangers they have passed through, George brings it down and shows it round, and the stirring tale is told anew, with fresh exaggerations every time.

Harris got off with merely a flesh wound.

After that I took the tin off myself, and hammered at it with the mast till I was worn out and sick at heart, whereupon Harris took it in hand.

We beat it out flat; we beat it back square; we battered it into every form known to geometry – but we could not make a hole in it. Then George went at it, and knocked it into a shape, so strange, so weird, so unearthly in its wild hideousness, that he got frightened and threw away the mast. Then we all three sat round it on the grass and looked at it.

There was one great dent across the top that had the appearance of a mocking grin, and it drove us furious, so that Harris rushed at the thing, and caught it up, and flung it far into the middle of the river, and as it sank we hurled our curses at it, and we got into the boat and rowed away from the spot, and never paused till we reached Maidenhead.

> Jerome K. Jerome

Lord Salisbury

His calibre is demonstrated by Malcolm's story of an incident which brought war very near, where Lord Salisbury was entertaining Princess Christian at Hatfield. 'It was a brilliant scene, a splendid old-fashioned Yule-tide festival. About the middle of dinner, a footman brought an "urgent" Foreign Office Box containing a despatch. Lord Salisbury unlocked it and read the contents. He apologised to the Princess who said she hoped it brought no disagreeable news.

' "No, not very. It is only to tell me that the Germans have sent two men-of-war into Delagoa Bay."

'One can imagine how a novelist might have dealt with the situation. He would have depicted an embarrassed silence, then general consternation, then the incontinent break-up of the feast; the ordering of a special train to London, and the hurried departure of the Secretary of State. Instead of which Lord Salisbury quietly re-locked the box and said casually to Her Royal Highness with a shrug of his massive shoulders: "What cheek, Madam, what cheek!" and the banquet went blithely on.'

> Anita Leslie

Rule by Gentlemen

Lord Salisbury was accustomed scrupulously to avoid calling a Cabinet when there was racing at Newmarket, and the House of Commons made a practice of adjourning for the Derby.

> Winston Churchill

1890–99

THE · WORKERS · MAY · POLE

[An offering for May-Day 1894 from Walter Crane]

On Killing: Paris

Ah, gentlemen, if the governing classes could go down among the unfortunates! But no, they prefer to remain deaf to their appeals. It seems that a fatality impels them, like the royalty of the eighteenth century, toward the precipice which will engulf them; for woe be to those who remain deaf to the cries of the starving, woe to those who, believing themselves of superior essence, assume the right to exploit those beneath them! There comes a time when the people no longer reason; they rise like a hurricane, and rush onward like a torrent. Then we see bleeding heads impaled on pikes.

Among the exploited, gentlemen, there are two classes of individuals. Those of one class, not realizing what they are and what they might be, take life as it comes, believe that they are born to be slaves, and content themselves with the little that is given them in exchange for their labour. But there are others, on the contrary, who think, who study, and, looking about them, discover social iniquities. Is it their fault if they see clearly and suffer at seeing others suffer? Then they throw themselves into the struggle, and make themselves the bearers of the popular claims.

I know very well that I shall be told that I ought to have confined myself to speech for the vindication of the people's claims. But what can you expect! It takes a loud voice to make the deaf hear. Too long have they answered our voices by imprisonment, the rope, and rifle-volleys. Make no mistake; the explosion of my bomb is not only the cry of the rebel Vaillant, but the cry of an entire class which vindicates its rights, and which will soon add acts to words. For, be sure of it, in vain will they pass laws. The ideas of the thinkers will not halt!

Auguste Vaillant, to his Judges

A Satire on German Mythologists

I am not disposed to run to the extravagant lengths reached by some of the most enthusiastic German scholars. A wholesome warning to these gentlemen was given some years ago by an ingenious French ecclesiastic, who wrote the following argument to prove that Napoleon Bonaparte was a mythological character.

Napoleon is, says the writer, an impersonification of the sun.

1. Between the name Napoleon and Apollo, or Apoleon, the god of the sun, there is but a trifling difference; indeed the seeming difference is lessened, if we take the spelling of his name from the column of the Place Vendôme, where it stands Néapoleó. But this syllable *Né* prefixed to the name of the sun-god is of importance; like the rest of the name it is of Greek origin, and is νη or ναι, a particle of affirmation, as though indicating Napoleon as the very true Apollo, or sun.

His other name, Bonaparte, makes this apparent connexion between the French hero and the luminary of the firmament conclusively certain. The day has its two parts, the good and luminous portion, and that which is bad and dark. To the sun belongs the good part, to the moon and stars belongs the bad portion. It is therefore natural that Apollo or Né-Apoleón should receive the surname of *Bonaparte*.

2. Apollo was born in Delos, a Mediterranean island; Napoleon in Corsica, an island in the same sea. According to Pausanias, Apollo was an Egyptian deity; and in the mythological history of the fabulous Napoleon we find the hero in Egypt, regarded by the inhabitants with veneration, and receiving their homage.

3. The mother of Napoleon was said to be Letitia, which signifies joy, and is an impersonification of the dawn of light dispensing joy and gladness to all creation. Letitia is no other than the break of day, which in a manner brings the sun into the world, and 'with rosy fingers opens the gates of Day'. It is significant that the Greek name for the mother of Apollo was Leto. From this the Romans made the name Latona which they gave to his mother. But *Lœto* is the unused form of the verb *Lœton* and signified to inspire joy; it is from this unused form that the substantive *Letitia* is derived. The identity, then, of the mother of Napoleon with the Greek Leto and the Latin Latona, is established conclusively.

4. According to the popular story, this son of Letitia had three

sisters, and was it not the same with the Greek deity, who had the three Graces?

5. The modern Gallic Apollo had four brothers. It is impossible not to discern here the anthropomorphosis of the four seasons. But, it will be objected, the seasons should be females. Here the French language interposes; for in French the seasons are masculine, with the exception of autumn, upon the gender of which grammarians are undecided, whilst Autumnus in Latin is not more feminine than the other seasons. This difficulty is therefore trifling, and what follows removes all shadow of doubt.

Of the four brothers of Napoleon, three are said to have been kings, and these of course are, Spring reigning over the flowers, Summer reigning over the harvest, Autumn holding sway over the fruits. And as these three seasons owe all to the powerful influence of the Sun, we are told in the popular myth that the three brothers of Napoleon drew their authority from him, and received from him their kingdoms. But if it be added that, of the four brothers of Napoleon, one was not a king, that was because he is the impersonification of Winter, which has no reign over anything. If however it be asserted, in contradiction, that the winter has an empire, he will be given the principality over snows and frosts, which, in the dreary season of the year, whiten the face of the earth. Well! the fourth brother of Napoleon is thus invested by popular tradition, commonly called history, with a vain principality accorded to him *in the decline of the power of Napoleon*. The principality was that of Canino, a name derived from cani, or the whitened hairs of a frozen old age – true emblem of winter. To the eyes of poets, the forests covering the hills are their hair, and when winter frosts them, they represent the snowy locks of a decrepit nature in the old age of the year:

'Cum gelidus crescit *canis* in montibus humor.'

Consequently the Prince of Canino is an impersonification of winter; – winter whose reign begins when the kingdoms of the three fine seasons are passed from them, and when the sun is driven from his power by the children of the North, as the poets call the boreal winds. This is the origin of the fabulous invasion of France by the allied armies of the North. The story relates that these invaders – the northern gales – banished the many-coloured flag, and replaced it by a white standard. This too is a graceful, but, at the same time, purely fabulous account of the Northern winds driving all the brilliant colours from the face of the soil, to replace them by the snowy sheet.

6. Napoleon is said to have had two wives. It is well known that the classic fable gave two also to Apollo. These two were the moon and the earth. Plutarch asserts that the Greeks gave the moon to Apollo for wife, whilst the Egyptians attributed to him the earth. By the moon he had no posterity, but by the other he had one son only, the little Horus. This is an Egyptian allegory representing the fruits of agriculture produced by the earth fertilized by the Sun. The pretended son of the fabulous Napoleon is said to have been born on the 20th of March, the season of the spring equinox, when agriculture is assuming its greatest period of activity.

7. Napoleon is said to have released France from the devastating scourge which terrorized over the country, the hydra of the revolution, as it was popularly called. Who cannot see in this a Gallic version of the Greek legend of Apollo releasing Hellas from the terrible Python? The very name *revolution*, derived from the Latin verb *revolvo*, is indicative of the coils of a serpent like the Python.

8. The famous hero of the nineteenth century had, it is asserted, twelve Marshals at the head of his armies, and four who were stationary and inactive. The twelve first, as may be seen at once, are the signs of the zodiac, marching under the orders of the sun Napoleon, and each commanding a division of the innumerable host of stars, which are parted into twelve portions, corresponding to the twelve signs. As for the four stationary officers, immovable in the midst of general motion, they are the cardinal points.

9. It is currently reported that the chief of these brilliant armies, after having gloriously traversed the Southern kingdoms, penetrated the North, and was there unable to maintain his sway. This too represents the course of the Sun, which assumes its greatest power in the South, but after the spring equinox seeks to reach the North, and after a *three months'* march towards the boreal regions, is driven back upon his traces, following the sign of Cancer, a sign given to represent the retrogression of the sun in that portion of the sphere. It is on this that the story of the march of Napoleon towards Moscow, and his humbling retreat is founded.

10. Finally, the sun rises in the East and sets in the Western sea. The poets picture him rising out of the waters of the East, and setting in the ocean after his twelve hours' reign in the sky. Such is

the history of Napoleon coming from his Mediterranean isle, holding the reins of government for twelve years, and finally disappearing in the mysterious regions of the great Atlantic.

S. Baring Gould

STAY YOUR ARMS

Stay your arms, O turning mill,
For the heath would now be still.
Ponds before the thaw are glooming
Rimmed with shining lance for lance,
And the little trees are looming
Like the varnished woodwax plants.

On the blind and frozen tide
Whiteclad children softly glide
Homeward from Communion, pray
Mutely: these to God whom learning
Rendered far aloof, and they
To the One who yields to yearning.

Did a whistle shrill below?
All the candles faintly flow.
Was it not like voices calling?
Ebon boys in deepness bound
Drew their brides into their thralling . . .
Bell, resound, O bell, resound!

Stefan George

To Laure Hayman

Here are fifteen chrysanthemums, twelve for your twelve when they are faded, three to round out your twelve; I hope the stems will be extremely long as I requested. And that these flowers – proud and sad, like you, proud of being beautiful, and sad that everything is so stupid – will please you. Thank you again (and if I had not had examinations Saturday, I should have come to tell you so) for your kind thought of me. It would have amused me so to go to this eighteenth-century fête, to see these young men, who you say are clever and charming, united in their love of you. How well I understand them! It is only natural that a woman who is desirable and nothing more, the mere object of lust, should exasperate her lovers, set them one against the other. But when, like a work of art, a woman reveals the utmost refinement of charm, the most subtle grace, the most divine beauty, the most voluptuous intelligence, a common admiration for her is bound to unite, to establish a brotherhood. Co-religionists are made in Laure Hayman's name. And since she is a very special divinity, since her charm is not accessible to everyone, since one must have very subtle tastes in order to understand it, like an initiation of the mind and the senses, it is only right that the faithful should love each other, that among the initiates there should be understanding. So your what-not of Saxe figures [an altar] seems to me one of the most charming things to be seen anywhere, and bound to be the rarest in existence since the days of Cleopatra and Aspasia. Therefore, I propose to call the present century the century of Laure Hayman and the ruling dynasty the Saxon line. – Forgive all this nonsense and allow me, when my examination is over, to bring you my tender respects.

Marcel Proust

A Wonder

It will be a marvellous thing – the true personality of man – when we see it. It will grow naturally and simply, flowerlike, or as a tree grows. It will not be at discord. It will never argue or dispute. It will not prove things. It will know everything. And yet it will not busy itself about knowledge. It will have wisdom. Its value will not be measured by material things. It will have nothing. And yet it will have everything, and whatever one takes from it, it will still have, so rich will it be. It will not be always meddling with others, or asking them to be like itself. It will love them because they will be different. And yet while it will not meddle with others, it will help all, as a beautiful thing helps us, by being what it is. The personality of man will be very wonderful. It will be as wonderful as the personality of a child.

Oscar Wilde

On Best-selling Writers of the 1890s

Will there never come a season
Which shall rid us from the curse
Of a prose which knows no reason
And an unmelodious verse:
When the world shall cease to wonder
At the genius of an Ass
And a boy's eccentric blunder
Shall not bring success to pass.

When mankind shall be delivered
From the clash of magazines,
And the inkstands shall be shivered
Into countless smithereens:
When there stands a muzzled stripling,
Mute, beside a muzzled bore;
When the Rudyards cease from kipling
And the Haggards ride no more?

      J. K. Stephen

THE GODS OF THE COPYBOOK HEADINGS

As I pass through my incarnations in every age and race,
I make my proper prostrations to the Gods of the Market-Place.
Peering through reverent fingers I watch them flourish and fall,
And the Gods of the Copybook Headings, I notice, outlast them
    all.

We were living in trees when they met us. They showed us each in
    turn
That Water would certainly wet us, as Fire would certainly burn:
But we found them lacking in Uplift, Vision and Breadth of Mind,
So we left them to teach the Gorillas while we followed the March
    of Mankind.

We moved as the Spirit listed. *They* never altered their pace,
Being neither cloud nor wind-borne like the Gods of the
    Market-Place;

But they always caught up with our progress, and presently word
   would come
That a tribe had been wiped off its icefield, or the lights had gone
   out in Rome.

With the Hopes that our World is built on they were utterly out of
   touch,
They denied that the Moon was Stilton; they denied she was even
   Dutch.
They denied that Wishes were Horses; they denied that a Pig had
   Wings.
So we worshipped the Gods of the Market Who promised these
   beautiful things.

When the Cambrian measures were forming, they promised
   perpetual peace.
They swore, if we gave them our weapons, that the wars of the
   tribes would cease.
But when we disarmed they sold us and delivered us bound to our
   foe,
And the Gods of the Copybook Headings said: '*Stick to the Devil
   you know.*'

On the first Feminian Sandstones we were promised the Fuller life
(Which started by loving our neighbour and ended by loving his
   wife)
Till our women had no more children and the men lost reason and
   faith,
And the Gods of the Copybook Headings said: '*The Wages of Sin
   is Death.*'

In the Carboniferous Epoch we were promised abundance for all,
By robbing selected Peter to pay for collective Paul;
But, though we had plenty of money, there was nothing our
   money could buy,
And the Gods of the Copybook Headings said: '*If you don't work
   you die.*'

Then the Gods of the Market tumbled, and their smooth-tongued
   wizards withdrew,

And the hearts of the meanest were humbled and began to believe
    it was true
That All is not Gold that Glitters, and Two and Two make Four –
And the Gods of the Copybook Headings limped up to explain it
    once more.

....

As it will be in the future, it was at birth of Man –
There are only four things certain since Social Progress began:
That the Dog returns to his Vomit and the Sow returns to her Mire,
And the burnt Fool's bandaged finger goes wabbling back to the
    Fire;
And that after this is accomplished, and the brave new world begins
When all men are paid for existing and no man must pay for his sins,
As surely as Water will wet us, as surely as Fire will burn,
The Gods of the Copybook Headings with terror and slaughter
    return!

        Rudyard Kipling

EMMY

Emmy's exquisite youth and her virginal air,
Eyes and teeth in the flash of a musical smile,
Come to me out of the past, and I see her there
As I saw her once for a while.

Emmy's laughter rings in my ears, as bright,
Fresh and sweet as the voice of a mountain brook,
And still I hear her telling us tales that night,
Out of Boccaccio's book.

There, in the midst of the villainous dancing-hall,
Leaning across the table, over the beer,
While the music madden'd the whirling skirts of the ball,
As the midnight hour drew near,

There with the women, haggard, painted and old,
One fresh bud in a garland wither'd and stale,
She, with her innocent voice and her clear eyes, told
Tale after shameless tale.

And ever the witching smile, to her face beguiled,
Paused and broaden'd, and broke in a ripple of fun,
And the soul of a child look'd out of the eyes of a child,
Or ever the tale was done.

O my child, who wrong'd you first, and began
First the dance of death that you dance so well?
Soul for soul: and I think the soul of a man
Shall answer for yours in hell.

        Arthur Symons

The Admiral, Eaton Place, Belgravia

On June 22, 1893, Lady Tryon was giving one of her 'At Home'
parties. The cream of Edwardian high society chatted and circulated
amid the elegant furniture. The ladies were resplendent in their frills
and laces and the gentlemen in tight-waisted frock coats when there
was a sudden hush in the conversation.

A commanding figure in full naval uniform had entered the room
without being announced. Glancing neither to the left nor to the right,
he strode across the room. The guests drew aside to let him pass, for
they all recognized Sir George Tryon.

At that very moment the body of Admiral Sir George Tryon was
lying in the wreckage of his flagship H.M.S. Victoria *at the bottom of*
the Mediterranean Sea, the result of a collision that remains a
mystery.

        Peter Underwood, 1973

On Prince Otto von Bismarck

Bismarck had the greatest contempt for principle of anyone who
ever lived . . .

Genius, saviour of the State, and sentimental traitor. Always Me,
Me, and, when things ceased to work, only tears about ingratitude,
and north German lachrymose sentimentality. Where I sense Bismarck as an instrument of Providence, I salute him; where he is
merely himself, Jupiter, dyke-supervisor and place-seeker, I find
him completely unsympathetic.

        Theodor Fontane, to his daughter

Science

Science is a match that man has just got alight . . . It is a curious sensation, now that the preliminary splutter is over and the flame burns up clear, to see his hands lit and just a glimpse of himself and the patch he stands on visible, and around him, in place of all that human comfort and beauty he had anticipated – darkness still.

H. G. Wells

On Women

First and foremost I should wish a woman I loved to be a mother . . . From the first I would impress on her the holiness of motherhood . . . But for the sake of that very motherhood I would teach her that she must be an intellectual being – that without a strong deliberate mind she is only capable of the animal office of bearing children, not of rearing them. It pains me to see a fine intelligent girl, directly she marries, putting aside intellectual things as no longer pertinent to her daily life.

Beatrice Webb

G.B.S.

I have got a sitting to-morrow from George Bernard Cocksure, as I call him, the G.B.S. of the *Saturday Review* and *Vanity Fair*.

Walter Sickert, to Lady Sybil Eden

Science is a bar of gold made by a quack alchemist.

Leo Tolstoy

A New Order

The ethical system of these men of the New Republic, the ethical system which will dominate the world state, will be shaped primarily to favour the procreation of what is fine and efficient and beautiful in humanity – beautiful and strong bodies, clear and powerful minds, and a growing body of knowledge – and to check the procreation of base and servile types, of fear-driven and cowardly souls, of all that is mean and ugly and bestial in the souls, bodies, or habits of men.

H. G. Wells

Any reasoned, intelligent battle against death – such as that waged by medicine – is unfortunate and evil in itself.

Leo Tolstoy

A Monarch

These are trying moments and it seems to me a defect in our much-famed Constitution to have to part with an admirable Govt like Lord Salisbury's for no question of any importance, or any particular reason, merely on account of the number of votes.

Queen Victoria

Another Monarch

I have listened to your words but can find no reason why I should obey you – I would rather die first. I have no relations with you and cannot bring it to my mind that you have given me as much as a fraction of a rupee or a quarter of even that or a needle or a thread. I look for some reason why I should obey you, and find not the smallest. If it should be friendship that you desire, then I am ready for it, today and always; but to be your subject, that I cannot be . . . If it should be war you desire, then I am ready, but never to be your subject . . . I do not fall at your feet, for you are God's creature just as I am . . . I am Sultan here in my land. You are Sultan there in yours. Yet listen, I do not say to you that you should obey me; for I know that you are a free man . . . As for me, I will not come to you, and if you are strong enough, then come and fetch me.

Chief Macemba, of the Yao, to General Hermann von Wissmann

On India

The future Viceroy must really shake himself more and more free from his red-tapist narrow-minded Council and Entourage. *He must be more independent, must hear for himself*, what the *feelings* of the Natives really are, and do what he thinks right and not be guided by the *snobbish* and vulgar, over-bearing and offensive behaviour of your Civil and Political Agents if we are to go on peaceably and happily in India, and to be liked and beloved by high and low – as well as respected, as we ought to be – and not trying to trample on the people and continually reminding them and making them feel that they are a conquered people.

Queen Victoria, to Lord Salisbury

IN THE ISLE OF DOGS

While the water-wagon's ringing showers
Sweetened the dust with a woodland smell,
'Past noon, past noon, two sultry hours,'
Drowsily fell
From the schoolhouse clock
In the Isle of Dogs by Millwall Dock.

Mirrored in shadowy windows draped
With ragged net or half-drawn blind,
Bowsprits, masts, exactly shaped
To woo or fight the wind,
Like monitors of guilt
By strength and beauty sent,
Disgraced the shameful houses built
To furnish rent.

From the pavements and the roofs
In shimmering volumes wound
The wrinkled heat;
Distant hammers, wheels and hoofs,
A turbulent pulse of sounds,
Southward obscurely beat,
The only utterance of the afternoon,
Till on a sudden in the silent street
An organ-man drew up and ground
The Old Hundredth tune.

John Davidson

The Time Traveller Visits the Future

I must confess that my satisfaction with my first theories of an automatic civilisation and a decadent humanity did not long endure.

Yet I could think of no other. Let me put my difficulties. The several big palaces I had explored were mere living places, great dining-halls and sleeping apartments. I could find no machinery, no appliances of any kind. Yet these people were clothed in pleasant fabrics that must at times need renewal, and their sandals, though undecorated, were fairly complex specimens of metal-work. Some-how such things must be made. And the little people displayed no vestige of a creative tendency. There were no shops, no workshops, no signs of importations among them. They spent all their time in playing gently, in bathing in the river, in making love in a half-playful fashion, in eating fruit and sleeping. I could not see how things were kept going.

Then, again, about the Time Machine; something, I knew not what, had taken it into the hollow pedestal of the White Sphinx. *Why?* For the life of me I could not imagine. Those waterless wells, too, those flickering pillars. I felt I lacked a clue. I felt – how shall I put it? Suppose you found an inscription, with sentences here and there in excellent plain English, and interpolated therewith, others made up of words, of letters even, absolutely unknown to you? Well, on the third day of my visit, that was how the world of Eight Hundred and Two Thousand Seven Hundred and One presented itself to me!

That day, too, I made a friend – of a sort. It happened that, as I was watching some of the little people bathing in a shallow, one of them was seized with cramp and began drifting downstream. The main current ran rather swiftly, but not too strongly for even a moderate swimmer. It will give you an idea, therefore, of a strange deficiency in these creatures, when I tell you that none made the slightest attempt to rescue the weakly crying little thing which was drowning before their eyes. When I realised this, I hurriedly slipped off my clothes and, wading in at a point lower down, I caught the poor mite and drew her safe to land.

    H. G. Wells

H. G. Wells . . . a romancer spoilt by romancing.

    Beatrice Webb

Emigration 1895

I was in the East End of London yesterday and attended a meeting of the unemployed. I listened to the wild speeches, which were just a cry for 'bread', 'bread', and on my way home I pondered over the scene and I became more than ever convinced of the importance of imperialism . . . My cherished idea is a solution for the social problem, i.e., in order to save 40,000,000 inhabitants of the UK from a bloody civil war, we colonial statesmen must acquire new lands to settle the surplus population . . .

Cecil Rhodes

From Tahiti

At the moment of receiving your kind letter I have not yet touched a brush, except to paint a glass window in my studio. I had to stop over in Papeete in temporary quarters and take a decision; finally to have a big Tahitian hut built for me in the country. A magnificent site, by the way, in the shade, at the roadside, with a stunning view of the mountains behind me. Imagine a huge bird-cage with bamboo bars and a roof of coconut-thatch, divided into two parts by my old studio curtains. One part serves as the bedroom, with very little light, so as to be cool. The other part has a big window overhead, to make a studio. On the floor there are some mats and my old Persian rug; the whole place is adorned with pieces of material, curios and drawings.

You see I am not too much to be pitied for the moment.

Every night my bed is invaded by little madcap girls; last night I had three of them at work. I am going to stop this giddy life, take a serious woman into the house and work steadily, more especially as I feel I'm in form and think I can do better things than before.

My former wife got married while I was away and I have been obliged to cuckold her husband, but she can't live with me, though she did run back to me for a week . . .

Paul Gauguin, to Georges Daniel de Monfried

Kissing

Of course though there's kissing and kissing. I'm a very 'kissing' person, but some girls kiss 'in conservatories'. (Oh don't you know what I mean – the dancer they have met an hour ago, and the next

one, probably, and the next *ad lib.*!) I never could have done that.
Very many women kiss two men at the same time. Pigs! I'll never
forget my first kiss. I made myself such a donkey over it, and always
laugh now when I remember. Mr Watts kissed me in the studio one
day, but sweetly and gently, all tenderness and kindness, and then I
was what they call 'engaged' to him and all the rest of it, and my
people hated it, and I was in Heaven, for I knew I was to live with
those pictures. 'Always,' I thought, and to sit next to that gentle Mr
W. and clean his brushes, and play my idiotic piano to him, and sit
with him there in wonderland (the Studio).

Ellen Terry, to George Bernard Shaw

An Aesthete of 1896

Suddenly we started, we had just seen a little pink butterfly, then
two, then five, leave the flowers of our shore and flutter over the
lake. Soon they were like an impalpable pink cloud blowing away,
then they reached the flowers of the other shore, came back and
gently recommenced the adventurous crossing, stopping sometimes
as if tempted above this lake delicately tinted with a great fading
flower. It was too much and our eyes filled with tears. These little
butterflies crossing the lake passed back and forth across our souls,
stretched with emotion before such beauty, ready to vibrate –
passed back and forth like the voluptuous bow of a violin. The light
movement of their flight did not graze the waters, but caressed our
eyes, our hearts, and at every stroke of their little wings we almost
fainted.

Marcel Proust

Duse

The reason why Duse is the greatest actress in the world is that she
has a more subtle nature than any other actress, and that she
expresses her nature more simply. All her acting seems to come
from a great depth, and to be only half telling profound secrets. No
play has ever been profound enough, and simple enough, for this
woman to say everything she has to say in it. When she has thrilled
one, or made one weep, or exalted one with beauty, she seems to be
always holding back something else. Her supreme distinction comes

from the kind of melancholy wisdom which remains in her face after the passions have swept over it . . .

To act as Duse acts, with an art which is properly the antithesis of what we call acting, is, no doubt, to fail in a lesser thing in order to triumph in a greater. Her greatest moments are the moments of most intense quietness; she does not send a shudder through the whole house, as Sarah Bernhardt does, playing on one's nerves as on a violin. 'Action', with her as with Rimbaud, 'is a way of spoiling something,' when once action has mastered thought, and got loose to work its own way into the world. It is a disturbance, not an end in itself; and the very expression of emotion, with her, is all a restraint, the quieting down of a tumult until only the pained reflection of it glimmers out of her eyes, and trembles among the hollows of her cheeks.

Arthur Symons

On Women

The great point is, not that they should understand us, but that they should worship and obey us.

Edward Burne-Jones

As long as men abolish only the external trappings of women's inequality and subjugation, as long as men continue in reality to demand that women be toys and objects of pleasure and therefore continue to regard her as such, as long as they continue to consider this as ultimately good and desirable, woman will remain what she has always been: an inferior being, a humiliated and depraved slave.

Leo Tolstoy

An Independent Man

To the devil with all philosophies of all great men. Every outstanding sage is as tyrannical as a general and as lacking in consideration because he knows he is immune. Diogenes spat in people's faces, knowing he was perfectly safe; and Tolstoy condemns all doctors as rogues and utterly disdains all important affairs of the day because he too is a Diogenes, safe from police arrest or newspaper assault.

Anton Chekhov, to Alexis Suvorin

For about seventeen years I was in thrall to Tolstoy's ideas. But now something in me protests; common sense and a feeling for justice have persuaded me that more love exists in electricity and steam than in chastity and vegetarianism.

Anton Chekhov, to Alexis Suvorin

Tolstoy has learned to ride a bicycle. Is this not inconsistent with the ideals of Christianity?

Vladimir Chertkov

On Captain Dreyfus

It would be strange if we Russians should bother ourselves with defending Dreyfus, an utterly undistinguished person, when so many outstanding people have been hanged, deported or imprisoned here at home.

Leo Tolstoy

The more that is given them the less will people work for themselves, and the less they work the more they will sink into poverty.

Leo Tolstoy

It is through disobedience that progress has been made, through disobedience and rebellion . . .

If Socialism is authoritarian; if there are Governments armed with economic power as they are now with political power; if, in a word, we are to have industrial tyrannies, then the last state of man will be worse than the first.

Oscar Wilde

From Reading Jail

On November 13th, 1895, I was brought down here from London. From two o'clock till half-past two on that day I had to stand on the centre platform of Clapham Junction in convict dress, and handcuffed, for the world to look at. I had been taken out of the hospital ward without a moment's notice being given to me. Of all possible objects I was the most grotesque. When people saw me they laughed. Each train as it came up swelled the audience. Nothing could exceed their amusement. That was, of course, before they knew who I was. As soon as they had been informed they laughed still more. For a half an hour I stood there in the grey November rain surrounded by a jeering mob.

Well, now I am really beginning to feel more regret for the people who laughed than for myself. Of course when they saw me I was not on my pedestal, I was in the pillory. But it is a very unimaginative nature that only cares for people on their pedestals. A pedestal may be a very unreal thing. A pillory is a terrific reality. They should have known also how to interpret sorrow better. I have said that behind sorrow there is always a soul. And to mock at a soul in pain is a dreadful thing. In the strangely simple economy of the world people only get what they give, and to those who have not enough imagination to penetrate the mere outward of things, and feel pity; what pity can be given save that of scorn?

>   Oscar Wilde

Prison

The poor are wiser, more charitable, more kind, more sensitive than we are. In their eyes prison is a tragedy in a man's life, a misfortune, a casualty, something that calls for sympathy in others. They speak of one who is in prison as of one who is 'in trouble' simply. It is the phrase they always use, and the expression has the perfect wisdom of love in it. With people of our own rank it is different. With us, prison makes a man a pariah. I, and such as I am, have hardly any right to air and sun. Our presence taints the pleasures of others. We are unwelcome when we reappear. To revisit the glimpses of the moon is not for us. Our very children are taken away. Those lovely links with humanity are broken. We are doomed to be solitary, while our sons still live. We are denied the one thing that might heal us and keep us, that might bring balm to the bruised heart, and peace to the soul in pain.

>   Oscar Wilde

Dinners

The Savoy dinners – the clear turtle soup, the luscious ortolans wrapped in their crinkled Sicilian vine-leaves, the heavy amber-coloured, indeed almost amber-scented champagne – Dagonet

1880, I think, was your favourite wine? – all have still to be paid for.
The suppers at Willis's, the special *cuvée* of Perrier-Jouet reserved
always for us, the wonderful *pâtés* procured directly from Strasburg,
the marvellous *fine champagne* served always at the bottom of great
bell-shaped glasses that its bouquet might be the better savoured by
the true epicures of what was really exquisite in life – those cannot
be left unpaid, as bad debts of a dishonest client.

    Oscar Wilde

Almost Everything

The gods had given me almost everything. I had genius, a distinguished name, high social position, brilliancy, intellectual daring; I
made art a philosophy and philosophy an art: I altered the minds of
men and the colours of things; there was nothing I said or did that
did not make people wonder. I took the drama, the most objective
form known to art, and made it as personal a mode of expression as
the lyric or sonnet; at the same time I widened its range and
enriched its characterization. Drama, novel, poem in prose, poem
in rhyme, subtle or fantastic dialogue, whatever I touched, I made
beautiful in a new mode of beauty: to truth itself I gave what is false
no less than what is true as its rightful province, and showed that the
false and the true are merely forms of intellectual existence. I
treated art as the supreme reality and life as a mere mode of fiction. I
awoke the imagination of my century so that it created myth and
legend around me. I summed up all systems in a phrase and all
existence in an epigram. Along with these things I had things that
were different. But I let myself be lured into long spells of senseless
and sensual ease. I amused myself with being a *flaneur*, a dandy, a
man of fashion. I surrounded myself with the smaller natures and
the meaner minds. I became the spendthrift of my own genius, and
to waste an eternal youth gave me a curious joy. Tired of being on
the heights, I deliberately went to the depths in the search for new
sensation. What the paradox was to me in the sphere of thought,
perversity became to me in the sphere of passion. Desire, at the end,
was a malady, or a madness, or both. I grew careless of the lives of
others. I took pleasure where it pleased me, and passed on. I forgot
that every little action of the common day makes or unmakes
character, and that therefore what one has done in the secret
chamber one has some day to cry aloud on the house-tops. I ceased

to be lord over myself. I was no longer the captain of my soul, and did not know it. I allowed pleasure to dominate me. I ended in horrible disgrace. There is only one thing for me now, absolute humility.

> Oscar Wilde

Yet lo! He was unchanged. He was still precisely himself. He was still playing with ideas, playing with emotions. 'There is only one thing left for me now,' he writes, 'absolute humility.' And about humility he writes many beautiful and true things. And, doubtless, while he wrote them, he had the sensation of humility. Humble he was not.

> Max Beerbohm

Become who you are.

> Friedrich Nietzsche

The Adventure

People thought it dreadful of me to have entertained at dinner the evil things of life, and to have found pleasure in their company. But they, from the point of view through which I, as an artist in life, approached them, were delightfully suggestive and stimulating. It was like feasting with panthers. The danger was half the excitement. I used to feel as the snake-charmer must feel when he lures the cobra to stir from the painted cloth or reed-basket that holds it, and makes it spread its hood at his bidding, and sway to and fro in the air as a plant sways restfully in a stream. They were to me the brightest of gilded snakes. Their poison was part of their perfection . . .

Clibborn and Atkins were wonderful in their infamous war against life. To entertain them was an astounding adventure. Dumas *frère*, Cellini, Goya, Edgar Allan Poe, or Baudelaire would have done just the same.

> Oscar Wilde

The Tragedy

Man survives earthquakes, epidemics, the horrors of disease, and all the agonies of the soul, but throughout all history his most tormenting tragedy has been, is, and will remain – the tragedy of the bedroom.

> Leo Tolstoy

It seems to me that my thoughts must always be of interest to everyone, and I am always prepared to thrust them on to the world in general.

> Leo Tolstoy

Art is the microscope that the artist focuses on the secrets of his own soul, and that reveals to men the secrets common to them all.

> Leo Tolstoy

The Barber

Watson, the late registrar of the Royal College of Music, went to get shaved in a provincial town. 'How easy it would be for me to cut your throat, sir!' said the barber as he was stropping the razor. Watson considered a moment and fled. The next day the barber did cut a customer's throat. He had become a homicidal maniac.

> Arnold Bennett

THE SOUNDING JOURNEYS

The sounding journeys you shall praise no more,
Where perilous and false the water leaps,
And where the chasm rears its rugged steeps
Around whose summits heaven's eagles soar.

Learn in these simple fields to apprehend
The breath that all-too frosty spring allays,
And that which renders less its sultry haze,
A willing ear their childish prattle lend!

You find the secret of eternal runes
Within these hills austerely drawn and pure,
Not only seas of stone with magic lure,
'No more the wonder beckons of lagoons,

Of great and ruined Rome, the world-wooed dream,
As vine and bitter scent of oaken grove,
As they who guard your people's treasure-trove:
Your waters, green with life, O surging stream!'

> Stefan George

On Leo Tolstoy

One day he was sorting his letters:
'They all make a great fuss about me,' he said, 'writing and so on.
But in the end, when I die, in a year or so, people will say: "Tolstoy?
Ah, that is the count who tried to make boots: and then something
curious happened to him. Is that the fellow you mean?" '

> Maxim Gorki

On Anton Chekhov

A lot could be written about Chekhov, but it would have to be done
in a fine and subtle way which I do not possess. It would be well to
write about him in the same manner as he himself wrote *The Steppe*,
a tale with a peculiar atmosphere, so light and so pensively sad in a
Russian way. A tale – just for oneself. It does one good to recall the
memory of such a man, it brings renewed energy into one's life, a
clear definite meaning.

Man is the axle of the world, in spite of his sins and defects. We all
hunger for the love of our fellow men, and when one is hungry even
an under-baked loaf is sweet.

> Maxim Gorki

Father and Son

With delight he followed every step in the growth of understanding
and yet it was not all pleasure to watch the mind outgrowing its
simplicity . . . At four years old Hughie had forgotten his primitive
language. The father regretted many a pretty turn of tentative
speech, which he was wont to hear with love's merriment. If a toy
were lost, a little voice might be heard saying, 'Where has it gone
now *to*?' And when it was found again – 'There is *it*!' After a tumble
one day, Hughie was cautious in running. 'I shall fall down and

break myself.' Then came distinction between days of the week.
'On Sunday I do' so and so; 'on Monday days I do' something else.
He said 'Do you bemember?' and what a pity it seemed when at last
the dull grown-up world was substituted. Never again, when rain
was falling, would Hughie turn and plead, 'Father, tell the sun to
come out!' Nor, when he saw the crescent moon in daytime, would
he ever grow troubled and exclaim, 'Someone has broken it!'

> George Gissing

The Actor Hermann Müller

Yet when the play was fading, and the curtain
Came down in silence like a painted eyelid
Over the magical cavern emptied now of life,
And he stepped out, a stage appeared before him
Like a wide, sleepless eye for ever open
On which no curtain mercifully falls:
The terrifying stage reality.
Then all the arts of transformation dropped
From him, and his poor soul walked quite unclothed
And gazed from a child's eyes.

> Hugo von Hofmannsthal

Civilization and Nature

In our northern country the physical sense seems to be dormant.
Our educational system too is a perpetual lesson of self-restraint
and suppression of the emotions. From the earliest age we are
taught that it is cowardly to cry, improper to laugh aloud, unseemly
to enjoy eating and feeble to love ease. Our whole nature is kept
back, possibly guided and possibly controlled, only pent up to break
out with irresistible force when the real overcomes the artificial and
we act from instinct and no longer from thought . . . Civilization is
against nature and we are surprised when nature gets the better of
the fight.

We must either pretend to have no sex or attempt to suppress it.
In most cases neither course is successful.

> Harley Rodney

A Marriage in Vienna

My mother's only friend was her shy and self-effacing elder brother. She fell in love with a young officer. Her stepmother laughed contemptuously: 'A mere boy, a mere nobody! You think that's a proper match for you?' Her father said: 'You'll have to get that out of your head. He's poor and he's much too young for you. No good can come of such a marriage. What you need is a *husband*, not a playmate.' The lieutenant was summoned to see my grandfather. Politely he was given to understand that it would be most undesirable were he to become involved with his superior's daughter. On 18 August there was a parade to celebrate the Emperor's birthday. My grandfather was watching it from the balcony with his wife and daughters. The young lieutenant was marching at the head of his company. He saluted, drew his revolver and shot himself. The band stopped playing. It was the time of psychological operettas, of *The Merry Widow*, of tragedy in everyday dress. Dust had begun to accumulate on the plush furniture and the artificial flowers. Lunch was eaten off tables where corpses had been laid out.

My mother was distraught, hardly aware of what she was doing. A respectable captain, complete with bald patch, moustache and *pince-nez*, appeared on the scene. Bearing a not-too-expensive bouquet, he fell on his knees before the young lady. '*Gnädiges Fräulein*,' he said, 'allow me to confess my love for you and to lay my heart at your feet.' The object of his address was all too aware of the absurdity both of his posture and his words; but she was defenceless, unsure of herself and the world; she begged to be given time to consider. 'That's the husband for you!' declared her stepmother, 'serious, staid, and correct.' 'An excellent officer,' put in my grandfather. 'And just the right difference in age – like us!' rejoined her stepmother. '*Quite* the best sort of marriage.' Whereupon my grandfather: 'He has worked his way up by earnestness of purpose and his own merits. In marriage, what counts is character, not charm.'

My mother did not dare say no. 'They want to get rid of me,' she thought, 'nobody cares about me.' The engagement was settled. Not until several days afterwards did she summon the courage to speak to her ever-busy father.

'I can't marry him. He repels me.'

'But you've given your consent,' my grandfather replied. 'You can't suddenly refuse now. You must stand by your word. He's a worthy man and he loves you. Besides which, there'd be a scandal.'

The word 'scandal' haunted her like a ghost. 'A scandal!' said her stepmother over her bare shoulder as she sat in front of her looking-glass. 'A scandal!' came the echo from the kitchen, the pantry, the stairs, from the creaking doors, from the whispering walls, from the ticking clocks. My mother contemplated suicide. But how? She had no revolver. Jump out of the window? Drown herself? It was too vulgar and distasteful. Run away, perhaps? But where? And what then? If only some gypsies would come along and take her away with them! If only the house would fall down! If only . . . if only . . . What finally decided her was the advice of her elder brother: 'I don't think he's really that bad. Or would you prefer to be a governess, a spinster, never have any children? It's not your style. By marrying him, at least you'll get away from here, from this enlightened despotism, this tyrannical kindliness that thwarts you at every turn.'

So she married the man she abominated.

'But why?' I asked. 'Why?'

'Don't ask me! I wasn't myself. Why do soldiers stand to attention when ordered to do so? Why do they throw themselves down into the mud and crawl about on all fours? Why do a dunderhead's subjects submit to him instead of forcing him to abdicate? Obedience and authority turn living men into dead things. And by the time the dead wake up, it's too late.'

Ernst Fischer

The Late-Victorian Grand Manner

So perished the French monarchy. Its dim origins stretched out and lost themselves in Rome; it had already learnt to speak and recognised its own nature when the vaults of the Thermae echoed heavily to the slow footsteps of the Merovingian kings. Look up that vast valley of dead men crowned, and you may see the gigantic figure of Charlemagne, his brows level and his long white beard tangled like an undergrowth, having in his left hand the globe and in his right the hilt of an unconquerable sword. There also are the short, strong horsemen of the Robertian house, half-hidden by their leather shields, and their sons before them growing in vestment and majesty, and taking on the pomp of the Middle Ages; Louis VII, all covered with iron; Philip the Conqueror; Louis IX, who alone is surrounded with light: they stand in a widening interminable procession, this great crowd of kings; they loose their armour, they take their ermine on, they are accompanied by their captains and their marshals; at last, in their attitude and in their magnificence they sum up in themselves the pride and achievement of the French nation. But time has dissipated what it could not tarnish, and the process of a thousand years has turned these mighty figures into insubstantial things. You may see them in the grey end of darkness, like a pageant all standing still. You look again, but with the growing light and with the wind that rises before morning they have disappeared.

Hilaire Belloc

Christmas

Your Christmas card made me very happy. If we were nothing more than creatures of the mind, we would not believe in anniversaries, in birthdays, in relics, in tombs. But since we are also composed of a small amount of matter, we like to believe that it, too, is a part of reality and has (we like to think that what we have room for in our hearts is round-and-about-us externally, too, a little), as the soul the body, its own material symbol. And then, as Christmas gradually loses for us its validity as an anniversary, it takes on a more and more intense reality, in which the light of its candles, its snow, that melancholy obstacle to some longed-for visitor, the odour of its tangerines steeping in the warmth of the rooms, the gaiety of its cold and its fires, the perfumes of the tea and the mimosa, come back to us coated in the delicious honey of our own personality, which we had unconsciously deposited there during the years, when, caught in the spell of our own egotistical designs, we were not aware of Christmas; and now, all of a sudden, it makes our heart beat faster.

Marcel Proust, to Marie Nordlinger

The Beauty of Light

This extraordinary Paris with its new – I mean more and more multiplied – manifestations of luxurious and extravagant entension, grandeur and general chronic *expositionism* . . . it strikes me as a monstrous massive flower of national decadence, the biggest temple ever built to material joys and the lust of the eyes, and drawing to it thereby all the forces of the nation as to a substitute for others – I mean other than Parisian – achievement. It is a strange great phenomenon – with a deal of beauty still in its great expansive symmetries and perspectives – and *such* a beauty of light.

Henry James, to Edward Warren

1900–09

THE YELLOW BOOK

AN ILLVSTRATED QVARTERLY.

BOOKS

PRICE
FIVE SHILLINGS

ELKIN MATHEWS
AND JOHN LANE,
THE BODLEY HEAD
VIGO ST. LONDON.

APRIL 15th
MDCCC XCIV.

Death of Nietzsche, 1900

The advance of European democracy is leading to the growth of a human species ready for slavery in the most exact sense.

    Friedrich Nietzsche

You say that a good cause justifies even war. I say unto you: a good war justifies any cause.

    Friedrich Nietzsche

Man is a rope stretched between the animal and the super-man – a rope over an abyss . . . I want to teach men the sense of their existence – the Super-Man – the lightning out of the dark cloud man.

    Friedrich Nietzsche

Whoever combats monsters should contrive that in doing so he does not himself become a monster. And when you gaze long into an abyss, that abyss also gazes into you.

    Friedrich Nietzsche

I call Christianity the one great curse, the one gigantic and innermost perversion, the one great instinct of revenge, for which no means are too poisonous, too cheating, too surreptitious and too petty – I call it the one eternal human blemish.

    Friedrich Nietzsche

Only he who lives dangerously, lives fully.

>Friedrich Nietzsche

He wrote that for me.

>Adolf Hitler, 1923

Nietzsche on Germans

I believe only in French culture, and regard all else in Europe calling itself 'Culture' as a misunderstanding. I do not regard even German culture seriously . . . Whenever Germany increases her power, she ruins culture . . . Man as artist is at home only in Paris . . . Germans are like women, you can scarcely ever fathom their depths – they possess no depths . . .

The Germans are always so badly deceived because they try to find a deceiver . . . Intoxication means more to them than nourishment . . . A popular leader must hold up to them the prospects of conquest and splendour, then he will be believed. They will always obey and will do more than obey, provided they get intoxicated on the way.

>Friedrich Nietzsche

Men should be trained for war and women for the recreation of the warrior: all else is folly.

>Friedrich Nietzsche

The State is the slow suicide of all that is called 'life'.

>Friedrich Nietzsche

Pure Will without the confusions of Intellect . . . how happy! how free!

>Friedrich Nietzsche

Nietzsche on Modern Man

Do not by any means imagine it desirable that the kingdom of righteousness and peace should be established on earth (because whatever happens it would be a kingdom of the utmost mediocrity and the Chinese ant-heap); we hail all who, like ourselves, love danger, war, adventure, who refuse compromise, refuse to be captured, refuted, stunted; we reckon ourselves among the Conquerors; we ponder the necessity for a new order, even a new slavery – for all strengthening and elevation of mankind simultaneously involves a new form of slavery.

Friedrich Nietzsche

If the organization of society is bad – as ours is – and a small number of people have power over the majority and oppress it, every victory over nature will inevitably serve only to increase that power and that oppression. This is what is actually happening.

Leo Tolstoy

To the German troops in China during the Boxer Rebellion

Give no quarter! Take no prisoners! Kill the foe when you capture him! Even as a thousand years ago the Huns under their King Attila made such a name for themselves as still resounds in terror through legend and fable, so may the name of Germans resound through Chinese history a thousand years hence.

Kaiser Wilhelm II

If your Emperor orders it, you must open fire on your own father and mother.

Kaiser Wilhelm II, to new recruits

On Kaiser Wilhelm II

Here His Majesty bagged a white cock pheasant, the fifty thousandth creature to fall at the hands of the All-Highest.

Inscribed in gold on a marble memorial

The only nations that have advanced to greatness have been those who do not flinch from war.

Kaiser Wilhelm II

The Future

From a European war a revolution may arise, and the ruling classes
would do well to consider this. But it may also result, over a long
period, in crises of counter-revolution, or furious reaction of dicta-
torships, of monstrous militarism, a long chain of retrograde violence.

Jean Jaurès

The Heretic

Zolotnitzki the priest was sentenced to thirty years' imprisonment
for heresy, and spent those thirty years in the prison of a monastery.
If I am not mistaken it was in Suzdal, in strict solitary confinement,
in a stone pit. During the languid course of eleven thousand days
and nights, the only consolation of this captive of a Christ-loving
Church, as well as his sole companion, was fire: the heretic was
granted permission to light the stove of his cell unaided by others.

In the early years of this century Zolotnitzki was released, for not
only had he forgotten all about his heresy, but his mind had ceased
to work altogether: the light in it was practically extinguished. Dried
to the bones by his rigorous imprisonment, he bore but a remote
resemblance to the inhabitants of the earth's surface. He walked
about with his head bent low, as though he were continually
descending, sinking into a pit, looking for a place wherein to hide his
weak, pitiful body. His dull eyes watered constantly, his head
shook, and his incoherent speech was impossible to understand.
The hairs of his beard, no longer grey but of a greenish decomposed
hue, stood out in sharp contrast with his pallid, withered face. He
was half-witted and evidently lived in terror of all men, but, fearing
them, tried to dissimulate his terror. When he was addressed by
anyone, he lifted his dry little childish hand as though he expected to
be struck a blow across the eyes and hoped to be able to protect
them with this weak, trembling hand. He was very quiet, talked
little and always in a whisper, in timid, rustling sounds.

He left prison a fire-worshipper, and grew animated only when he
was allowed to light a wood-pile in the stove and sit in front of it,
watching it. Seating himself on a low little stool, he lit the logs
lovingly, making the sign of the cross over them, and murmured,
shaking his head, all the words that still lived in his memory:

'Thou, who art . . . Eternal fire . . . Burning the sinners
. . . Omnipresent . . . '

He pushed the burning logs gently with a small poker, swayed
backwards and forwards as though about to poke his head into the
fire, while the wind drew the thin green hairs of his beard inside the
stove.

'Thy will be done . . . Thy image be blessed for ever and ever
. . . And they fly . . . So they fly . . . From the image of the
fire . . . Thy name be praised . . . Unquenchable . . . '

He was surrounded by kind-hearted people who wondered how
men could torture a man so much, and how pertinacious is the vital
spark.

Zolotnitzki's horror was great when he first saw an electric lamp,
when the white, colourless light, imprisoned in the glass, flared up
before him mysteriously. Having stared at it for some moments
intently, the old man waved his hands in despair and began muttering plaintively:

'What! the fire imprisoned too! . . . oh-oh! . . . What for? The
devil's not in it, is he? Oh-oh! Why have they done it?'

It took some time to comfort him. Tears streamed from his dull,
colourless eyes, he trembled all over, and, sighing sorrowfully, cried
appealingly to the people round him:

'Oh, you slaves of God, why do you do it? Imprison a sunbeam!
Oh, you sinful people, beware of the fire's wrath!'

He sobbed, lightly touching the shoulders of those who stood
close to him with his small, dry, trembling hand: 'Oh – let it go – set
it free!'

Maxim Gorki

The Prophet

One must admit that it is impossible to show why certain things
should not utterly destroy and end the entire human race and story;
why night should not presently come down and make all our dreams
and efforts vain . . . e.g. something from space, or pestilence, or
some great disease of the atmosphere, some trailing cometary
poison, some great emanation of vapour from the interior of the
earth, or new animals to prey on us, or some drug or wrecking
madness into the minds of men . . . I have come to believe in other
things: in the coherency and purpose in the world, and in the

greatness of human destiny. Worlds may freeze and suns may
perish, but I believe there stirs something within us now that can
never die again . . . It is possible to believe that all the past is but
the beginning of a beginning, all that the human mind has accomplished is but the dream before the awakening. A day will come
when beings now latent in our thoughts and hidden in our loins will
stand upon this earth as one stands upon a footstool, and laugh, and
reach out their hands amid the stars.

    H. G. Wells

On Van Gogh, 1901

At first sight these [paintings] seemed to me loud and restless, quite
crude, quite strange . . . in order to see the first of them as pictures
at all, as a unity, I had to prepare myself – but then I saw, then I saw
them all thus, each single one and all together, and Nature in them,
and the strength of the human soul which had transformed Nature,
and tree and bush and field and slope which were painted here, and
also that other strength, that which was behind the paint, the
essence, that indescribable sense of fate . . . There is an incredible
blue, most powerful of blues, which constantly reappears, a green
like that of molten emeralds, a yellow that deepens into orange. But
what are colours if the innermost life of objects doesn't break
through them? And this innermost life was there, tree and stone and
wall and gorge gave of themselves their innermost, almost casting it
at me . . . the impact of its existence, the ferocious wonder of its
existence surrounded by incredibility, made a dead set at my soul.
How can I make it clear . . . That here each Being – the Being of
each tree, each strip of yellow or greenish field, each fence, each
gorge cut into the stony hill, the Being of the pewter jug, the
earthenware bowl, the table, the clumsy armchair lifted itself
toward me as though newly born from the frightful chaos of
Non-living, from the abyss of Non-Being, so that I felt – nay, that I
knew – how each of these objects, these creatures, was born from a
terrible doubting of the world, and how with its existence it now
covered over forever the dreadful chasm of yawning nothingness
. . . And now I could, from picture to picture, feel a something,
could feel the mingling, the merging of formation, how the innermost life broke forth into colour and how the colours live one for the
sake of the others, and how one, mysteriously, powerfully, carried

all the others; and in all this I could sense a heart, the soul of the man who had created it, who with his vision did himself answer the spasms of his own most dreadful doubts.

Hugo von Hofmannsthal

On the French Impressionists

An art which transgresses the laws and barriers outlined by me, ceases to be an art; it is merely a factory product, a trade, and art must never become such a thing.

Kaiser Wilhelm II

On Plays

Shakespeare's plays are bad enough, but yours are even worse! My dear friend, I implore you, do stop writing plays!

Leo Tolstoy, to Anton Chekhov

On Giving Help to the Starving

There are dozens of customers for this sort of thing: people who have lived their lives oblivious to the common people, often repelled by them, despising them, and who are then suddenly consumed by enormous care for their inferior brothers. Their motives are self-importance, vanity and fear of popular anger . . .

To combat famine, all that is necessary is for men to do more good deeds. A good deed does not consist in handing bread to the starving, but in loving the starving as much as the over-fed. Loving is more important than handing out food . . . Therefore, as you ask me what is to be done. I reply: arouse, if you can – and you can – the love of men for one another, not now when there is a famine, but always and everywhere.

Leo Tolstoy, to Nikolai Leskov

An Austrian Journalist

If I must choose the lesser of two evils I will choose neither.

Karl Kraus

The English are not idealists. Despite their devotion to commerce, they would not sacrifice their entire lives to it.

> Karl Kraus

Prussia is a place where you are free to move, but with a gagged mouth: Vienna is an isolation cell in which you are permitted to scream.

> Karl Kraus

Who can see much of importance where he roams?
Yet whoever utters 'Evening' says a great deal,
A word from which flows rare thought, rare sadness,
Like honey dripping from hollow combs.

> Hugo von Hofmannsthal

Edward Bowen: A Harrow Master

He delighted in all sorts of unusual and quaint methods of teaching and of exacting penalties. He believed that everyone should possess at least one piece of absolutely useless information, for instance, to know the seven mouths of the Nile. If people failed this test, he would say, 'O boy, do a map of the Nile in five paints, boy.' Once for ignorance of the whereabouts of the Cocytus, which I think I placed in Asia Minor, I did 'a map of hell in five paints, boy.'

> G. M. Trevelyan

The Trusted Servant

A former servant of ours, a sickly, quiet man with dark and tired eyes, whose duty it was to drive a paralysed lady in a wheelchair, one fine and beautiful morning drew from his pocket a razor and cut his sad mistress's withered throat.

> Fedor Stepun, 1947

A Portent

The Myth is a corpus of images capable of evoking instinctively all the sentiments which correspond to the various manifestations of the war undertaken by Socialism . . .

Strikes have created in the proletariat the noblest, profoundest and most moving feelings that they possess.

> Georges Sorel

Socialists should be respectable.

> Beatrice Webb

A Ballade of Genuine Concern

A child at Brighton has been left to drown:
  A railway train has jumped the line at Crewe:
I haven't got the change for half-a-crown:
  I can't imagine what on earth to do . . .
  Three bisons have stampeded from the Zoo,
A German fleet has anchored in the Clyde.
  By God the wretched country's up the flue!
– The ice is breaking up on every side.

What! Further news? Rhodesian stocks are down?
  England, my England, can the news be true!
Cannot the Duke be got to come to town?
  Or will not Mr Hooper pull us through?
  And now the Bank is stopping payment too,
The chief cashier has cut his throat and died,
  And Scotland Yard has failed to find a clue:
– The ice is breaking up on every side.

A raging mob inflamed by Charley Brown
  Is tearing up the rails of Waterloo;
They've hanged the Chancellor in wig and gown,
  The Speaker, and the Chief Inspector too!
  Police! Police! Is this the road to Kew?
I can't keep up: my garter's come untied:
  I shall be murdered by the savage crew.
– The ice is breaking up on every side.

ENVOI

Prince of the Empire, Prince of Timbuctoo,
Prince eight foot round and nearly four foot wide,

Do try to run a little faster, do.
– The ice is breaking up on every side.

Hilaire Belloc

Undressing the Cocotte

It was no small affair: full armour, shield, yoke, sheath, whalebone, shoulder-pieces, thigh-pieces – gauntlets, corselet, halters of pearls, shields of feathers, baldrics of satin, velvet and jewels, coats of mail – these knights bristling with tulle, and eyelashes, these sacred scarabs armed with asparagus tongs, these samurais of sable and ermine, these dreadnaughts of pleasure from dawn to dusk harnessed and caparisoned by sturdy wenches – seemed strangely stiff in front of their host as if unable to extract from an oyster anything except its pearl . . . The idea of undressing one of these ladies seemed an expensive enterprise which would have to be organised like a household furniture removal.

Jean Cocteau

At Mrs George Wyndham's

There is something about an open fire, bread and butter sandwiches, very strong tea, a yellow fog without, and the cultural drawl of English voices which makes London very attractive, and, if I had been fascinated before, from that moment I loved it dearly. There was in this house a magic atmosphere of security and comfort, of culture and ease, and I must say I felt as much as home as a fish that has found the water to which it belongs. The beautiful library, too, attracted me very much.

It was in this house that I first noticed the extraordinary demeanour of good English servants, who move about with a sort of assured aristocratic manner of their own, and, far from objecting to being servants, or wishing to rise in the social scale as they do in America, they are proud of working 'for the best families'. Their fathers did it before them, and their children will do it after them. This is the kind of thing that makes for the calm and security of existence.

Isadora Duncan

The Volunteer Doctor in South Africa

You would have smiled if you could have seen me in my pink
undershirt, breeches and helmet, burned red and covered with dirt.
Ah, if you could have seen the men! I mean the troops. A whole
brigade passed us today, such splendid chaps, bearded and fierce,
picturesque brigands, my word! – they look like fighting. How I
would love to march them down the Strand just as they are. London
would go mad. The Gordons passed me. 'Good old Gordons,' I
yelled. 'What cheer mate!', they cried back, seeing in the dirty man
a brother tommy. They are splendid. We are not depressed by the
recent cavalry reverse. Last night it was rumoured that the Boers
would raise the town, but we saw nothing except our own . . .

> Sir Arthur Conan Doyle, to his wife

A British View

It was the supreme instant of the Natal campaign, as, wave after
wave, the long lines of infantry went shimmering up the hill. On the
left the Lancasters, the Lancashire Fusiliers, the South Lancashires,
the York and Lancasters, with a burr of north country oaths went
racing for the summit. Spion Kop with a thousand comrades were
calling for vengeance. 'Remember, men, the eyes of Lancashire are
watching you,' cried the gallant MacCarthy O'Leary. The old 40th
swept on, but his dead body marked the way which they had taken.
On the right the East Surrey, the Cameronians, the 3rd Rifles, the
1st Rifle Brigade, the Durhams, and the gallant Irishmen, so sorely
stricken and yet so eager were all pressing upwards and onwards.
The Boer fire lulls, it ceases – they are running! Wild hatwaving
men upon the Hlangwane uplands see the silhouette of the active
figures of the stormers along the skyline and know that the position
is theirs. Exultant soldiers dance and cheer upon the ridge. The sun
is setting in glory over the great Drakensberg mountains, and so also
that night set for ever on the hopes of the Boer invaders of Natal.
Out of doubt and chaos, blood and labour, had come at last the
judgment that the lower should not swallow the higher, that the
world is for the man of the twentieth and not of the seventeenth
century.

> Sir Arthur Conan Doyle

Christmas Day, Groenkop Hill, South Africa, 1901

The Boers charged rapidly, yelling madly through the camp, and a terrible hand to hand fight took place. But trench after trench was overpowered until the whole Kopje was in the enemy's hands. Then, according to some writers, disgraceful things happened, but of this there is no need to speak here. At any rate, everything was ransacked and pillaged and what could not be carried off was set on fire. The Kopje was piled high with dead and wounded.

Trooper Archie 'Jacko' Bowers

On the veldt the natives live simply. When a man has worked and purchased several bullocks, he buys a wife and his working days are over. He smokes and directs the labours of his spouse, till he can afford more wives; for he counts his wealth in wives and cattle, not gold.

Trooper Archie 'Jacko' Bowers

I am a Nationalist and not a cosmopolitan. A Nationalist believes that competition between nations is the Divine Order of the World, a Law of Life and Progress . . . If I am also an imperialist, it is because the destiny of the English race has been to strike fresh roots in distant parts of the world. My patriotism knows no geographical but only racial limits.

Lord Milner

The South African War

In this war the old terror of a visible foe gave way to the paralysing sensation of advancing on an invisible one, which fostered the suspicion that the enemy was everywhere. A universal terror, rather than a localized danger, now enveloped the attacker, while the defender, always ready to protect himself by some rough earth or stone-work, was enabled through the rapidity of rifle-fire to use extensions unheard of in past fighting, and in consequence to overlap every frontal attack. Thus, at the battle of the Modder River, the Boers extended three thousand men on a frontage of seven thousand seven hundred yards; at Magersfontein, five thousand on eleven thousand; and at Colenso, four thousand five hundred on thirteen thousand. Yet in spite of this human thinness, these fronts could not be penetrated. This spelt the end of successful frontal rifle attacks.

> J. F. C. Fuller, 1954

That the sunshine of England is pale,
And the breezes of England are stale,
An' there's somethin' gone small with the lot.

> Rudyard Kipling

We've had an imperial lesson. It may make us an Empire yet.

> Rudyard Kipling, from 'The Volunteer'

The Boers

A horrid people, cruel and overbearing.

> Queen Victoria

The craving for the large and lonely spaces in the outlandish corners of the world, the incurable intermittent fever to be moving, ever-moving among strange people and under strange skies . . .

> A. E. W. Mason

FOLLOWING BRITISH FAILURES EXPOSED BY THE BOER WAR

And ye vaunted your fathomless powers, and ye flaunted
  your iron pride,
Ere – ye fawned on the Younger Nations for the men who
  could shoot and ride!
Then ye returned to your trinkets; then ye contented
  your souls
With the flannelled fools at the wicket or the muddied
  oafs at the goals.

> Rudyard Kipling

Bernard Shaw was to talk of Englishmen drinking golf instead of wisdom.

The Empire

Alec had seen many men lose their heads under the influence of that climate. The feeling of an authority that seemed so limited, over a race that was manifestly inferior, the subtle magic of the hot sunshine, the vastness, the remoteness from civilization, were very apt to throw a man off his balance. The French had coined a name for the distemper and called it *Folie d'Afrique*. Men seemed to go mad from a sense of power, to lose all the restraints which had kept them in the way of righteousness.

W. Somerset Maugham

There was a vast amount of red [on the map] – good to see at any time, because one knows that some real work is being done.

Joseph Conrad

Doubted are they, and defamed
By the tongues their act set free.

Rudyard Kipling

Englishmen in Canada

Why do Canadians dislike English immigrants? Because we are sick of remittance-men and loafers sent out here. Because the English are rotten with Socialism . . . they carry frills.

Rudyard Kipling

The English rule in India is surely one of the more extraordinary accidents that ever happened in history. We are there like a man who has fallen off a ladder on to the neck of an elephant and doesn't know what to do or how to get down. Unless something happens he remains. Our functions in India are absurd. We English do not own that country, we do not even rule it. We make nothing happen; at the most we prevent things happening. We suppress our own literature there. Most English people cannot even go to this land they possess; the authorities would prevent it. If Messrs Perowne or Cook organised a cheap tour of Manchester operatives, it would be stopped. No one dare bring the average English voter face to face with the reality of India, or let the Indian native have a glimpse of the English voter . . . A sort of magic inconclusiveness . . . Our flag is spread over the peninsula, without plans, without intentions – a vast preventative.

H. G. Wells

Marlowe Remembers

Now when I was a little chap I had a passion for maps. I would look for hours at South America, or Africa, or Australia, and lose myself in all the glories of exploration. At that time there were many blank spaces of the earth, and when I saw one that looked particularly inviting on a map (but they all look that) I would put my finger on it and say, When I grow up I will go there. The North Pole was one of these places, I remember. Well, I haven't been there yet, and shall not try now. The glamour's off. Other places were scattered about the Equator, and in every sort of latitude all over the two hemispheres. I have been in some of them, and . . . well, we won't talk about that. But there was one yet – the biggest, the most blank, so to speak – that I had a hankering after.

True, by this time it was not a blank space any more. It had got filled since my boyhood with rivers and lakes and names. It had ceased to be a blank space of delightful mystery – a white patch for a boy to dream gloriously over. It had become a place of darkness. But there was in it one river especially, a mighty big river, that you could see on the map, resembling an immense snake uncoiled, with its head in the sea, its body at rest curving afar over a vast country, and its tail lost in the depths of the land. And as I looked at the map of it in a shop-window, it fascinated me as a snake would a bird – a silly little bird. Then I remembered there was a big concern, a Company for trade on that river. Dash it all! I thought to myself, they can't trade without using some kind of craft on that lot of fresh water – steamboats! Why shouldn't I try to get charge of one? I went on along Fleet Street, but could not shake off the idea. The snake had charmed me.

Joseph Conrad

Tribal Rebellion in German East Africa

It was, and is, my policy to use force with terror and even brutality. I shall exterminate the rebellious tribes in torrents of blood.

General von Trotha

*Out of 80,000, 65,000 Hereros were slaughtered, and 10,000 Namas,
out of 20,000.*

Death of Queen Victoria

*From the unrolling mists of oblivious babyhood, the strains drift
back to me of 'We're Soldiers of the Queen, me lads!' and 'Good-bye
Dolly, I must leave you.' An organ was triumphantly playing the first
of these tunes in a Macclesfield street one cold spring morning when I
noticed that banners and gay streamers were hanging from all the
windows.*

*'It's because of the Relief of Ladysmith,' my mother explained in
response to my excited questioning; 'Now Uncle Frank will be
coming home.'*

*But Uncle Frank – a younger brother of my father's who had been
farming in South Africa when the War began and had joined the
Queen's forces as a trooper – never came home after all, for he died
of enteric in Ladysmith half an hour before the relief of the town.*

*I had quite forgotten him on a grey January afternoon nearly a year
later, when I sat snugly in our warm kitchen, drawing birds and
dragons and princesses with very long hair, while the old lady whose
Diamond Jubilee had made such an impression upon my three-year-
old consciousness sank solemnly into her grave. In front of the fire,
the little plump cook read the evening paper aloud to the housemaid.*

*'The Queen is now asleep,' she quoted in a sepulchral tones, while
I, absorbed with my crayons, remained busily unaware that so much
more than a reign was ending, and that the long age of effulgent
prosperity into which I had been born was to break up in thirteen
years' time with an explosion which would reverberate through my
personal life to the end of my days.*

                   Vera Brittain, 1933

Queen Victoria was like a great paper-weight that for half a century
sat upon men's minds, and when she was removed their ideas began
to blow about all over the place haphazardly.

                   H. G. Wells

1902 – A Reply to Darwin and Huxley

The first thing which strikes us as soon as we begin studying the

struggle for existence under both its aspects – direct and meta-
phorical – is the abundance of facts of mutual aid, not only for
rearing progeny, as recognized by most evolutionists, but also for
the safety of the individual, and for providing it with the necessary
food. With many large divisions of the animal kingdom mutual aid is
the rule. Mutual aid is met with even amidst the lowest animals, and
we must be prepared to learn some day, from the students of
microscopical pond-life, facts of unconscious mutual support, even
from the life of micro-organisms.

> Peter Kropotkin

The Vogue

Some time ago a man named Martin had relations, *comme ma-
quereau*, with a courtesan. She found a rich protector, and told
Martin frankly that she could only see him on the quiet in the future,
as the rich protector would be jealous. Martin got into her apartment, stood behind the door, and struck her dead with one blow of a
knife in the heart as she entered one night. She was only a *fille*, and
the affair was considered as a *crime passionnel*, and Martin was
acquitted (*Doux Pays!*). I was told yesterday that Martin, handsome and well dressed, frequents the *Folies Bergères* and other
places, and has relations with other women. There are a number of
women who are proud to shake hands with, to drink with, and to be
the mistress of an assassin. 'He killed a woman at one stroke!' In
certain circles, Martin is the vogue! This is one of the most curious,
and yet natural, things I have heard about Paris.

> Arnold Bennett

Paris Streets

The day before yesterday, or a bit earlier, two children were born in
the streets of Paris the same day. C. explained to me that the thing
occurred not infrequently. *Accouchement* in a 'maison' was an
expensive affair, comparatively. Hence women, at the very last
moment, went to the *poste de police* and demanded the assistance
which the law binds itself to give.

> Arnold Bennett

Imagination

Last night, when I went into the Duval for dinner, a middle-aged woman, inordinately stout and with pendent cheeks, had taken the seat opposite to my prescriptive seat. I hesitated, as there were plenty of empty places, but my waitress requested me to take my usual chair. I did so, and immediately thought: 'With *that* thing opposite to me my dinner will be spoilt!' But the woman was evidently also cross at my filling up her table, and she went away, picking up all her belongings, to another part of the restaurant, breathing hard. Then she abandoned her second choice for a third one. My waitress was scornful and angry at this desertion, but laughing also. Soon all the waitresses were privately laughing at the goings-on of the fat woman, who was being served by the most beautiful waitress I have ever seen in any Duval. The fat woman was clearly a crotchet, a 'maniaque', a woman who lived much alone. Her dress (she displayed on taking it off a simply awful light puce flannel cloak) and her parcels were continually the object of her attention and she was always arguing with her waitress. And the whole restaurant secretly made a butt of her. She was repulsive; no one could like or sympathize with her. But I thought – she has been young and slim once. And I immediately thought of a long 10 or 15 thousand words short story, 'The History of Two Old Women'. I gave this woman a sister, fat as herself. And the first chapter would be in the restaurant (both sisters) something like tonight – and written rather cruelly. Then I would go back to the infancy of these two, and sketch it all. One would have lived ordinarily, married prosaically, and become a widow. The other should have become a whore and all that; 'guilty splendour'. Both are overtaken by fat. And they live together again in old age, not too rich, a nuisance to themselves and to others. Neither has any imagination. For 'tone' I thought of *Ivan Ilyitch*, and for technical arrangement I thought of that and also of *Histoire d'une fille de ferme*. The two lives would have to intertwine. I saw the whole work quite clearly, and hope to do it.

Arnold Bennett

Clouds

They represent the spirit of play, the wrath of heaven and the power of death; they are a comfort to the eye, a blessing and a gift of God, as tender, yielding and gentle as the souls of new-born children. They are as handsome, rich and prodigal as Good Angels; as sombre, inescapable and merciless as messengers of death. They sweep by in silvery wisps, sail along, white, jocund masses lined with gold; they hang poised, tinged with yellow, red and blue. Darkly and slowly they glide past like murderers; chase helter-skelter like mad horsemen, linger sad and dreamily on the pale heights like melancholy hermits. They assume the shapes of the blessed isles and of guardian angels, of threatening hands, fluttering sails, cranes in flight. They journey between God's heaven and our poor earth, glorious images of all man's yearning, and belonging to both – dreams of the earth in which its blemished soul cleaves to the pure heaven above. They are the eternal symbol of all voyaging, all questing, all yearning for home. Like they who are suspended, faint-hearted yet defiant and nostalgic between heaven and earth, the souls of human beings sharing the same emotions are suspended between time and eternity.

O lovely, restless floating clouds! I was an ignorant child but I loved and contemplated them, little knowing that I too should go through life like a cloud, wandering, everywhere a stranger, floating between time and eternity. Ever since childhood days they have been my dear friends and sisters. I cannot even cross the road without exchanging a greeting with them while we linger a moment and gaze at each other. Nor did I ever forget what I learned at that time; their features, shapes, colours, games and frolics; their strange, fantastic tales. Most of all I remember the Snow Princess. Her stage is on the lower mountains in early winter, among the warm undercurrents of air. The Snow Princess appears with a small retinue, descending from the great heights, and seeks a resting-place for herself in distant mountain-hollows or upon a broad summit. Envious, the false North wind sees the innocent maiden lie down to rest, in secret lust leaps up the mountain and suddenly falls upon her in rage and fury, hurls torn shreds of black cloud in the beautiful Princess's direction, shouts at her and tries to drive her away. For a while the Princess is ill at ease, waits patiently and often climbs back to her heights, shaking her head in gentle scorn. Often too, however, she gathers her frightened maids-in-waiting around her, unveils her dazzlingly regal countenance and waves the evil spirit boldly back. He hesitates, howls and flees away. And she lies down quietly, shrouds her throne in white mist, and when the mist has withdrawn, valleys and mountain-tops lie bright and gleaming in their covering of pure, soft new snow.

Hermann Hesse

Youth

I did not think of myself as a great poet. What I wrote was magazine verse, not poetry. Inwardly however, I cherished the secret hope that one day I was destined to write real poetry, a daring and ambitious song of life and longing. The bright and cheerful mirror of my soul was clouded at intervals by a kind of melancholy; otherwise it was not seriously troubled. I was overwhelmed sometimes for a day, sometimes a night, by an indefinable loneliness and gloom which vanished without a trace, only to return weeks or months later. In time I became as accustomed to it as a trusted friend until it seemed less of a torment than a disquieting weariness which had its own particular sweetness. When it assailed me at night, instead of sleeping, I lay by the window for hours on end, gazed at the dark waters of the lake, the mountains silhouetted against the pale sky and the lovely stars above them. On such occasions I was often overcome by a tormentingly exquisite sensation as if all this nocturnal loveliness viewed me with justifiable reproach. As if stars, mountains and lake were longing for someone who could understand and voice their beauty and the suffering of their inarticulate existence, as if I were this person whose vocation was to interpret the silence of nature in my poetry. I did not get so far as to consider how I could possibly achieve it. I merely felt the lovely, solemn night waiting impatiently for me with unexpressed longing. Nor in this mood did I ever compose anything. All the same I was aware of a kind of responsibility towards these dark voices, and after such nights I usually took lonely walks that lasted several days. It was, I felt, my way of showing a little affection to the earth which was offering itself to me with dumb entreaties – an idea which caused me to laugh at myself. These journeys became one of the foundations of my later life, for since then I have spent the greater part of my life wandering for weeks or months through many countries. I grew accustomed to walking far afield with little money and a hunk of bread in my pocket, spending entire days in solitude and frequently passing the night in the open.

Hermann Hesse

Breakfast in Lucca

For all my early start, the intolerable heat had again taken the ascendant before I had fairly entered the plain. Then, it being yet but morning, I entered from the north the town of Lucca, which is the neatest, the regularest, the exactest, the most fly-in-amber little town in the world, with its uncrowded streets, its absurd fortifications, and its contented silent houses – all like a family at ease and at rest under its high sun. It is as sharp and trim as its own map, and that map is as clear as a geometrical problem. Everything in Lucca is good.

I went with a short shadow, creeping when I could on the eastern side of the street to save the sunlight; then I came to the main square, and immediately on my left was the Albergo di Something-or-other, a fine great hotel, but most unfortunately right facing the blazing sky. I had to stop outside it to count my money. I counted it wrong and entered. There I saw the master, who talked French.

'Can you in an hour,' said I, 'give me a meal to my order, then a bed, though it is early day?' This absurd question I made less absurd by explaining to him my purpose. How I was walking to Rome, and how, being northern, I was unaccustomed to such heat; how, therefore, I had missed sleep, and would find it necessary in future to walk mainly by night. For I had now determined to fill the last few marches up in darkness, and to sleep out the strong hours of the sun.

All this he understood; I ordered such a meal as men give to beloved friends returned from wars. I ordered a wine I had known long ago in the valley of the Saone in the old time of peace before ever the Greek came to the land. While they cooked it I went to their cool and splendid cathedral to follow a late Mass. Then I came home and ate their admirable food and drank the wine which the Burgundians had trodden upon the hills of gold so many years before. They showed me a regal kind of a room where a bed with great hangings invited repose.

All my days of marching, the dirty inns, the forests, the nights abroad, the cold, the mists, the sleeplessness, the faintness, the dust, the dazzling sun, the Apennines – all my days came over me, and there fell on me a peaceful weight, as his two hundred years fell upon Charlemagne in the tower of Saragossa when the battle was done; after he had curbed the valley of Ebro and christened Bramimonde.

Hilaire Belloc

Gordon Craig

Craig then took me up to his studio at the top of a high building in Berlin. There was a black, waxed floor with roseleaves, artificial roseleaves, strewn all over it.

Here stood before me brilliant youth, beauty, genius; and, all inflamed with sudden love, I flew into his arms with all the magnetic willingness of a temperament which had for two years lain dormant, but waiting to spring forth. Here I found an answering temperament, worthy of my metal. In him I had met the flesh of my flesh, the blood of my blood. Often he cried to me, 'Ah, you are my sister.'

I do not know how other women remember their lovers. I suppose it is the correct thing to stop always at a man's head, shoulders, hands, etc., and then describe his clothes, but I always see him, as that first night in the studio, when his white, lithe, gleaming body emerged from the chrysalis of clothes and shone upon my dazzled eyes in all his splendour.

So must Endymion, when first discovered by the glistening eyes of Diana, in tall, slender whiteness, so must Hyacinthus, Narcissus, and the bright, brave Perseus have looked. More like an angel of Blake than a mortal youth he appeared. Hardly were my eyes ravished by his beauty than I was drawn toward him, entwined, melted. As flame meets flame, we burned in one bright fire. Here, at last, was my mate; my love; my self – for we were not two, but one, that one amazing being of whom Plato tells in the *Phaedrus*, two halves of the same soul.

This was not a young man making love to a girl. This was the meeting of twin souls. The light covering of flesh was so transmuted with ecstasy that earthly passion became a heavenly embrace of white, fiery flame.

There are joys so complete, so all perfect, that one should not survive them. Ah, why did not my burning soul find exit that night, and fly, like Blake's angel, through the clouds of our earth to another sphere?

His love was young, fresh, and strong, and he had neither the nerves nor nature of a voluptuary, but preferred to turn from love-making before satiety set in, and to translate the fiery energy of his youth to the magic of his Art.

In his studio was no couch, no easy chair, and no dinner. We slept on the floor that night. He was penniless, and I didn't dare go home for money. I slept there for two weeks. When we wanted a dinner, he ordered one to be sent up, on credit, and I hid on the balcony until it came, then crept in and shared it.

Isadora Duncan

Isabelle Eberhardt Dies, 1904

Everything about her was extraordinary. She was a woman, dressed as a man. A European turned Arab. A Russian who transposed 'nitchevo' into 'mektoub', whose untidy mystical torments, l'âme slave, found peace in Islam's faith – and flesh. She was born on the prim, pale lake-side of Geneva. She died on the burning desert. She was an expatriate wanderer whose nomadic Slav background led her to range the desert insatiably: yet she dreamed of a petit-bourgeois *haven, a grocer's shop in some obscure little Algerian town where she and her Arab husband and all his hordes of relatives could conduct a modest business. She adored her insignificant husband, but her sensual adventures were without number. Her behaviour was outrageous; she drank, she smoked hashish, but* déclassée, *she remained* racée. *She was the outcast, despised and rejected by French Administration and the colony in general. But she was General Lyautey's trusted friend. She was a writer who was almost unrecognized, and quite penniless till after her death, when, ironically, posthumous editions of her books earned a small fortune – for others. Her death was strangest of all, for she was drowned in the desert.*

Lesley Blanche, 1954

Edwardian Party Games

They began, sedately enough, with partial unpacking and tea; but by Sunday night the entire house would be strewn with dozens of pairs of white shoes which had been used from store in every kind of outdoor game, with discarded costumes hunted out of great chests and closets for the exacter verisimilitude of charades, and with the general litter of a tempestuous assembly. No late nights were kept; but from nine o'clock in the morning until ten or eleven in the evening . . . the pace was terrific. And through it all was Mr Wells, leader in every activity from lawn tennis, hockey, quoits, and dancing to bridge and a frightful pastime known as Demon Patience; Mr Wells, full of

hospitality and the high spirits always engendered in him by the
society of young, active, laughing people; Mr Wells, above all, the
animated, unexhausted, and inexhaustible talker, who to the last
moment of the day would receive with every word dropped by
another person, and every small incident that occurred or was
described, fresh inspiration . . .

Frank Swinnerton, 1937

On Henry James's Novels

It is like a church lit but without a congregation to distract you, with
every light and line focused on the high altar. And on the altar, very
reverently placed, intensely there, is a dead kitten, an egg-shell, a
bit of string . . . And the elaborate copious emptiness of the whole
Henry James exploit is only redeemed and made endurable by the
elaborate, copious wit . . . He spares no resource in the telling of
his dead inventions . . . He splits his infinitives and fills them up
with adverbial stuffing. His vast paragraphs sweat and struggle
. . . And all for tales of nothingness . . . It is a magnificent but
painful hippopotamus resolved at any cost, even at the cost of its
dignity, upon picking up a pea which has got into the corner of its
den.

H. G. Wells

Paris

In the garden of the Tuileries he had lingered, on two or three spots,
to look; it was as if the wonderful Paris spring had stayed him as he
roamed. The prompt Paris morning struck its cheerful notes – in a
soft breeze and a sprinkled smell, in the light flit, over the garden-
floor, of bareheaded girls with the buckled strap of oblong boxes, in
the type of ancient thrifty persons basking betimes where terrace-
walls were warm, in the blue-frocked brass-labelled officialism of
humble rakers and scrapers, in the deep references of a straight-
pacing priest or the sharp ones of a white-gaitered, red-legged
soldier. He watched little brisk figures, figures whose movement
was as the tick of the great Paris clock, take their smooth diagonal
from point to point; the air had a taste as of something mixed with
art, something that presented nature as a white-capped master-

chef. The palace was gone, Strether remembered the palace; and when he gazed into the irremediable void of its site the historic sense in him might have been freely at play – the play under which in Paris indeed it so often winces like a touched nerve. He filled out spaces with dim symbols of scenes; he caught the gleam of white statues at the base of which, with his letters out, he could tilt back a straw-bottomed chair. But his drift was, for reasons, to the other side, and it floated unspent up the rue de Seine and as far as the Luxembourg.

In the Luxembourg Gardens he pulled up; here at last he found his nook, and here, on a penny chair from which terraces, alleys, vistas, fountains, little trees in green tubs, little women in white caps, and shrill little girls at play all sunnily 'composed' together, he passed an hour in which the cup of his impressions seemed truly to overflow.

Henry James

Portent

At seven o'clock in the evening, in the Rue Royale, I saw a regiment of the line march past, the 104th, the band at its head. It was returning from a camp at Châlons, after a month of marches and manoeuvres. Their uniforms dusty from the road, the men were marching well in excellent rank and file, sunburned, in fine fettle: the classical type of French soldier. From a military point of view, our nation had not degenerated.

What is no less satisfactory, as a spectacle, is the crowd lining the pavement, standing on benches, watching the soldiers marching past. Plenty of emotion there, vibrant warmth, cheers when the colours passed, and repeated cries of 'Long live France! Long live the Army!'

There is no doubt that national sentiment is reawakening. This morning my tailor was saying to me, 'Ah, monsieur, how much longer are these Germans going to be allowed to bother us? Why don't we give them one on the nose, eh? A good, hearty one. If they declare war, well, we'll fight.'

'And how do your men feel about it?'

'Every working man will say exactly what I have said, monsieur.'

Maurice Paléologue

A Boy's Vigil at the Dinner Table

General Feversham, himself jogged by the unlucky mention of a name, suddenly blurted out –

'Lord Wilmington. One of the best names in England, if you please. Did you ever see his house in Warwickshire? Every inch of the ground you would think would have a voice to bid him play the man, if only in remembrance of his fathers . . . It seemed incredible and mere camp rumour, but the rumour grew. If it was whispered at the Alma, it was spoken aloud at Inkermann, it was shouted at Balaclava. Before Sebastopol the hideous thing was proved. Wilmington was acting as galloper to his General. I believe upon my soul the General chose him for the duty, so that the fellow might set himself right. There were three hundred yards of bullet-swept flat ground, and a message to be carried across them. Had Wilmington toppled off his horse on the way, why, there were the whispers silenced for ever. Had he ridden through alive he earned distinction besides. But he didn't dare, he refused! Imagine it if you can! He sat shaking on his horse, and declined. You should have seen the General. His face turned the colour of that Burgundy. "No doubt you have a previous engagement," he said, in the politest voice you ever heard – just that, not a word of abuse. A previous engagement on the battle-field! For the life of me I could hardly help laughing. But it was a tragic business for Wilmington. He was broken, of course, and slunk back to London. Every house was closed to him, he dropped out of his circle like a lead bullet you let slip out of your hand into the sea. The very women in Piccadilly spat if he spoke to them; and he blew his brains out in a back bedroom off the Haymarket. Curious that, eh? He hadn't the pluck to face the bullet when his name was at stake, yet he could blow his own brains out afterwards.'

Lieutenant Sutch chanced to look at the clock as the story came to an end. It was now a quarter to one. Harry Feversham still had a quarter of an hour's furlough, and that quarter of an hour was occupied by a retired surgeon-general with a great wagging beard, who sat nearly opposite to the boy.

'I can tell you an incident still more curious,' he said.

'The man in this case had never been under fire before, but he was of my own profession. Life and death were part of his business. Nor was he really in any particular danger. The affair happened during a hill campaign in India. We were encamped in a valley, and a few Pathans used to lie out on the hillside at night and take long shots into the camp. A bullet ripped through the canvas of the hospital tent – that was all. The surgeon crept out to his own quarters, and his orderly discovered him half an hour afterwards lying in his blood stone dead.'

'Hit?' exclaimed the Major.

'Not a bit of it,' said the surgeon. 'He had quietly opened his instrument-case in the dark, taken out a lancet, and severed his femoral artery. Sheer panic, do you see, at the whistle of a bullet.'

> A. E. W. Mason

An Indian Assassin, Condemned for Attacking Sir Curzon Wylie and Dr Lalcasa, 1904

I admit the other day I attempted to shed English blood as an humble revenge for the inhuman hangings and deportations of patriotic Indian youths. In this attempt I have consulted none but my own conscience. I have conspired with none but my own duty.

I believe that a nation held down by foreign bayonets is in a perpetual state of war, since open battle is rendered impossible to a disarmed race. I attacked by surprise; since guns were denied to me I drew my pistol and fired.

As a Hindoo I felt that wrong to my country is an insult to God. Her cause is the cause of Shri Ram, her service is the service of Shri Krishna. Poor in wealth and intellect, a son like myself has nothing else to offer to the Mother but his own blood, and so I have sacrificed the same on her altar.

The only lesson required in India at present is to learn how to die, and the only way to teach it is by dying ourselves. Therefore I die, and glory in my martyrdom.

> Dhingra, at the Old Bailey

On Lenin

Lenin's ultra-centralism in its essence is carried not by a positive, creative spirit but by the sterile spirit of a night-watchman. His thoughts are mainly directed to controlling the party activity and not to stimulating it, to narrowing down the movement and not to developing it . . . Nothing delivers a still young movement more readily to the lust for power of academicians than the imprisonment of this movement in the iron casing of a bureaucratic centralism which degrades the fighting worker to become a pliant tool of a committee.

In the effort to prevent the Russian workers' movement from mistakes by putting it under the tutelage of an all-knowing and all-present Central Committee, there seems to appear a subjectivism which had already often tricked Russian socialism . . . The great Ego, crushed and smashed by Russian absolutism, takes revenge by placing itself in its revolutionary fantasy upon the throne and declaring itself . . . to be the almighty Lord of history – this time in the autocratic majesty of a Central Committee of the Social-Democratic Workers' Movement.

Rosa Luxemburg, 1904

We need the real, nation-wide terror which reinvigorates the country and through which the Great French Revolution achieved glory.

Lenin, 1908

Modern Art

Allow me to repeat what I said when you were here: deal with nature by means of the cylinder, the sphere and the cone, all placed in perspective, so that each side of an object or a plane is directed towards a central point. Lines parallel to the horizon give breadth, a section of nature or, if you prefer, of the spectacle spread before our eyes by the *Pater Omnipotens Aeterne Deus*. Lines perpendicular to that horizon give depth. But for us men, nature has more depth than surface, hence the need to introduce in our vibrations of light, represented by reds and yellows, enough blue tints to give a feeling of air.

Paul Cézanne, to Émile Bernard

Man's Behaviour When Alone

Today while I was watching a fair little lady in cream-coloured stockings, with the immature features of a child, who stood on the Triotzki bridge, holding the balustrade with her grey-gloved hands as though preparing to jump into the Neva, I saw her stick out a sharp, pink little tongue at the moon.

The old man in the moon, the sly fox of the skies, was stealthily making his way through a cloud of dirty smoke. He was very large and his cheeks were crimson, as though he had had too much to drink. The young lady was teasing him very earnestly and even revengefully – so it seemed to me at least.

She recalled to my mind the memory of certain 'peculiarities' which had puzzled me for a long time. Whenever I watch how a man behaves when he is alone, I always conclude that he is 'insane' – I can find no other word for it.

I first noticed this when I was still a boy: a clown named Rondale, an Englishman, who was walking along the dark and deserted passages of a circus, took off his top hat to a mirror and bowed respectfully to his own reflection. There was no one in the passage but himself. I was sitting on a cistern over his head and so was invisible to him, and had thrust out my head just at the moment when he made his respectful bow. This action of the clown plunged me into dark and unpleasant speculations. He was a clown, and what is more, an Englishman, whose profession – or art – lay in his eccentricity.

Then I noticed a neighbour, A. Chekhov, sitting in his garden, try unsuccessfully to catch a sunbeam with his hat and to place both on his head. I could see that his failure annoyed the sunbeam-hunter; his face grew redder and redder, and he ended by slapping his hat on his knee, putting it on his head with a quick movement and impatiently pushing his dog away. Then, half-closing his eyes and looking stealthily at the sky, he stalked towards the house. Seeing me in the porch, he smiled and said:

'Good-morning, Have you read Belmont's verses, "The sun smells of grass"? Silly, isn't it? In Russia it smells of Kazan soap, and here – Tartar sweat.'

It was Chekhov, too, who tried conscientiously to poke a thick red pencil into the neck of a small medicine-bottle, thereby breaking a certain law of physics as well as the bottle. He persisted with the quiet obstinacy of a scientist making an experiment.

Leo Tolstoy once said to a lizard in a low whisper: 'Are you happy, eh?'

The lizard was warming itself on a stone among the shrubs that grew on the road to Dulber, while he stood watching it, his hands thrust inside his belt. Then, cautiously looking round, the great man confided to the lizard: 'As for me – I'm not!'

Professor Tikhvinsky, the chemist, sitting in my dining-room, addressed his own reflection in the copper tea-tray: 'Well, old boy, how is life?'

The image made no reply; so Tikhvinsky sighed deeply and began carefully rubbing it off with his palm, puckering his brows and twitching his nose, which resembled the trunk of an embryo elephant.

I was told that someone once found N. S. Leskoff occupying himself by sitting at the table and lifting a tuft of cottonwool into the air, then letting it fall into a china bowl and stooping over it, listening, evidently expecting that the wool would produce a sound as it fell on the china.

The priest F. Vladimirsky once placed a boot in front of him, and said to it impressively: 'Now then – go!' Then, 'Ah, you can't?' Then, with dignity and conviction, he added: 'You see! You can't go anywhere without me!'

'What are you doing, Father?' I asked, entering the room at this moment.

He looked at me attentively and explained: 'It's this boot. It's all worn down at the heel. Nowadays they make such poor boots!'

> Maxim Gorki

The Prophet

Under the banner of learning, art and persecuted freedom of thought, Russia will one day be ruled by such toads and crocodiles as were unknown even in Spain under the Inquisition. Yes, you just wait. Narrow-mindedness, enormous pretensions, excessive self-importance, a total absence of any literary or social conscience, these things will do their work.

> Anton Chekhov

Anton Chekhov

He refused to march under any political banner – a thing, let it be remembered, of almost inconceivable courage in his country; he submitted to savagely hostile attacks for his political indifference; yet he spent more than half his life and energy in doing more active good to his neighbour than most of the high-souled professors of liberalism and social reform. He undertook an almost superhuman journey to Sahalin in 1890 to investigate the conditions of the prisoners there; in 1892 he spent the best part of a year as a doctor devising preventive measures against the cholera in the country districts where he lived, and although he had no time for writing on which his living depended, he refused the government pay in order to preserve his own independence of action; in another year he was the leading spirit in organizing practical measures of famine relief about Nizhni-Novgorod. From his childhood to his death, moreover, he was the sole support of his family. Measured by the standards of Christian Morality, Chekhov was a Saint. His self-devotion was boundless.

J. Middleton Murry

Anton Chekhov Dies, 1904

Even in death Chekhov was not spared ironies such as had long haunted both his life and his plots. The coffined corpse was delivered to St Petersburg in a railway wagon labelled as if to inspire some newly arisen Antasha Chekhonte: FRESH OYSTERS.

Ronald Hingley, 1976

The Murder of the Russian Minister of the Interior, Viacheslar Plehve, St Petersburg, 1904

The usual guards were posted all the way to the station – police on foot and on horseback, secret agents in every possible disguise, some dressed as beggars, others as fine gentlemen. Some stood in the thoughtful pose of men absorbed in ethereal dreams, others sauntered along in leisurely, aristocratic fashion. All their faces, however, betrayed the mark of Cain. They all cast inquisitive, questioning, furtive glances around. I had to work my way through this barricade of guards with the greatest possible care, for at any moment a sudden shove might cause me to be prematurely blown up.

The minister's carriage came speeding along like an arrow. I went quickly to meet it and block the way. I saw Plehve quickly changing his position and bowing at the carriage window. I took my bomb and flung it at the window-pane. What happened next I neither saw nor heard. Everything disappeared.

But the next moment consciousness returned. I was lying on the pavement. My first thought was astonishment at being still alive. I tried to get up, but my body felt as if it were not there; I felt as if nothing were left but thought. I passionately wanted to know the result of my deed. Somehow I managed to raise myself on my elbow and look round. Through the smoke I saw a red general's cloak lying on the ground, and something else, but neither carriage nor horses. According to eye-witnesses I shouted: 'Long live freedom!' Without knowing how badly I was wounded, I was filled with the wish not to be caught by my enemies. The thought, 'I may get delirious,' ran through my mind. 'Rather commit *hara-kiri* in the Japanese manner than die at the filthy hands of the gendarmes.' I tried to take my revolver from my pocket, but my hands would not obey me. In the meantime one of the police who always escorted Plehve's carriage on bicycles rushed up, attracted by my cry. He fell upon me and held me down with the weight of his body. And then there began the scenes that are usual in these cases. The first man started hitting me. Then others turned up and started belabouring me in every possible way with their fists, with kicks, with the butts of their revolvers. Yet I felt no pain and no resentment. Everything was indifferent to me. In the blessedness of victory and the peace of approaching death everything faded into insignificance. I heard shouts of 'Where's the other bomb?'

            Yegor Sazonov, from prison

Anarchists who commit dastardly murders very badly, die like saints, and leave beautiful letters behind 'em . . . People whose conduct is inexplicable to me, and yet their spiritual life is higher than most.

            Robert Louis Stevenson

Life's Challenge

To die young, clean, ardent; to die swiftly, in perfect health; to die saving others from death, or worse – disgrace – to die scaling heights; to die and to carry with you into the fuller, ampler life beyond, untainted hopes and aspirations, unembittered memories, all the freshness and gladness of May – is not that the cause for joy rather than sorrow?

H. A. Vachell

Plan of Attack, 1905

The neutrality of Luxemburg, Belgium and the Netherlands must be violated. The violation of Luxemburg will have no important consequences save protests. The Netherlands regard England allied to France no less as an enemy than does Germany. It will be possible to come to an agreement with them. Belgium will probably show resistance.

Count von Schlieffen

'Bloody Sunday', St Petersburg, January 22, 1905

A Peaceable Crowd Petitions the Tsar:
We working men of St Petersburg, our wives and children, and our parents, helpless and aged men and women, have come to you, our ruler, in quest of justice and protection. We are beggars, we are oppressed and overburdened with work; we are insulted, we are not regarded as human beings but are treated as slaves who must suffer their bitter lot in silence. We have suffered but are driven further and further into the abyss of poverty, injustice and ignorance; we are strangled by despotism and tyranny, so that we can breathe no longer. We have no strength at all, O Sovereign. Our patience is at an end. We are approaching that terrible moment when death is better than the continuance of intolerable sufferings . . .

The troops fired into the unarmed masses outside the Winter Palace, leaving perhaps 1,000 dead.

Sinking of the Imperial Russian Fleet by the Japanese at Tsu-Shima, May, 1905

I have sworn to God to accomplish my task. He has already strengthened my nerve, and has in His infinite mercy protected us in the stress of the operations we have already accomplished. I pray that God may strengthen my right hand. He may purge my country from shame with my blood.

Admiral Petrovitch Rozhestvensky's order to Fleet

The Admiral had sailed a half-derelict fleet 18,000 miles in seven months, rounding the Cape, enduring breakdowns, groundings, fiascos, mutinies, world opinion forcing him to coal in mid-ocean, with men going mad and killing themselves, with news of the Winter Palace massacre and final military disaster in Manchuria. His great voyage, first ridiculed, then applauded, ended in one of the most spectacular naval disasters ever known, he himself wounded thirteen times.

The Great Principles of Conduct

The Tsu-Shima victory is the outcome of Bushido, of the whole training of the Japanese people in the great fundamental principles of human conduct. That training is not a veneer which can be put on for a given purpose. It is a thing which must begin with the cradle, and which must be universal in a nation which hopes to come through the last ordeal as the Japanese have now come. Which thing may well give this nation pause, and set it considering whether there are not greater ideals than buying in the cheapest market and obtaining the greatest average return upon capital.

    The Times

You have all heard of the bravery of the Japs in their war against Russia, how they feared nothing and willingly went to their death in order that their country might win. This spirit of sacrificing themselves is called Bushido and is just the spirit which every fellow must have if he means to be a real true Scout.

    Robert Baden-Powell

A Last Word from a Frenchman

You know now who I am; a revolutionary living by the fruits of brigandage. Moreover, I have set fire to several hotels and I have defended my liberty against the aggression of the agents of authority.

    I have laid bare my whole life of struggle; I submit it as a problem for your intelligence. Not recognising that anyone has the right to judge me, I ask neither for pardon nor for merciful treatment. I don't beg from those whom I hate and despise. You are the stronger party; dispose of me as you like, send me to the penal settlement or to the scaffold, it doesn't matter much to me! But before we part let me say a last word to you.

Since you reproach me above all with being a thief it is useful to define what theft is.

Theft is restitution, it is the act of taking possession again. Rather than be cloistered in a factory as though I were in a penal settlement, rather than beg for that which is my right . . . I preferred to rebel and fight every inch of the ground with my enemies by making war on the rich and attacking their belongings. Of course, I understand that you would have preferred that I should submit myself to your laws, that as a docile and browbeaten worker I should create wealth in exchange for a ridiculous wage, and that with my body played out and my brain stultified I should go and die like a dog in the gutter. Then you would not call me a 'cynical bandit' but an 'honest worker'. Using flattery, you would even have awarded me the 'médaille de travail'. . . . The priests promise their dupes Paradise: you are less abstract, you offer them a scrap of paper!

I thank you very much for so much kindness, for so much gratitude, gentlemen! I prefer to be a cynic aware of his rights than an automaton, a caryatid.

> Alexandre Jacob, to the Jury

The Optimist

When the masons, and carpenters, and all who are concerned in house building, know that their daily bread is secured to them, they will ask nothing better than to work at their old trades a few hours a day. They will adapt the fine houses which absorbed the time of a whole staff of servants, and in a few months homes will have sprung up, infinitely healthier and more conveniently arranged than those of today. And to those who are not yet comfortably housed the anarchist Commune will be able to say: 'Patience, comrades! Palaces fairer and finer than any the capitalists built for themselves will spring from the ground of our enfranchised city. They will belong to those who have most need of them. The anarchist Commune does not build with an eye to revenues. These monuments erected to its citizens, products of the collective spirit, will serve as models to all humanity; they will be yours.'

> Peter Kropotkin

A Jesus for the New Century

Many people are shocked on learning that the historical Jesus must be accepted as 'capable of error' because the supernatural Kingdom of God, the manifestation of which He announced as imminent, did not appear.

What can we do in face of what stands clearly recorded in the Gospels? Are we acting in the spirit of Jesus if we attempt with hazardous and sophisticated explanations to force the sayings into agreement with the dogmatic teaching of His absolute universal incapability of error. He Himself never made any claim to such omniscience. Just as He pointed out to the young man who addressed Him as 'Good Master' that God alone is good, so He would also have set His face against those who would have liked to attribute to Him a divine infallibility. Knowledge of spiritual truth is not called upon to prove its genuineness by showing further knowledge about the events of world-history and matters of ordinary life. Its province lies on a quite different level from the latter's, and it is quite independent of it.

The historical Jesus moves us deeply by His subordination to God. In this He stands out as greater than the Christ personality of dogma which, in compliance with the claims of Greek metaphysics, is conceived as omniscient and incapable of error.

> Albert Schweitzer

The Beggars

What we see now is a fat man in a funny hat enthroned on a sort of four-legg'd stool, but he has only stumps for legs, holds a stick in walking-stick position a little behind him in his left hand, while in his other hand he brandishes a longer stick, handle-upward, like a croquet-mallet. He is one of the static, the immovable ones, who has to be carried out and lifted home at evening, and must be some kind of Roi d'Yvetot, or beggar-king. Waddling away from him with his back to us, another fat figure in a like furry hat, guitar on back, almost round of circumference – there are fat as well as thin ones! – pegging away from us upon his pair of stumps. Their ladies, whether queens or beggar-women, wear the high head-dresses of cambric and lace of the Payes de Caux.

Then in a kind of pointless frenzy, reeling from side to side and

half-staggering sideways and backwards, a victim of chorea, but of
course this is before the disease has been given its collector's name.
And a pair of cripples, both on crutches, hurrying, hurrying, and
they have got their two pairs of legs crossed and entangled. There is a
beggar, also on crutches, trailing a deformed leg like a thin, bent stalk
behind him. And a 'hopper', guitar or mandoline on his back,
hopping and jumping on his one leg and a stick; and two of the
quick-moving sort, they can go nearly as fast as skaters so long as they
are on level ground, their feet on bits of board which they have
learned not to knock against each other, while they dart forward by
means of what looks like a flat-iron on four points which they hold in
either hand.

Sacheverell Sitwell, 1973

The New Journalism

God made the people read so that I could fill their brains with facts,
facts, facts – and later tell them whom to love, whom to hate, and
what to think.

Lord Northcliffe

The only drawback to democracy was Demos – a jealous God of
primitive tastes and despotic tendencies.

Rudyard Kipling

Looking Back

The Dreyfus Affair can only be explained by the need for heroism
which periodically seizes this people, this race – seizes a whole
generation of us. The same applies to those other great ordeals:
wars . . . when a great war or great revolution erupts, it is because
people have had enough, particularly enough of peace. It means too
that the masses feel a violent need, a mysterious need for a great
movement . . . a sudden need for glory, war, history, which causes
an explosion, a break-out.

Charles Péguy

On Jews

There are far too many in my country. They want stamping out. If I did not restrain my people there would be a pogrom.

Kaiser Wilhelm II, to Sir Edward Grey

On a Politician

He seems to set great reliance on his Parliamentary and national reputation. He has rather misread the Constitution. If I am satisfied with him, that is sufficient, and nothing else matters.

Kaiser Wilhelm II

The principles of democracy can only create weak and often corrupt social institutions. A society is strong only if it recognizes the fact of natural superiorities, in particular the superiorities of birth.

Kaiser Wilhelm II

Socialism

Let us be clear about one thing: that Socialism means revolution, that it means a change in the everyday texture of life. It may be a very gradual change but it will be a very complete one. You cannot change the world, and at the same time not change the world. You will find Socialists about, or at any rate men calling themselves Socialists, who will pretend that this is not so, who will assure you that some odd little jobbing about municipal gas and water is Socialism, and backstairs intervention between Conservative and Liberal is the way to the millennium. You might as well call a gas jet in the lobby of a meeting-house the glory of God in heaven.

H. G. Wells

Imperialism

For where else in the world has a race gone forth and subdued, not a country or a kingdom, but a continent, and that continent peopled, not by savage tribes, but by races with traditions and a civilisation older than our own, with a history not inferior to ours in dignity or romance; subduing them not to the law of the sword, but to the rule of justice, bringing peace and order and good government to nearly one-fifth of the entire human race, and holding them with so mild a restraint that the rulers are the merest handful amongst the ruled, a tiny speck of white foam upon a dark and thunderous ocean.

> Lord Curzon, Viceroy of India, to the Prince and Princess of Wales

The Passing of the Great Cricketer, W. G. Grace

And then, in 1906, came what was almost the end. He was now fifty-eight, and Mr Leveson-Gower asked him to play once again for the Gentlemen at the Oval.

'Yes, Snipe,' he said. 'Yes – I'll do it.'

'And what if you fail?' he was asked, and he answered, 'I've been well advertised all my life. If I fail it'll be passed over, but if I do well it'll be a great exit.'

And a supremely great exit it was. Once again his birthday had come round, and, forty-one years after he had first played for the Gentlemen, he made 74 runs. Then, tired but happy, he lumbered into the pavilion, threw his bat on the table, and said, 'I shan't play any more.'

He never did play any more against the Players, but in 1907 he played for the Gentlemen against Surrey, the opening match of the season, and in 1908 he played in the same match on an April day of snow-showers. He made 15 and 25, and bowled twelve balls for five runs and no wicket. That was the end of his first-class cricket. He played afterwards in a number of minor matches for the M.C.C., and for local sides, and his very last match of all was a few days before the beginning of the war, for Eltham against Grove Park on July 25th, 1914. He made 31 runs on a fiery and impossible wicket, and the last bowlers who ever bowled to him could not get him out.

> Bernard Darwin, 1934

Latin Races

The whole of these pathetic and degenerate Latin races are becoming tools in England's hands, tools with which to block Germany's Mediterranean trade . . .

This eunuch people bred from the ethnic chaos of ancient Rome hates us from the depths of its soul.

> Kaiser Wilhelm II, on King Edward VII's meeting with King Alphonso XIII of Spain, 1905

On a Political Opponent

If he had a few more brains he would be a half-wit.

> A. J. Balfour

On the Achievements of Modern Science

Physics has now come to an end.

> Lord Kelvin

On Jews

I decide who is a Jew.

> Karl Lueger, Mayor of Vienna

Private Education, 1907

I would suggest that schools should assemble once a day for the practice of traditional songs and other music in unison. Then twice a week for half an hour's sight-reading and ear-training, but the school must be divided into the musical and the non-musical. We should find alternatives for the non-musical, but there must be no soft options for them like carpentering or modelling; I usually make them do drill or read the lives of the Archbishops.

> *Preparatory Schools Review*

Private Life

Be alone always. Be gentle with her when she is gentle, but if she tries to impose her will on you, beat her.

> D. H. Lawrence, to a youth before marriage

Sunning

*It was still the custom, in some Bradford mills, for the women to seize
a newly-arrived lad, and 'sun' him, that is, pull his trousers down and
reveal his genitals. But all this not unwholesome and perhaps traditional female bawdiness – there was a suggestion of mythology,
ancient worship, folklore, about that queer 'sunning' ritual – was far
removed from cynical whoring. There was nothing sly, nothing
hypocritical, about those coarse dames and screaming lasses, who
were devoted to their own men, generally working in the same mill,
and who kept on 'courting', though the actual courtship stage was
over early, for years and years, until a baby was due, when they
married.*

     J. B. Priestley, 1964

FRANKISH LANDS

Most evil was this forking of my ways:
There, from the chasm, tongues of baneful fire,
Here, regions to be shunned where loathing festered
In me for everything they praised and practised.
I scoffed at their gods, mine they taunted! Where is
Your poet, poor and boastful people? None
Is here: for This One spends his days in exile,
And That One's frantic head is veiled in frost.

The West then called with fabled voice . . . so rang
The sire's praise of his forever lavish
Young land, whose glory thrilled, whose travail moved him
To tears, though he was distant, of the Mother
Of aliens, of the unesteemed and banished . . .
The heir was greeted by a surge when luring
In kindliness and plenitude, the basins
Of Meuse and Marne were spread beneath the sunrise.

And in the town of merry grace, in gardens
Of wistful charm, near nightly gleaming towers
With magic arches, youth was all about me
And swept away with all the things I cherish –
There bard and hero fended for the Secret:

VILLIERS who thought himself the peer of kings,
VERLAINE in fall and shrift devout and childlike,
And bleeding for his concept, MALLARMÉ.

Though dream and distance give us strength and nurture –
Air that we breathe, the Living only proffer.
So friends who still are singing there, I thank you
And forebears that to graves I since have followed . . .
When I had gained a foothold – late – how often
As in my dreary land I strove, uncertain
Of victory, this whisper gave new vigors:
RETOURNENT FRANC EN FRANCE DULCE TERRE.

       Stefan George

A POEM OF MY TIMES

I am your conscience, I your voice pervading
Your malcontent that curses and condemns:
'The base alone still rule, the noble perished,
Belief is washed away and love is wilted.
How can we flee the foulness of the earth?'
Let torches show you where the era's ruin
Consumes you, where you shape it with the fevers
Of your own senses, with your ravelled heart.

You turned until you saw the Great no longer,
The Beautiful – in order to deny them,
And you dethroned their new, their ancient statues.
Beyond the Body and the Soil your structures
Of smoke and dust and fog you lifted, tower
And wall and arch began to grow gigantic –
But clouds that floated higher could have presaged
The hour long before when this would fall.

You crawled to caves: 'there is no day,' you clamoured,
'And only he who killed the fleshly in
Himself is free and so he earns endurance.'
So seekers after gold once, pale and fevered,
Their ore in crucibles with tinctures melted,
And just without were many sunlit courses . . .

When you concocted souls from filth and poison
You spilled the residue of healthy saps.

I saw the Pharaohs gazing through millennia
With eyes of stone, by tears of ours burdened,
By dreams of ours weighted . . . as we, they also
Knew: deserts shift with gardens, frost with blaze,
Night comes for sun – atonement for delight.
And though despair and dark engulf us: One Thing
That ever was – none knows it – is eternal,
And youth and flowers laugh and songs resound.

        Stefan George

CHILDHOOD

The school's long stream of time and tediousness
winds slowly on, through torpor, through dismay.
O loneliness, O time that creeps away . . .
Then out at last: the streets ring loud and gay,
and in the big white squares the fountains play,
and in the parks the world seems measureless. –
And to pass through it all in children's dress,
with others, but quite otherwise than they: –
O wondrous time, O time that fleets away,
O loneliness!

And out into it all to gaze and gaze:
men, women, women, men in blacks and greys,
and children, brightly dressed, but differently;
and here a house, and there a dog, maybe,
and fear and trust changing in subtle ways: –
O grief uncaused, O dream, O dark amaze,
O still-unsounded sea!

And then with bat and ball and hoop to playing
in parks where the bright colours softly fade,
brushing against the grown-ups without staying
when ball or hoop their alien walks invade;
but when the twilight comes, with little, swaying
footsteps going home with unrejected aid: –

O thoughts that fade into the darkness, straying
alone, afraid!

And hours on end by the grey pond-side kneeling
with little sailing-boat and elbows bare;
forgetting it, because one like it's stealing
below the ripples, but with sails more fair;
and, having still to spare, to share some feeling
with the small sinking face caught sight of there: –
Childhood! Winged likenesses half-guessed at, wheeling,
oh, where, oh, where?

       Rainer Maria Rilke

GOD IN THE MIDDLE AGES

And they'd got him in themselves upstored,
and they wanted him to reign forever,
and they hung on him (a last endeavour
to withhold his journey heavenward

and to have him near them in their slumbers)
their cathedrals' massive weights. He must
merely wheel across his boundless numbers
pointingly and, like a clock, adjust

what they daily toiled at or transacted.
But he suddenly got into gear,
and the people of the stricken town

left him – for his voice inspired such fear –
running with his striking-words extracted,
and absconded from his dial's frown.

       Rainer Maria Rilke

LATE AUTUMN IN VENICE

The city drifts no longer like a bait now,
upcatching all the days as they emerge.
Brittlier the glassy palaces vibrate now
beneath your gaze. And from each garden verge

the summer like a bunch of puppets dangles,
headforemost, weary, made away.
Out of the ground, though, from dead forest tangles
volition mounts: as though before next day

the sea-commander must have rigged and ready
the galleys in the sleepless Arsenal,
and earliest morning air be tarred already

by an armada, oaringly outpressing,
and suddenly, with flare of flags, possessing
the great wind, radiant and invincible.

      Rainer Maria Rilke

From SECOND BEST

Exile of immortality, strongly wise,
Strain through the dark, with undesirous eyes
To what may lie beyond it. Sets your star,
O heart, for ever! Yet behind the night,
Waits for the great unborn, somewhere afar,
Some white tremendous daybreak. And the light,
Returning, shall give back the golden hours,
Ocean a windless level, Earth a lawn
Spacious and full of sunlit dancing-places,
And laughter, and music, and, among the flowers,
The gay child-hearts of men, and the child-faces,
O heart, in the great dawn!

      Rupert Brooke

Socialist Conference at Stuttgart

However radical the men's speeches, whatever 'insane' resolutions
they might have adopted, the bourgeoisie could always be consoled
by the knowledge that one sure resource was available to them:
to break the opposition of the 'hotheads' and replace them
with submissive women workers. But then, look, what a surprise!
From all corners of the earth women representatives of the working
class got together . . . And if only recently the bourgeoisie sought

comfort in the isolation of the female half of the proletariat, that
sweet hope was dashed after the Stuttgart Congress.

      Alexandra Kollontai

The Young Writer

I have just finished reading a book by Elizabeth Robins, *Come and
Find Me*. Really, a clever, splendid book; it creates in me such a
sense of power. I feel that I do now realise, dimly, what women in
the future will be capable of. They truly as yet have never had their
chance. Talk of our enlightened days and our emancipated country – pure nonsense! We are firmly held with the self-fashioned
chains of slavery. Yes, now I see that they *are* self-fashioned chains,
and must be self-removed. Eh bien – now where is my ideal and
ideas of life? Does Oscar – and there is a gardenia yet alive beside
my bed – does Oscar now keep so firm a strong-hold in my soul?
No; because I am growing capable of seeing a wider vision – a little
Oscar, a little Symons, a little Dolf Wyllarde – Ibsen, Tolstoi,
Elizabeth Robins, Shaw, D'Annunzio, Meredith. To weave the
intricate tapestry of one's own life, it is well to take a thread from
many harmonious skeins – and to realise that there must be har-
mony. Not necessary to grow the sheep, comb the wool, colour and
brand it – but joyfully take all that is ready, and with that saved
time, *go* a great way further. Independence, resolve, firm purpose,
and the gift of discrimination, *mental clearness* – here are the
inevitables. Again, Will – the realisation that Art is absolutely
self-development. The knowledge that genius is dormant in every
soul – that that very individuality which is at the root of our being is
what matters so poignantly.

    Here then is a little summary of what I need – power, wealth and
freedom. It is the hopelessly insipid doctrine that love is the only
thing in the world, taught, hammered into women, from generation
to generation, which hampers us so cruelly. We must get rid of that
bogey – and then, then comes the opportunity of happiness and
freedom.

      Katherine Mansfield

Reading Habits in 200 Middlesbrough Homes

There are:

17 women who cannot read.
8 men who cannot read.
28 houses where no one cares to read.
8 men who actually dislike reading.
3 women who actually dislike reading.
7 women who say they 'have no time for it'.
50 houses where they only read novels.
58 houses where they read the newspapers only.
37 houses where they are 'fond of reading' or 'great readers'.
25 houses where they read books that are absolutely worth reading
   (this includes the men who read books about their work).

> Lady Florence Bell

Death of the Head of the Kaiser's Military Chancellery

At Donaueschingen, on November 10, 1908, the Emperor had watched the trial trip of the new airship; when it was over, he was loud in his praises of Count Zeppelin. He had by that time forgotten that, in his intimate circle a few months previously, he had spoken of him as 'the most stupid of all South Germans'. Now he was in the highest spirits. A triumph of German ingenuity! The Emperor's support could be fully relied upon.

After the fatigues of the official display, it was pleasant to relax in the company of a close friend in his neighbouring castle. Count Fürstenberg knew that the Emperor intended visiting him and had made his preparations: he had invited guests for a modest entertainment.

An hour of easy conversation in the drawing-room of the luxuriously appointed castle followed the dinner, after which the guests gathered in the main hall where, to the left of the stairway, a small orchestra was playing melodious waltzes, the overture to a cabaret show given 'by amateur talent drawn from the assembled company', according to the programme.

There was much laughter and applause; the gaiety reached its height with the last number: a solo dance by an unnamed ballet dancer – Count Hülsen-Haseler, giving a female impersonation, twirling in a stately dance on long thin legs emerging from the short ballet-dancer's skirt. The Head of the Military Chancellery, encouraged by the laughter, danced and leapt most comically. His performance was the hit of the evening. With a profound bow he withdrew behind the screen of palms concealing the side gallery, which had been transformed into the artistes' dressing-room.

A minute later, a dull thud was heard, the unmistakable sound of a falling body. The Count had collapsed, face downward, in a sudden heart attack, his delicate hands already taking on the livid hue of death. The gay music continued for a little while, until an adjutant of Count Fürstenberg announced that Count Hülsen had been taken ill. Servants dressed their dead master in his uniform; he lay on his death-bed impeccably attired when the hastily summoned priest arrived – too late, however, to administer the last sacraments. 'I have lost my best friend,' Wilhelm telegraphed to the Empress. He was soon to lose others.

P. J. Bouman, 1951

The Prophet

Look at it from any point of view you like, and I say you will come to the conclusion in regard to the relations between England and Germany, that there is no cause of difference between them, and although there may be snapping and snarling in the newspapers and in the London clubs, these two great people have nothing to fight about, have no prize to fight for, and have no place to fight in . . .

I say we honour that strong, patient, industrious German people, who have been for many centuries a prey to European intrigue and a drudge amongst the nations of the Continent. Now in the fullness of time, after many tribulations, they have by their virtues and valour won themselves a foremost place in the front of civilization.

Winston Churchill, to Swansea miners

Your Swansea speech was tiptop and pleased the Germans immensely.

David Lloyd George, to Winston Churchill

On Marriage

It would be a hundred times easier to struggle against physical desire if carnal relations and the feelings that lead to them were not made to look poetical; if marriage were not presented as an admirable institution that makes people happy, whereas in at least nine thousand nine hundred and ninety-nine cases out of ten thousand, if not in all, it ruins their entire lives; if, from childhood to adulthood, people were persuaded that the sexual act (merely imagining a loved person in that posture is enough!) is an ignoble and bestial one that is meaningless unless it is uppermost in the minds of both partners that they are going to assume the heavy and complex responsibility of bearing a child and raising it to the best of their ability as a result of their intercourse.

Leo Tolstoy

The Genius

Count Leo Tolstoy is an artist of genius, perhaps our Shakespeare. But although I admire him, I do not like him. He is not a sincere person; he is exaggeratedly self-preoccupied, he sees nothing and knows nothing outside himself. His humility is hypocritical and his desire to suffer repellent! Usually, such a desire is a symptom of a sick and perverted mind but in his case it is a great pride, wanting to be imprisoned solely in order to increase his authority. He lowers himself in my eyes, by his fear of death and his pitiful flirtation with it; as a rabid individualist, it gives him a sort of illusion of immortality to consolidate his authority . . . What comic greed! Exactly, comic! For more than twenty years this bell has been tolling a paean from the steeple-top that is contrary to my beliefs in every respect; for more than twenty years this old man has been talking of nothing but transforming young and lovely Russia into a province of China and young and gifted Russians into slaves. No, that man is a stranger to me, in spite of his very great beauty.

Maxim Gorki, to Vengerov

Young Gentlemen

Other trials and tribulations the young gentlemen at Temple Grove had to face were:
  1 An almost unending diet of flogging, and one Headmaster who, after each flogging, made a point of kissing his victim to convince him that all was now atoned and forgiven.

2 *Football to be played:*
  (a) in full everyday clothing except for the jacket.
  (b) with a bandage round your head if you happened to have mumps.
  (c) on a very rough pitch shared with cattle.
3 *Snow frequently piling up on the blankets in the dormitories, and ice in the water-jugs.*
4 *Lavatories that would not have passed in a slum tenement.*
5 *Excessive bullying, though some relief and protection was afforded by two memorable matrons, whose names are still honoured in the school. (One of them to the end of her days always referred to the dormitories as 'dromedaries'.)*

Arthur Harrison, 1977

Mr X and Mr Y

'A very fine term – cricket at Battersea Park on Wednesdays and Fridays, Swedish Drill through the term in Captain Wardle's gymnasium, swimming at Chelsea Baths – Decide for various reasons that Mr X had better leave at the end of term – have appointed Mr Y to succeed him.'

Next term: 'I decide that for various reasons Mr Y had better leave at the end of the term – a most successful school play performed by the boys, a selection from *Shockheaded Peter* – a number of children and nurses came to the Dress Rehearsal. A successful dancing class of thirty children is held by Miss Sturgess, also a Tango class for grown-up people on Thursdays.'

Orlando Wagner, Headmaster

Next year they found themselves unable to put on a play 'owing to lack of talent among the boys' – this was odd at a time when John Gielgud was a member of the school.

Arthur Harrison, 1977

A School Dispute

Mike unlocked the door, and flung it open. Framed in the entrance was a smallish, freckled boy, wearing a pork pie hat and carrying a bag. On his face was an expression of mingled wrath and astonishment.

Psmith rose courteously from his chair, and moved forward with slow stateliness to do the honours.

'What the dickens,' inquired the newcomer, 'are you doing here?'

'We are having a little tea,' said Psmith, 'to restore our tissues after our journey. Come in and join us. We keep open house, we Psmiths. Let me introduce you to Comrade Jackson. A stout fellow. Homely in appearance, perhaps, but one of us. I am Psmith. Your own name will doubtless come up in the course of general chit-chat over the tea-cups.'

'My name's Spiller, and this is my study.'

Psmith leaned against the mantelpiece, put up his eyeglass, and harangued Spiller in a philosophical vein.

'Of all sad words of tongue or pen,' said he, 'the saddest are these: "It might have been." Too late! That is the bitter cry. If you had torn yourself from the bosom of the Spiller family by an earlier train, all might have been well. But no. Your father held your hand and said huskily, "Edwin, don't leave us!" Your mother clung to you weeping, and said, "Edwin, stay!" Your sisters – '

'I want to know what – '

'Your sisters froze on to your knees like little octopuses (or octopi), and screamed, "Don't go, Edwin!" And so,' said Psmith, deeply affected by his recital, 'you stayed on till the later train; and, on arrival, you find strange faces in the familiar room, a people that know not Spiller.' Psmith went to the table, and cheered himself with a sip of tea. Spiller's sad case had moved him greatly.

The victim of Fate seemed in no way consoled.

'It's beastly cheek, that's what I call it. Are you new chaps?'

'The very latest thing,' said Psmith.

'Well, it's beastly cheek.'

Mike's outlook on life was of the solid, practical order. He went straight to the root of the matter.

'What are you going to do about it?' he asked.

Spiller evaded the question.

'It's beastly cheek,' he repeated. 'You can't go about the place bagging studies.'

'But we do,' said Psmith. 'In this life, Comrade Spiller, we must be prepared for every emergency. We must distinguish between the unusual and the impossible. It is unusual for people to go about the place bagging studies, so you have rashly ordered your life on the assumption that it is impossible. Error! Ah, Spiller, Spiller, let this be a lesson to you.'

'Look here. I tell you what it – '

'I was in a car with a man once. I said to him: "What would happen if you trod on that pedal thing instead of that other pedal thing?" He said, "I couldn't. One's the foot-brake, and the other's the accelerator." "But suppose you did?" I said. "I wouldn't," he said. "Now we'll let her rip." So he stamped on the accelerator. Only it turned out to be the foot-brake after all, and we stopped dead, and skidded into a ditch. The advice I give to every young man starting life is: "Never confuse the unusual and the impossible." Take the present case. If you had only realised the possibility of somebody some day collaring your study, you might have thought out dozens of sound schemes for dealing with the matter. As it is, you are unprepared. The thing comes on you as a surprise. The cry goes round: "Spiller has been taken unawares. He cannot cope with the situation." '

'Can't I! I'll – '

'What *are* you going to do about it?' said Mike.

'All I know is, I'm going to have it. It was Simpson's last term, and Simpson's left, and I'm next on the house list, so, of course, it's my study.'

'But what steps,' said Psmith, 'are you going to take? Spiller, the Man of Logic, we know. But what of Spiller, the Man of Action? How do you intend to set about it? Force is useless. I was saying to Comrade Jackson before you came in, that I didn't mind betting you were an insignificant-looking little weed. And you *are* an insignificant-looking little weed.'

P. G. Wodehouse

A Suffragette in Holloway Prison, 1909

We remained quite still when ordered to undress, and when they told us to proceed to our cells we linked arms and stood with our backs to the wall. The Governor blew his whistle and a great crowd of wardresses reappeared, falling upon us, forcing us apart and dragging us towards the cells. I think I had twelve wardresses for my share, and among them they managed to trip me so that I fell helplessly to the floor. One of the wardresses grasped me by my hair, wound the long braid around her waist and literally dragged me along the ground. In the cell they fairly ripped the clothing from my back, forcing on me one coarse cotton garment and throwing others on the bed for me to put on myself. Left alone exhausted by the dreadful experience I lay for a time gasping and shivering on the floor. By and by a wardress came to the door and threw me a blanket. This I wrapped around me, for I was chilled to the bone by this time. The single cotton garment and the rough blanket were all the clothes I wore during my stay in prison. Most of the prisoners refused everything but the blanket. According to agreement we all broke our windows and were immediately dragged off to the punishment cells. There we hunger struck, and after enduring great misery for nearly a week, we were one by one released.

Lucy Burns

Congo Atrocities

Sir,

There are many of us in England who consider the crime which has been wrought in the Congo lands by King Leopold of Belgium and his followers to be the greatest which has ever been known in human annals. Personally I am strongly of that opinion. There have been great expropriations like that of the Normans in England or of the English in Ireland. There have been massacres of populations like that of the South Americans by the Spaniards, or of subject nations by the Turks. But never before has there been such a mixture of wholesale expropriation and wholesale massacre, all done under an odious guise of philanthropy, and with the lowest commercial motives as a reason. It is this sordid cause, and the unctuous hypocrisy which make the crime unparalleled in its horror.

Sir Arthur Conan Doyle, to the American Press, 1909

Bayreuth, 1909

It has been possible, during these last performances, to step out of the opera-house and find oneself in the midst of a warm summer evening. From the hill above the theatre you look over a wide land, smooth and without hedges; it is not beautiful, but it is very large and tranquil. One may sit among rows of turnips and watch a gigantic old woman, with a blue cotton bonnet on her head and a figure like one of Dürer's, swinging her hoe. The sun draws out strong scents from the hay and the pine trees, and if one thinks at all, it is to combine the simple landscape with the landscape of the stage. When the music is silent the mind insensibly slackens and expands, among happy surroundings: heat and the yellow light, and the intermittent but not unmusical noises of insects and leaves smooth out the folds. In the next interval, between seven and eight, there is another act out here also; it is now dusky and perceptibly fresher; the light is thinner, and the roads are no longer crossed by regular bars of shade. The figures in light dresses moving between the trees of the avenue, with depths of blue air behind them, have a curiously decorative effect. Finally, when the opera is over, it is quite late; and half way down the hill one looks back upon a dark torrent of carriages descending, their lamps wavering one above another, like irregular torches.

> Virginia Woolf

Sunset, 1909

At such a point as the Marble Arch you may see conflagrations of jewels, a sky of burning lavender, tossed abroad like a crumpled cloak, with broad bands of dull purple and smoky pink, slashed with bright gold and decked with grey streamers.

> Arthur Symons

The wind, the wind, the wind blows high
The snow is falling from the sky
Maisie Drummond says she'll die
For want of the Golden City.

> Children's Song

The Policeman

A police-sergeant knows the history of hundreds of criminals in his district. He knows how much 'time' they have behind them, the houses they 'use', and, as a rule, where to lay his hand upon them at any hour of the night and day.

When a young man was arrested on suspicion of being concerned with his brother in the murder of an old couple in High Street, Deptford, the police-officer just looked into a public-house and said, 'Alf, I want you.'

George Robert Sims

1910–14

Austria

We youngsters, utterly absorbed in our literary ambitions, noticed little of the dangerous changes in our country; we looked only at books and paintings. We had not the least interest in political and social reforms; what did those squabbles mean in our lives?

> Stefan Zweig

What if the star that glitters
Constantly above that modish shop
Were suddenly to plunge
A long hat-pin into my heart?

> Osip Mandelstam

All night huge hordes of suicides venture out,
Those who pursue their lost selves;
Crookbacked they haunt south, west, east, north,
And with their arms for brooms they sweep the dust.

> Georg Heym

On the Wireless

What a marvellous invention it is! How privileged we are to be alive in an age of such scientific miracles!

> Dr H. H. Crippen, on SS *Montrose*

Dr Crippen was arrested for murder, on arrival at New York harbour, as a result of a wireless message to the Captain from Scotland Yard.

When the heart is breaking, and the way is long
In seeking rest, with no accompanying song,
Scorned by the world by cruel fate undone,
Friendless, yet not alone – for there is one –

Who truly loves this soon admitted clay
Who truly dreads this sure and awful day
When mortal soul shall fly to realms aloft
In life – in death – she still shall speak me soft.

> Dr H. H. Crippen from the Condemned Cell, Pentonville
> Prison, to Ethel LeNeve

Farewell

This is my farewell letter to the world. After many days of anxious
expectation that my innocence might be proved, after enduring the
agony of a long trial and the suspense of an appeal, and after the
final endeavour of my friends to obtain a reprieve, I see that at last
my doom is sealed and that in this life I have no more hope.

With all the courage I have I face another world and another
Judge – from Whom I am sure of justice greater than that of this
world and of mercy greater than that of men.

I have no dread of death, no fear of the hereafter, only the dread
and agony that one whom I love best may suffer when I have
gone . . .

About my unhappy relations with Belle Elmore I will say nothing.
We drifted apart in sympathy; she had her own friends and pleasures, and I was a rather lonely man and rather miserable. Then I
obtained the affection and sympathy of Miss Ethel LeNeve.

I confess that according to the moral laws of Church and State we
were guilty, and I do not defend our position in that respect. But
what I do say is that this love was not of a debased and degraded
character.

It was, if I may say so to people who will not, perhaps, understand
or believe, a good love. She comforted me in my melancholy
condition. Her mind was beautiful to me. Her loyalty and courage
and self-sacrifice were of a high character. Whatever sin there
was – and we broke the law – it was my sin, not hers.

In this farewell letter to the world, written as I face eternity, I say
that Ethel LeNeve has loved me as few women love men, and that

her innocence of any crime, save that of yielding to the dictates of the heart, is absolute.

To her I pay this last tribute. It is of her that my last thoughts have been. My last prayer will be that God may protect her and keep her safe from harm and allow her to join me in eternity . . .

I make this defence and this acknowledgment – that the love of Ethel LeNeve has been the best thing in my life – my only happiness – and that in return for that great gift I have been inspired with a greater kindness towards my fellow-beings, and with a greater desire to do good.

We were as man and wife together, with an absolute communion of spirit. Perhaps God will pardon us because we were like two children in the great unkind world, who clung to one another and gave each other courage . . .

I myself have endeavoured to be equally courageous, yet there have been times during her visits to me when an agony of intense longing has taken possession of me, when my very soul has cried out to clasp her hand and speak those things which are sacred between a man and a woman who have loved.

Alas! We have been divided by the iron discipline of prison rules, and warders have been the witnesses of our grief.

Why do I tell these things to the world? Not to gain anything for myself – not even compassion. But because I desire the world to have pity on a woman who, however weak she may have seemed in their eyes, has been loyal in the midst of misery, and to the very end of the tragedy, and whose love has been self-sacrificing and strong.

These are my last words.

I belong no more to the world.

In the silence of my cell I pray that God may pity all weak hearts, all the poor children of life, and His poor servant.

Dr H. H. Crippen, Pentonville Prison

A Home Secretary Speaks

The mood and temper of the public in regard to the treatment of crime and criminals is one of the most unfailing tests of civilization of any country. A calm and dispassionate recognition of the rights of the accused against the State, and even of convicted criminals against the State, a constant heart-searching by all charged with the

duty of punishment, a desire and eagerness to rehabilitate in the
world of industry all those who have paid their dues in the hard
coinage of punishment, tireless efforts towards the discovery of
regenerating processes, and an unfaltering faith that there is a
treasure, if you can only find it, in the heart of every man – these are
the things which in the treatment of crime and criminals make and
measure the stored-up strength of a nation, and are the sign and
proof of the living virtue in it.

> Winston Churchill, to the House of Commons

A Voice from Greece

DESIRES

Like beautiful bodies of the dead who had not grown old
and they shut them, with tears, in a magnificent mausoleum,
with roses at the head and jasmine at the feet –
that is how desires look that have passed
without fulfilment; without one of them having achieved
a night of sensual delight, or a moonlit morn.

> C. P. Cavafy

VOICES

Ideal and dearly beloved voices
of those who are dead, or of those
who are lost to us like the dead.

Sometimes they speak to us in our dreams;
sometimes in thought the mind hears them.

And for a moment with their echo other echoes
return from the first poetry of our lives –
like music that extinguishes the far-off night.

> C. P. Cavafy

CANDLES

The days of our future stand before us

like a row of little lighted candles –
golden, warm, and lively little candles.

The days gone by remain behind us,
a mournful line of burnt-out candles;
the nearest ones are still smoking,
cold candles, melted and bent.

I do not want to look at them; their form saddens me,
and it saddens me to recall their first light.
I look ahead at my lighted candles.

I do not want to turn back, lest I see and shudder –
how quickly the sombre line lengthens,
how quickly the burnt-out candles multiply.

   C. P. Cavafy

THE GOD FORSAKES ANTONY

When suddenly at the midnight hour
an invisible troupe is heard passing
with exquisite music, with shouts –
do not mourn in vain your fortune failing you now,
your works that have failed, the plans of your life
that have all turned out to be illusions.
As if long prepared for this, as if courageous,
bid her farewell, the Alexandria that is leaving.
Above all do not be fooled, do not tell yourself
it was only a dream, that your ears deceived you;
do not stoop to such vain hopes.
As if long prepared for this, as if courageous,
as it becomes you who are worthy of such a city;
approach the window with firm step,
and listen with emotion, but not
with the entreaties and complaints of the coward,
as a last enjoyment listen to the sounds,
the exquisite instruments of the mystical troupe,
and bid her farewell, the Alexandria you are losing.

   C. P. Cavafy

THE KNEE

A knee is roaming, through the world;
No more; it's just a knee.
It's not a tent; it's not a tree;
It is a knee; no more.

There was a man once in a war
Got killed and killed and killed.
Alone, unhurt, remained the knee
Like a saint's relics, pure.

Since then, it roams the whole world, lonely;
It is a knee, now, only;
It's not a tent; it's not a tree;
Only a knee, no more.

Christian Morgenstern

To cherish only children's books
Childish dreams and cogitations; throw
Out anything grown-up and clocks;
Grow out of deeply-rooted sorrow.

I am tired to death
of life, and welcome nothing it can give me.
But I adore the poor earth:
There is no other earth to see.

In a garden far-off I swung
On a simple wooden swing,
And I remember dark tall firs
In hazy fevers.

Osip Mandelstam

PIERROTS
(*Scène courte mais typique*)

Your eyes! Since I lost their incandescence
Flat calm engulfs my jibs,
The shudder of *vae soli* gurgles beneath my ribs.

You should have seen me after the affray,
I rushed about in the most agitated way
Crying: My God, my God, what will she say?!

My soul's antennae are prey to such perturbations,
Wounded by your indirectness in these situations
And your bundle of mundane complications.

Your eyes put me up to it.
I thought: Yes, divine, these eyes, but what exists
Behind them? What's there? Her soul's an affair for oculists.

And I am sliced with loyal aesthetics.
Hate tremolos and national frenetics.
In brief, violet is the ground tone of my phonetics.

I am not 'that chap there' nor yet 'The Superb'
But my soul, the sort which harsh sounds disturb,
Is, at bottom, distinguished and fresh as a March herb.

> Jules Laforgue (translated by Ezra Pound)

Ezra Pound in London

Ezra would approach with the steps of a dancer, making passes with a cane at an imaginary opponent. He would wear trousers made of green billiard cloth, a pink coat, a blue shirt, a tie hand-painted by a Japanese friend, an immense sombrero, a flaming beard cut to a point and a single, large blue ear-ring.

> Ford Madox Ford, 1931

L'Art, 1910

Green arsenic smeared on an egg – white cloth,
Crushed strawberries! Come, let us feast our eyes.

> Ezra Pound

Freud and Jung in Vienna

Freud had a dream . . . I interpreted it as best I could, but added that a great deal more could be said about it if he would supply me with

some additional details from his private life. Freud's response to these
words was a curious look – a look of the utmost suspicion. Then he
said 'But I cannot risk my authority!' At that moment he lost it
altogether. That sentence burned itself into my memory; and in it the
end of our relationship was already foreshadowed. Freud was plac-
ing personal authority above truth.

> C. J. Jung, 1963

Freud himself had told me that he never read Nietzsche; now [1910] I
saw Freud's psychology as, so to speak, an adroit move on the part of
intellectual history compensating for Nietzsche's deification of the
power principle.

> C. J. Jung

The Invention

The aeroplane is all very well for sport; for the Army it is useless.

> Ferdinand Foch

Women's Clothes

The influences of beauty and of reason are always fighting in a
woman's clothes; reason has won some remarkable triumphs, in
Germany for the most part, but generally submits to a weak
compromise. When we talk of fashion, however, we mean something definite though hard to define. It comes from without; we
wake in the morning and find the shops alive with it; soon it is
abroad in the streets. As we turn over the pictures in these volumes
we see the spirit at work. It travels all over the body ceaselessly.
Now the skirt begins to grow, until it trails for six feet upon the
ground, suddenly the spirit leaps to the throat, and creates a gigantic
ruff there, while the skirt shrinks to the knees; then it enters the
hair, which immediately rises in the pinnacles of Salisbury Cathedral; a slight swelling appears beneath the skirt; it grows, alarmingly;
at last a frame has to support the flounces; next the arms are
attacked; they imitate Chinese pagodas; steel hoops do what they
can to relieve them. The hair, meanwhile, has subsided. The lady
has outgrown all cloaks, and only a vast shawl can encompass her.

> Virginia Woolf

News of King Edward VII's Death Reaches Ireland, May 1910

As I was dressing one morning at a Cork hotel, I received a telegram informing me that King Edward had died during the night. We did not leave Cork till ten or eleven o'clock, but up to that hour, although the news was well known, I saw no indication of public mourning. No bells were rung, and no flags flew at half-mast. This may have been mere carelessness, or it may have been – something else.

> H. Rider Haggard

The Socialist

The National flag is for us a rag to plant on a dunghill.

> Benito Mussolini

Let us hear no more talk of battleships, barracks, cannon, at a time when thousands of villages have no schools, roads, electricity, or doctors, but still live tragically beyond the pale of civilized life.

> Benito Mussolini

The Futurist

Let us jeer at the exhausted prototypes of the Beautiful, the Grand, the Solemn, the Religious, the Ferocious, the Seductive and the Terrifying.

The Variety Theatre destroys the Solemn, the Sacred, the Serious, and the Sublime in Art with a Capital A.

> Filippo Tommaso Marinetti

Destroy the Museums. Crack syntax. Sabotage the adjective. Leave nothing but the verb.

> Filippo Tommaso Marinetti

A lady having a large acquaintance should keep a visiting book in which to enter the names of her acquaintances, and the date when their cards were left upon her, and the date of her return cards left

upon them, that she might know whether a card were due to her
from them, or whether it were due from them to her.

A Member of the Aristocracy

The Essence of Socialism

Determined revolutionary action together with a deep feeling for
humanity – that alone is the essence of Socialism. A world must
be overturned, but every tear that flows and might have been
staunched is an accusation; and a man hurrying to achieve some
great deed and who knocks down a child out of insensitive carelessness commits a crime.

Rosa Luxemburg

Freedom only for the supporters of the Government, only for the
members of a single party – however large – is no freedom at all.
Freedom is always and exclusively freedom for whoever thinks
differently.

Rosa Luxemburg

Danger

Strange regions exist, strange minds, strange worlds of the fancy,
lofty and spare. At the edges of large cities, where street-lighting is
sparse and policemen walk in twos, are houses where you mount to
the very top, up and up, into garrets under the roof, where pale
young geniuses, criminals of the dream, sit brooding with folded
arms; up into cheap studios adorned with symbols, where solitary
and rebellious artists, inwardly consumed, hungry and proud,
wrestle in clouds of tobacco with ideals appallingly final. Here is the
end: ice, celibacy, sterility. Here the atmosphere is so thin that life's
mirages have vanished. Here reign defiance and unyielding consis-
tancy, the ego unshaken amid despair; here freedom, madness, and
death rule undisputed.

Thomas Mann

Without Judah, without Rome,
We will build Germania's Dome.

Georg von Schönerer

Votes for Women, 1911

I want to see women have the vote because I believe the vote may be a useful educational symbol (even if it has to be a temporary political nuisance) in the necessary work of establishing the citizenship of women . . . At present women are not regarded as citizens; they do not regard themselves as citizens, they behave accordingly and most of the troubles of life ensue. Apart from a natural opposition of sex, I believe there is very little difference between men and women that is not imposed on them through the sex-mania of our social system. Humanity is obsessed by sex. I have always been disposed to take sex rather lightly and to think that we make a quite unnecessary amount of fuss about it . . . I do my best to avoid the present suffrage agitation because it over-accentuates all those sexual differences I want to minimise and shakes my faith in the common humanity of women.

H. G. Wells

Mr Brope

'Who and what is Mr Brope?' demanded the aunt of Clovis suddenly.

Mrs Riversedge, who had been snipping off the heads of defunct roses, and thinking of nothing in particular, sprang hurriedly to mental attention. She was one of those old-fashioned hostesses who consider that one ought to know something about one's guests, and that the something ought to be to their credit.

'I believe he comes from Leighton Buzzard,' she observed by way of preliminary explanation.

'In these days of rapid and convenient travel,' said Clovis, who was dispersing a colony of green-fly with visitations of cigarette smoke, 'to come from Leighton Buzzard does not necessarily denote any great strength of character. It might only mean mere restlessness. Now if he had left it under a cloud, or as a protest against the incurable and heartless frivolity of its inhabitants, that would tell us something about the man and his mission in life.'

Saki

International Crisis at Agadir, 1911

So now the Admiralty wireless whispers through the ether to the tall

*masts of ships, and captains pace their decks absorbed in thought. It
is nothing. It is less than nothing. It is too foolish, too fantastic to be
thought of in the twentieth century. Or is it fire and murder leaping
out of the darkness at our throats, torpedoes ripping the bellies of
half-awakened ships, a sunrise on a vanished naval supremacy, and
an island well-guarded hitherto, at last defenceless? No, it is nothing.
No one would do such things. Civilization has climbed above such
perils. The interdependence of nations in trade and traffic, the sense
of public law, the Hague Convention, Liberal principles, the Labour
Party, high finance, Christian charity, common sense, have rendered
such nightmares impossible. Are you quite sure?*

Winston Churchill, 1923

IN THE MORNING

A strong wind sprang up.
Opens the blood-red gates of the iron sky.
Beats against the towers.
Brightly ringing blows lithe over the city's brazen plain.

The morning sun sooty. On embankments thunder trains.
Through clouds plough golden angel ploughs.
Strong wind over the pale city.
Steamers and cranes awake by the murkily flowing river.

Morosely bells clap on the weather-beaten cathedral.
Many women you see and girls going to work.
In the pale light. Wild from the night. Their skirts flap.

Limbs made for love.
To the machine and grudging drudgery.
Look into the tender light,
Into the trees' tender green.
Listen! The sparrows shriek.
And outside in the wilder fields
Larks are singing.

Jakob van Hoddis

And the Horns of Summer Fell Silent . . .

And the horns of summer fell silent in the death of the meadows,
Into the darkness cloud upon cloud floated off.
But remotely the bordering forests were shrinking,
Muffled in mourning like men that follow a hearse.

Loud sang the gale in the terror of fields that were fading;
It drove into poplars to shape a white tower between boughs.
And like the sweepings of wind there lay in the waste land
Below, a village, drab roofs in a huddle of gray.

But on and on, as far as the pallid horizon
The tents of autumn extended their fabric of corn,
The numberless cities, but empty, forgotten.
And no one was walking about in the streets.

And the shade of the night sang. Only the ravens still drifted
Here and there under leaden clouds in the rain,
Alone in the wind, as down in the dark of our foreheads
Black thoughts revolve and recede in disconsolate hours.

> Georg Heym

Proud Songsters

The thrushes sing as the sun is going,
And the finches whistle in ones and pairs,
And as it gets dark loud nightingales
    In bushes
Pipe, as they can when April wears,
    As if all Time were theirs.

These are brand-new birds of twelve-months' growing,
Which a year ago, or less than twain,
No finches were, nor nightingales,
    Nor thrushes,
But only particles of grain,
    And earth, and air, and rain.

> Thomas Hardy

A German Voice

A nation must learn to act on behalf of its convictions, as in
Revolutionary France or Civil War England, even if bloodshed
ensues: for future casualties will only be greater if it refuses. A
nation that voluntarily surrenders rights and representations to its
kings and heroes – to Kaiser and Bismarck – does itself the worst
injustice whatever temporary advantages follow. Without genuine,
live democracy people will always project themselves into the
figures of their leaders, will talk themselves into the conception of
superman, while their personal human growth is dangerously
stunted.

Heinrich Mann

Beware! The dead are powerful persuaders. One must pay attention
to the dead.

Dr Georges Clemenceau

The Explorer

In all times and countries we have seen the known world lose itself in
the fogs of cloudland – never uniformly, it is true, but in constantly
changing proportions. Here and there we have a glimpse, now and
again a vision over wider regions; and then the driving mists once
more shut out our view. Therefore all that human courage and
desire of knowledge have wrested in the course of long ages from
this cloudland remains vague, uncertain, full of riddles. But for this
very reason it is all the more alluring . . .

What a vast amount of labour lies sunk in man's knowledge of the
earth, especially in those remote ages when development proceeded at such an immeasurably slower pace, and when man's
resources were so infinitely poorer. By the most manifold and
various ways the will and intelligence of man achieve their object.
The attraction of long voyages must often enough have been the
hope of finding riches and favoured lands, but still deeper lay the
imperious desire of getting to know our own earth. To riches men
have seldom attained, to the Fortunate Isles never; but through all
we have won knowledge.

Fridtjof Nansen

Eleanora Duse

One day Duse and I were walking by the sea when she turned to me. The setting sun made a fiery halo about her head. She gazed at me long and curiously.

'Isadora,' she said in a choking voice, 'don't, don't seek happiness again. You have on your brow the mark of the great unhappy ones of the earth. What has happened to you is but the prologue. Do not tempt Fate again.'

Ah, Eleanora, if I had but heeded your warning! But hope is a hard plant to kill, and, no matter how many branches are knocked off and destroyed, it will always put forth new shoots.

Duse was then a magnificent creature, in the full power of her life and intelligence. When she walked along the beach she took long strides, walking unlike any other woman I have ever seen. She wore no corset, and her figure, at that time very large and full, would have distressed a lover of fashion, but expressed a noble grandeur. Everything about her was the expression of her great and tortured soul. Often she read to me from the Greek tragedies, or from Shakespeare, and when I heard her read certain lines of Antigone I thought what a crime it was that this splendid interpretation was not being given to the world. It is not true that Duse's long retirement from the stage in the fullness and ripeness of her Art was due, as some people prefer to think, to an unhappy love or some other sentimental reason, nor even to ill-health, but she had not the help or the necessary capital to carry out her ideas of Art as she wished – that is the simple, shameful truth. The world that 'loves Art' left this greatest actress in the world to eat her heart out in solitude and poverty for fifteen long years. When Morris Gest finally came to the realisation of this, and arranged a tour for her in America, it was too late, for she died on that last tour, pathetically endeavouring to amass the money necessary for her work, for which she had waited all those long years.

Isadora Duncan

Resisting D'Annunzio

The third time I resisted D'Annunzio was years afterwards, during the war. I came to Rome and stayed at the Hotel Regina. By a strange chance, D'Annunzio had the room next to me. Every night he used to go and dine with the Marquesa Casati. One night she invited me to dine. I went to the palace and walked into the antechamber. It was all done out in Grecian style, and I sat there awaiting the arrival of the Marquesa, when I suddenly heard a most violent tirade of the most vulgar language you could possibly imagine directed at me. I looked round and saw a green parrot. I noticed he was not chained. I got up and leaped into the next salon. I was sitting there awaiting the Marquesa, when I suddenly heard a noise – brrrr – and I saw a white bulldog. *He* wasn't chained, so I leaped up into the next salon, which was carpeted with white bear rugs and had bear skins even on the walls. I sat down there and waited for the Marquesa. Suddenly I heard a hissing sound. I looked down and saw a cobra in a cage sitting up on end and hissing at me. I leaped into the next salon, all lined with tiger-skins. *There* was a gorilla, showing its teeth. I rushed into the next room, the dining-room, and there I found the secretary of the Marquesa. Finally the Marquesa descended for dinner. She was dressed in transparent gold pyjamas. I said:

'You love animals, I see.'

'Oh, yes, I adore them – especially monkeys,' she replied, looking at her secretary.

Strange to say, after this exciting aperitif, the dinner passed off with the utmost formality.

Isadora Duncan

Bavarian Tyrol

We stayed in the Gasthaus zur Post. In the morning we used to have breakfast under the thick horse-chestnut trees, and the red and white flowers fell on us. The garden was on a ledge, high over the river, above the weir, where the timber rafts floated down. The Loisach – that's the river – is pale jade green, because it comes from glaciers. It is fearfully cold and swift. The people were all such queer Bavarians. Across from the inn, across a square full of horse-chestnut trees, was the church and the convent, so peaceful, all whitewashed, except for the minaret of the church, which has a black hat. Every day, we went out for a long, long time. There are flowers so many they would make you cry for joy – Alpine flowers. By the river, great hosts of globe flowers, that we call bachelor's buttons – pale gold great bubbles – then primulas, like mauve cowslips, somewhat – and queer marsh violets, and orchids, and lots of bell-flowers, like large, tangled, dark-purple hare-bells, and stuff like larkspur, very rich, and lucerne, so pink, and in the woods, lilies of the valley – oh, flowers, great wild mad profusion of them, everywhere. One day we went to a queer old play done by the peasants – this is the Ober-Ammergau country. One day we went into the mountains, and sat, putting Frieda's rings on our toes, holding our feet under the pale green water of a lake, to see how they looked.

D. H. Lawrence, to Mrs S. A. Hopkin

A View from an Airship

Paris unfurls beneath us. It has been photographed so often from the sky that I recognize it easily, the complicated network of its streets, its star-shaped squares, its rivers and islands form a plan which is already familiar. It is these details of colour and contour that I like, roofs that are strangely blue or angry and red; the lakes in the public parks glitter and go out, a train begins to curl round like an irritated caterpillar . . . It is the compactness of the town that delights me, the fact of finding it 'almost small and untidy . . . Its stifling confusion only stops in respectful fashion to leave a little air round the handsome edifices: the Louvre and its clear-cut gardens are restful to the eye, the outline of the Luxembourg can be read like a clear picture. Abundant young trees in regular rows make each cemetery into an attractive enclosure . . .

But through what wretched gaps among the modern close-set houses do the laden air and miserly light come down? How shapeless our houses are, how close to the colour of dirty butter, beside the old buildings which are delicately eternally grey. The old quarters are the most beautiful, those which time, soot, worn stone and coal-laden rain have covered with a subtly-coloured ash. I lean down, regretting that we must pass them so quickly, over the last few gardens, shut off in the depths of black buildings, unsuspected by passers-by, languishing and adorned like valuable captives . . . During the first moments, did I not fly over one of these flowerbeds, the one where an acacia flowered, near a long strip of grass, the one where a glass-roof glitters? . . . I didn't think of it in time . . . The idea that I have – down there where the Seine glitters and curves – a place of shelter which includes everything I love, touches me for a moment but without warmth and without force. My pleasure, which is too new and too potent, forgets in inhuman fashion *those down there* . . .

    Colette

The Titanic Disaster

Captain Edward J. Smith: Mr Murdoch, what was that?
First Officer William Murdoch: An iceberg, Sir. I hard-a-starboarded, and I was going to hard-a-port around it, but she was too close. I couldn't do any more.
Smith: Close the emergency doors.
Murdoch: The doors are already closed.

God Himself couldn't sink this ship.

    A deck-hand

The Titanic was the last stand of wealth and society in the centre of public affection. In 1912 there were no movie, radio or television stars. The public depended on socially prominent people for all the vicarious glamour that enriches drab lives. The New York American broke the news with a leader devoted almost entirely to John Jacob Astor. At the end it mentioned that 1,800 others were also lost.

    Walter Lord, 1956

Senator William Alden Smith Reports

No sufficient tests were made of boilers or bulkheads or gearing or equipment, and no life-saving or signal devices were reviewed. Officers and crew were strangers to one another . . . neither was familiar with the vessel or its tools. No drill or helpful discipline disturbed the tranquillity of the voyage; and when the crisis came, a state of *absolute unpreparedness* stupefied the passengers and crew.

The Question

Mr Lowe, what is an iceberg made of?
Fifth Officer H. G. Lowe: Ice.

    W. A. Smith Investigation

Mr Ismay, White Star Chairman

Mr J. Bruce Ismay is responsible for the lack of lifeboats, he is responsible for the Captain who was so reckless, and for the sailing directions given to the Captain which probably caused his recklessness. In the face of all this he saves himself, leaving fifteen hundred men and women to perish. I know of nothing at once so cowardly and so brutal in recent history. The one thing he could have done was to prove his honesty and his sincerity by giving his life.

Brooks Adams, to Senator Francis G. Newlands

The Titanic *had everything on board – except sufficient lifeboats, and binoculars for the crow's nest.*

Senator Smith's Report certainly offers no balm to Anglo-Saxon pride. All those racial qualities which have been assumed to distinguish the Anglo-Saxon from the emotional races of Southern Europe and the heathen breeds were wanting in that tragic test among the ice-floes of the North Atlantic.

Gaelic-American

Following the disaster, the American feminist, Anna Shaw, and a British Fabian, Millicent Murby, denounced the saving of women and children first. Some American blacks welcomed the sinking as a blow at white self-importance.

The Captain

The mystery of his indifference to danger when other and less pretentious vessels doubled their look-out or stopped their engines, finds no reasonable hypothesis in conjecture or speculation. Science in shipbuilding was supposed to have attained perfection and to have spoken her last word. Mastery of the ocean had at last been achieved. And over-confidence seems to have dulled the faculties usually so alert, with the atmosphere literally charged with warning signals and wireless messages registering their last appeal, the stokers in the engine-room fed their fires with fresh fuel, registering her *fastest speed* in that dangerous place.

W. A. Smith Report

We shall leave to the honest judgment of England its painful chastisement of the British Board of Trade, to whose laxity of regulation and hasty inspection the World is largely indebted for this awful fatality. Of contributing causes there were very many. In the face of warning signals, speed was increased; and messages of danger seemed to stimulate her to action rather than stimulate her to fear.

Senator W. A. Smith

THE CONVERGENCE OF THE TWAIN
(Lines on the loss of the 'Titanic')

In a solitude of the sea
Deep from human vanity,
And the Pride of Life that planned her, stilly couches
she.

Steel chambers, late the pyres
Of her salamandrine fires,
Cold currents thrid, and turn to rhythmic tidal lyres.

Over the mirrors meant
To glass the opulent
The sea-worm crawls – grotesque, slimed, dumb,
indifferent.

Jewels in joy designed
To ravish the sensuous mind
Lie lightless, all their sparkles bleared and black
and blind.

Dim moon-eyed fishes near
Gaze at the gilded gear
And query: 'What does this vaingloriousness down
here?' . . .

Well: while was fashioning
This creature of cleaving wing,
The Immanent Will that stirs and urges everything

Prepared a sinister mate
For her – so gaily great –
A Shape of Ice, for the time far and dissociate.

And as the smart ship grew
In stature, grace, and hue,
In shadowy silent distance grew the Iceberg too.

Alien they seemed to be:
No mortal eye could see
The intimate welding of their later history,

Or sign that they were bent
By paths coincident
On being anon twin halves of one august event,

Till the Spinner of the Years
Said 'Now!' And each one hears,
And consummation comes, and jars two hemispheres.

Thomas Hardy

Echoes of the Titanic *disaster may perhaps be discerned in T. S. Eliot's 'The Dry Salvages', 1943.*

From a Girl Guide

While boys and girls are learning
To be their Empire's fence,
We needn't really be afraid
Of National decadence.

Dorothea Moors

From the South Pole

We are showing that Englishmen can still die with a bold spirit, fighting it out to the end. I think this makes an example for Englishmen of the future.

Captain Robert Falcon Scott

I do not think we can hope for better things now. We shall stick it out
to the end, but we are getting weaker, of course, and the end cannot
be far.

It seems a pity, but I do not think I can write more.

For God's sake look after our people.

> Captain Robert Falcon Scott

DOMUS CAEDAT ARBOREM

Ever since the great planes were murdered at the end of the gardens
The City, to me, at night has the look of a spirit brooding crime;
As if the dark houses watching the trees from dark windows were
    simply biding their time.

> Charlotte Mew

A Satirical Drama

There's a feeling in the air that *something* ought to be suppressed,
isn't there? But they aren't quite sure what. Wells said so in the
N.L.C. yesterday afternoon. I want to tell you about the Dramatisa-
tion of the Minority Report. *He* talked about it for three hours. He
and Chesterton did it one Sunday. It's an admirable thing, but they
say Granville Barker's very angry, and says it's not the sort of thing
he meant when he advocated the 'presentation on the stage of
urgent social problems'.

The first curtain rises on a workhouse ward. 'Pauper imbecile
nursing pauper child (upside down).' A notice is displayed over the
window 'Paupers are forbidden to look out of this window,' and
over the door 'Visitors are earnestly requested not to give tobacco
or buns to the paupers.'

The ultimate curtain falls on a scene strangely similar. Belloc
nursing a child ('still upside down, but not quite so upside down').
Over the window and the door the same two notices, only that
'Paupers' is crossed out and 'Workers (No. 3 grade) under disciplin-
ary training' is written over the top . . . Between every two scenes
there's an interlude, and Belloc and Chesterton are shown drinking,
the number of empty bottles increasing gradually through the
play . . . There's a great scene on the Death of Bumble. The
murder takes place off the stage, and then leading Fabians come on

dancing to triumphal music, James and Dr Dodd, Pease and Mrs Hylton-Dale, Tina and Ben and Jesse Holiday, each carrying on a pitchfork a piece of Bumble . . . These are put into a boiling cauldron, and clouds of steam rise . . . On the clouds are discovered sitting the Gods of the English, Mill and Bentham and Herbert Spencer, throned and crowned, and . . . S. and B. Webb.

Hugh Dalton, to Rupert Brooke

GRAND BALLET

I saw you dance that summer before the war.
One thunderous night it was, at Covent Garden,
When we, who walked, beneath the weighted trees,
Hot metropolitan pavements, might have smelt
Blood in the dust, and heard the traffic's cry
Ceaseless and savage like a prophecy.

As by a sunrise sea I saw you stand,
Your sylphides round you on the timeless strand,
White, pure, delicious poisèd butterflies,
The early nineteenth century in their eyes,
And Chopin ready for their silver toes.
(Oh sighs unsatisfied, and one red rose!)

The fountain of all movement ready to flow
Seemed prisoned in your entrancèd body. So
You stood, their Prince, most elegantly fair,
Swan-sleeved, black-jacketed, with falling hair
And hands half-raised in ravishment. O there,
You Grecian arrow fitted to the bow,
You beech-tree in a legendary wood,
You panther in a velvet bolero,
There you for one immortal moment stood –

One moment like a wave before it flows,
Frozen in perfectness. Then one hand rose
And tossed a silver curl, demurely light
(O grace, O rose, O Chopin and all delight),
And the enchantment broke.
        That thunderous night

We saw Nijinsky dance.
          Thereafter fell
On the awaiting world the powers of Hell,
Chaos, and irremediable pain;
And utter darkness on your empty brain,
Not even grief to say, No more, no more.

But tell me, when my mortal memories wane
As death draws near, and peace is mine and pardon,
Where will it like an escapèd dove repair?
To what Platonic happy heaven – where? – where? –
Untouchable by Fate and free of Time,
That one immortal moment of the mime
We saw Nijinsky dance at Covent Garden?

          Frances Cornford, 1934

In Europe, the epoch of conquest is over, and save in the Balkans
and perhaps on the fringes of the Austrian and Russian empires, it is
as certain as anything in politics that the frontiers of our national
states are finally drawn. My own belief is that there will be no more
wars among the six Great Powers.

          H. N. Brailsford, 1913

The motor-car will help solve the congestion of traffic.

          A. J. Balfour

Once more, once more,
I am for you
A star.
Alas the sailor
Whose course is set askew
By such a star:
He will be smashed on rocks
Or scraped on shallows.
Woe, too, to you –
Your heart at sea –
Whose false course is
Set by me:
You will be smashed on rocks –

Rocks which will laugh at you,
As you have laughed at me.

> Viktor Khlebnikov

My house on the hill-top in Ireland will become a ruin and many
houses in England will too; another fifty years will see the end of life
as we know it.

> George Moore, to Lady Sybil Eden

Still we know how Day the Dyer
Works, in dims and deeps and dusks and darks.

> James Joyce

A Royal Occasion, May 30, 1913

Emily Wilding Davison, who had been associated with the militant
movement since 1906, gave up her life for the Women's Cause by
throwing herself in the path of the thing which, next to property, is
held most sacred to Englishmen – sport. Miss Davison went to the
races at Epsom, and breaking through the barriers . . . rushed in
the path of the galloping horses and caught the bridle of the King's
horse, which was leading all the others. The horse fell, throwing his
jockey and crushing Miss Davison in such shocking fashion that she
was carried from the course in a dying condition . . .

She had suffered many imprisonments, had been forcibly fed and
most brutally treated. On one occasion when she had barricaded her
cell against the prison doctors, a hose pipe was turned on her from
the window and she was drenched and all but drowned in the icy
water while workmen were breaking down her cell door. Miss
Davison, after this experience, expressed to several of her friends
the deep conviction that now, as in days called uncivilized, the
conscience of the people would awaken only to the sacrifice of a
human life. At one time in prison she tried to kill herself by throwing
herself headlong from one of the upper galleries, but she succeeded
only in sustaining cruel injuries. Ever after that time she clung to her
conviction that one great tragedy, the deliberate throwing into the
breach of a human life, would put an end to the intolerable torture
of women. And so she threw herself at the King's horse, in full view
of the King and Queen and a great multitude of their Majesties'

subjects, offering up her life as a petition to the King, praying for the
release of suffering women throughout England and the World.

> Emmeline Pankhurst

Mother and Daughter

*On the way to golf, I induced Mother to disclose a few points on
sexual matters which I thought I ought to know, though the information is always intensely distasteful to me and most depressing – in fact
it quite put me off my game!*

> Vera Brittain, 1933

A Cabinet Minister on the Kaiser's Germany

The high-minded, benignant and virile guardian of the European
peace.

> John Morley

The Prime Minister's Wife on the Naval Estimates for 1914

Don't let Winston have too much money – it will hurt our party in
every way – Labour and even Liberals. If one can't be a little
economical when all foreign countries are peaceful I don't know
when we can.

> Margot Asquith, to David Lloyd George

Astrology

The planet Jupiter represents the body, which term is here meant to
include the etheric double as well as the dense physical . . . The
Auric Egg itself, regarded as a vehicle, is under the dominant
influence of Jupiter, as are all the finer substances composing the
inner vehicles of Consciousness.

> Alan Leo

RETURN OF THE VILLAGE LAD

When I was young the world was a little pond

Grandmother and red roof, the lowing
Of oxen and a bush made up of trees.
And all around was the great green meadow.

Lovely it was, this dreaming-into-the-distance,
This being nothing at all but air and wind
And bird-call and fairy-tale book.
Far off the fabulous iron serpent whistled –

      Alfred Lichenstein

ASH WEDNESDAY

Only yesterday powdered and lustful I walked
In this various and resonant world.
Today how long ago the lot was drowned.

Here is a thing.
There is a thing.
Something looks like this.
Something else looks different.
How easily one can blow out
The whole blossoming earth.

The sky is cold and blue.
Or the moon is yellow and flat.
A wood contains many single trees.

Nothing now worth weeping for.
Nothing now worth screaming for.
Where am I –

      Alfred Lichenstein

CHILDREN IN FRONT OF A LONDON SOUP KITCHEN

I saw children, a long line of them, arranged in pairs, stand in front
   of the building where the poor are fed.
They waited, untalkative, weary, for their turn at the nightly
   spread.
They were dirty and in rags, squeezed up against housefront and
   railing.

Little girls around pale babies cupped hands that were failing.

Hungry, intimidated they stood among lamps being lighted,
Many with delicate faces by marks and dark bruises blighted.
Their clothing smelled of basements, ill-lit rooms, of scolding and
     poverty,
Their bodies were scarred by deprivation and premature drudgery.

They waited: soon the others would be through, they'd be
     admitted to the hall,
Served with bread and vegetables, the soup in tin cups and all.
Oh, and then they'd grow sleepy and their twisted limbs would be
     untied
And night and good sleep would bring them to rocking-horses, to
     soldiers, the rooms of marvellous dolls' houses open wide.
          Ernst Stadler

Awe

Few live for Always
But if the passing moment makes you anxious
Your lot is terror and your house precarious.
          Osip Mandelstam

The shy speechless sound
of a fruit falling from its tree,
and around it the silent music
of the forest, unbroken . . .
          Osip Mandelstam

The Admiralty

In the northern capital a dusty poplar languishes.
The translucent clockface is lost in the leaves,
and through the dark green a frigate or acropolis
gleams far away, brother of water and sky.

An aerial ship and a touch-me-not mast,
a yardstick for Peter's successors, teaching

that beauty is no demi-god's whim,
it's the plain carpenter's fierce rule-of-eye.

The four sovereign elements smile on us,
but man in his freedom has made a fifth.
Do not the chaste lines of this ark
deny the dominion of space?

The capricious jellyfish clutch in anger,
anchors are rusting like abandoned ploughs –
and behold the locks of the three dimensions are sprung
and all the seas of the world lie open.

      Osip Mandelstam

THE CASINO
(Unpremeditated Happiness)

The wind is playing with a corrugated cloud,
The anchor scrapes the ocean bottom;
Lifeless as linen, my wine-struck mind
Hangs over nothingness.

But I revel in the Casino on the dunes:
The vast view from the misty window,
A thin ray of light on the crumpled table cloth.

And, with greenish water suspended all around,
When the wine flashes crystal like a rose,
I like to soar – the grey gull's shadow.

      Osip Mandelstam

A YOUNG FACE ONE DAY APPEARS

A young face one day appears
before our house.
We tell her: why do you return
to the old home?
She opens a window and all the fields
in light and fragrance waft inside.
On the white path

the tree trunks grow black;
the top leaves
are green smoke dreaming far away.
A pond seems
like a broad river in the white mist
of morning. Across the livid mountains
another chimera.

Antonio Machado

NAKED IS THE EARTH

Naked is the earth,
and the soul howls to the pale horizon
like a hungry she-wolf. Poet, what do you seek
in the sunset?

Bitter walking, for the road
weighs upon the heart. The frozen wind
and coming night, and the bitterness
of distance! On the white road

a few stiff trees blacken;
in the distant mountains there is gold
and blood. The sun is dead. Poet, what do you seek
in the sunset?

Antonio Machado

AND HE WAS THE DEVIL OF MY DREAMS

And he was the devil of my dreams,
the handsomest angel. His eyes
of victory shone like steel,
and bloody flames from his torch
lighted the deep crypt of my soul.

'Will you come with me?' 'Never.
Tombs and the dead terrify me.'
Yet the ferrous fingers
seized my right arm.

'Will you come with me?' – And in my dream
I went forward, blinded by his red lantern.
And in the crypt I heard the ringing chains
and the stirring of imprisoned beasts.

> Antonio Machado

THE FAREWELL

I picked this fragile sprig of heather
Autumn has died long since remember
Never again shall we see one another
Odour of time sprig of heather
And remember I await our life together

> Apollinaire

THE BETROTHAL

I no longer have pity for myself
Nor can I express my torment of silence
All the words I have to say have become stars
An Icarus tries to rise as high as each of my eyes
And like a sun god I flame between these two nebulae
What have I done to the theological beasts of the mind
At one time the dead came back to revere me
And I hoped for the end of the world
But mine arrived whistling like a hurricane.

I have had the courage to look behind me
At the corpses of my days
Which strew my path and I mourn them
Some rot inside Italian churches
Or else in little lemon groves
Which blossom and bear fruit
At the same time and in all seasons
Other days cried before they died in taverns
Where vivid bouquets were wheeling about
Before the eyes of a mulatto woman who improvised poetry
And the roses of electricity still open
In the garden of my memory

Templars I blaze among you on your pyre
Let us prophesy together O it is
For you Grand Master that I am on fire
And spin the night itself in this wild gyre

Flame frees my bonds Only my breath
Can snuff the tongues that lick at forty dead
I sight both shame and glory in my death
And tilt at the quintain that the future holds

Doubt swooped like a feigned and painted bird
Love frolicked with the sun in the village street
Their gay outlandish children built and lit
This pyre of passion where my courage nests

                Apollinaire, to Picasso

HUNTING HORNS

Our past is noble and tragic
Like the mask of a tyrant
No trick of chance or of magic
Nothing quite insignificant
Makes our love seem pitiful

And Thomas de Quincey drinking his
Sweet and chaste and poisoned glass
Dreaming went to see his Ann
Let us since all passes pass
I shall look back only too often

Memories are hunting horns
Whose sound dies among the wind

        Apollinaire

THE INSANE

THEY are silent because the division walls
are broken down in the brain,
and hours when they might be understood at all
begin and leave again.

Often when they go to the window at night,
suddenly everything seems right:
their hands touch something tangible,
the heart is high and can pray,
the calmed eyes gaze

down on this unhoped-for, oft-distorted
garden in this peaceful square at rest,
which in the reflex of this foreign world
grows ever larger, never to be lost.

        Rainer Maria Rilke

ONCE MORE

Once more, swept by an ancient grief,
The cotton-grass is bent to earth,
Once more beyond the misty stream,
You call upon me from afar.

Droves of wild horses on the steppe
Flash by and vanish, leave no mark,
And savage passions are unloosed
Beneath the high moon's crescent yoke.

I too am swept by an ancient grief,
A wolf beneath the crescent moon,
All power over myself is lost,
How can I fly to follow you!

I hear the clash of bloody strife,
Afar the Tartar trumpet brays,
I see the distant spreading fires
And Russia's fields softly ablaze.

        Alexander Blok

Jean Jaurès

This one is a jet of words. Like the water in the stone jet on the
fountain in Brussels, words which cost him no effort seem to be torn

from him by a convulsion. He seems to speak with his head, his shoulders, his chest, his fists, his back which is that of an old coal-heaver. There emerges from him a terrible sound, which frightens sleep away. His voice rolls along like a jolting carriage and encounters everything on its way: clichés, lies, talk, even the well-devised period, balanced, resonant and solid, which he rushes through in order to dash further on and find something better or worse.

He drinks quickly and speaks. He wipes his forehead and speaks. He defies a heckler who has said nothing. He cries: 'I' and on his lips that is spelt 'I-y' like a bark. He says, unnecessarily: 'Ah!' in order to take the field and launch into a sentence further on. He states, after sixty-five minutes of resounding speech, 'I'm at the end of my tether!' . . . but it is not yet time to register this vague promise . . . After that he speaks. He looks up and shows a face resembling a thunderstruck Titan, on which one can see that he has a bristly beard and a soft nose. He speaks; what am I saying? His tone rises to the level of the most prophetic lamentations, and buries us in ruins beneath his voice, vast and tumultuous as the sea: 'Hear me, hear me, all of you! I have climbed the mountain so that you shall hear me, I shall speak the truth, even if it has cost me my life. I rend my garments, I strip the hairs from my face, I weep, I shout, I offer my forehead to bullets, and my breast to the knife, so that I may come here and swear, oh men, that . . . the barometer is going down and the spring will be wet!'

Colette

The American Ambassador at the German Court

On the arrival at the Palace with these and all the members of the Embassy staff and their wives, we were shown up a long staircase, at the top of which a guard of honour, dressed in costume of the time of Frederick the Great, presented arms to all Ambassadors, and ruffled kettledrums.

Through long lines of cadets from the military schools, dressed as pages, in white, with short breeches and powdered wigs, we passed through several rooms where all the people to pass in review were gathered. Behind these, in a room about sixty feet by fifty, on a throne facing the door were the Emperor and Empress, and on the broad steps of this throne were the Princes and their wives, the

Court ladies-in-waiting, and all the other members of the Court. The wives of the Ambassadors entered the room first, followed at intervals of about twenty feet by the ladies of the Embassy and the ladies to be presented. As they entered the room and made a change of direction toward the throne, pages in white straightened out the ladies' trains with long sticks. Arrived opposite the throne and about twenty feet from it, each Ambassador's wife made a low curtsey, and then stood on the foot of the throne, to the left of the Emperor and Empress, and as each lady of the Embassy not before presented, and each lady to be presented, stopped beside the throne and made a low curtsey, the Ambassadress had to call out the name of each one in a loud voice; and when the last one had passed she followed her out of the room, walking sidewise so as not to turn her back on the royalties – something of a feat when towing a train about fifteen feet long!

James W. Gerard

The Officers

For years officers of the army, both in the discharge of their duties and outside, have behaved in a very arrogant way towards the civil population. Time and again while I was in Germany waiting in line at some ticket office an officer shoved himself ahead of all others, without even a protest from those waiting. On one occasion I went to the races at Berlin with my brother-in-law and bought a box. While we were out looking at the horses between the races, a Prussian officer and his wife seated themselves in our box. I called the attention of one of the ushers to this, but the usher said he did not dare ask a Prussian officer to leave, and it was only after sending for the head usher and showing him my Jockey Club badge and my pass as an Ambassador that I was able to secure possession of my own box. There have been many instances in Germany where officers having a slight dispute with civilians have instantly cut the civilian down. Instances of this kind of harsh treatment of Germans by officers and under-officers while serving in the army undoubtedly created in Germany a spirit of antagonism not only to the army itself but to the whole military system of Prussia.

James W. Gerard

An American View

The short war against Denmark in 1864, against Austria, Bavaria, etc., in 1866, and against France in 1870, enormously increased both the pride and prestige of the Prussian army. It must not be forgotten that at all periods of history it seems as if some blind instinct had driven the inhabitants of the inhospitable plains of North Germany to war and to conquest. The Cimbri and Teutones, the tribes defeated by Marius; Ariovistus, who was defeated by Julius Caesar; the Goths and the Visi-Goths, the Franks and the Saxons, all have poured forth from this infertile country for the conquest of other lands. The Germans of today express this longing of the North Germans for pleasanter climes in the phrase in which they demand 'a place in the sun'. The nobles of Prussia are always for war. The business men and manufacturers and shipowners desired an increasing field for their activities. The German colonies were uninhabitable by Europeans. All his life the glittering Emperor and his generals had planned and thought of war; and the Crown Prince, surrounded by his remarkable collection of relics and reminders of Napoleon, dreamed only of taking the lead in a successful war of conquest. Early in the winter of 1913–14 the Crown Prince showed his collection of Napoleona to a beautiful American woman of my acquaintance, and said that he hoped war would occur while his father was alive; but, if not, he would start a war the moment he came to the throne.

                        James W. Gerard

First Night

First Production of Rosenkavalier *in England* Covent Garden. Began at 8.20 (20 minutes late) and finished at midnight, with many cuts. Then 30 minutes' wait nearly, for motor in procession of motors. The thing was certainly not understood by stalls and grand circle. What its reception was in the amphitheatre and gallery I was too far off to judge. First act received quite coldly. Ovation as usual at end – and an explosive sort of shout when Thomas Beecham came to bow. The beauty and symmetry of the book came out even more clearly than on reading it. An entirely false idea of this opera so far in England. Not sensual, nor perverse, nor depraved. It is simply the story of a young man providing a tragedy for an ageing woman by ceasing to love her, and an ecstatic joy for a young woman by beginning to love her. All the main theme is treated with gravity and beauty. The horseplay, and the character of Ochs, and the eighteenth-century colour is incidental. It seemed to me to be a work of the first order.

Arnold Bennett

Unconscious Motivations

As can sometimes be demonstrated by analysis, the dropping of objects or the overturning and breaking of the same are very frequently utilized as the expression of unconscious streams of thought, but more often they serve to represent the superstitious or odd significances connected therewith in popular sayings. The meanings attached to the spilling of salt, the overturning of a wineglass, the sticking of a knife dropped to the floor, and so on, are well known. I shall discuss later the right to investigate such superstitious interpretations; here I shall simply observe that the individual awkward acts do not by any means always have the same meaning, but, depending on the circumstances, they serve to represent now this or that purpose.

Recently we passed through a period in my house during which an unusual number of glass and china dishes were broken. I myself largely contributed to this damage. This little endemic was readily explained by the fact that it preceded the public betrothal of my eldest daughter. On such festivities it is customary to break some dishes and utter at the same time some felicitating expression. This custom may signify a sacrifice or express any other symbolic sense.

Sigmund Freud

The Zulus

It is I am sure the greatest mistake to suppose that the native does not feel or forgets harsh treatment. On the contrary, I believe that at the bottom of that secret mind of his, which so few of alien race have the imagination and the sympathy to understand at all, he feels a great deal. Also his memory is very long. Listen to some old Zulu describing events which took place in the day of Chaka or Dingaan, when his nation was great and ruled the land. He quotes the very words that were said, the very deeds that were done. No syllable, no gesture is overlooked. It is all there written upon the book of the mind, and much else is there also, of which he does not speak to the white man – as yet. But a day may dawn when he, or his son, or his grandson will do so and then it will be found that no single blow or curse, or humiliation or act of robbery or injustice has been overlooked. Deaths in war he will take no account of, for he springs from a race of soldiers and is prepared to accept what he gives without complaint or malice. Death is, so to speak, the coin of his trade, as victory and defeat are its stakes but with the rest it is otherwise. For these in some shape, probably one that is quite unforeseen, an hour of reckoning will surely strike. It is not possible in this or any other human affair, continually and with intent, to sow the wind and always escape the reaping of the whirlwind.

I think that even now, at the eleventh hour, much might be done to give these people something to replace all they have lost.

The reign of chiefs is finished, the pageant, the spoils, and the pomp of battle have gone with it to the limbo of the past. A new condition has appeared. The son of him who slew our soldiers by the fatal mound of Isandhlwana, or rushed through a storm of bullets until he fell pierced upon Ulundi's plain, often the man himself, walks along the hills and valleys of Zululand, with greasy trousers for his kilted uniform, holding a tattered parasol in the hand that once grasped the shield or the stabbing spear . . .

Their crimes and errors for the most part are those of kings and chiefs, and of the witch doctors preying upon the superstitions of a primitive race. Their virtues are their own, and if encouraged with understanding these should in the end give them no mean place among the coloured subjects of the Crown. If, however, they are embittered by injustices and ill treatment, if their proffered loyalty and trust are scorned and rejected; if in the place of help, education and good counsel, they receive from the white man, their master, little save his dislike, his disease and his drink, if their lands continue to be taken from them and the morality of their women corrupted; ultimately they will add all his vices to their own.

      H. Rider Haggard, to the Colonial Office

Never has the sky been more perfectly blue.
      David Lloyd George, January 1914

Assassination of Archduke Franz-Ferdinand, Heir to the Austro-Hungarian Empire, and his Wife, by Slav Nationalists, at Sarajevo

The Almighty does not allow Himself to be challenged with impunity. A Higher Power has restored the order I was unable to uphold.

Emperor Franz-Josef

Austrian Ultimatum to Serbia Accepted Almost in Entirety

A brilliant achievement; it removes all reason for war . . . the reservations made on a few points of detail can in my view be cleared up by negotiation.

Kaiser Wilhelm II

The future belongs to Russia; she grows and grows, and weighs upon us like a nightmare.

German Imperial Chancellor Bethmann Hollweg

There's talk of war. It will never happen. The Germans haven't the credits.

The Governor of the Bank of England

Russian Mobilization

This seemed to darken our world and we looked glumly at each other. Curiously enough that news gave me the first sense of foreboding I had, and I can feel it still. Even then we were not sure, but our hopes were ill-founded for they rested mainly on the Germans by-passing Belgium. Against this was a growing conviction that we must be involved anyway, even if only at sea at first.

When we got back to our lines and were discussing this new event, our platoon commander came up. He was a popular Master and we told him our anxious thoughts, but he would have none of them: 'There won't be any war,' he said, 'the City would never allow it. Even if fighting did break out, it couldn't last more than a few days, the money would run out.'

Anthony Eden, 1976

The Schoolboy

In the closing days of July the Eton College Officers Training Corps was in camp together with contingents from other schools. Years later Hitler was to cite these activities to me as proof of the military training of British youth . . .

In that year the talk was all of war, would there be one, would our country be involved, how long would it last and, only occasionally because the contingency seemed comparatively remote, should we personally have any part in it? The general expectancy was that the war, if it came, would be brief and over in a matter of six weeks. There were no Kitcheners among us.

While each boy had his individual angle, the general mood was not of eagerness for war. There was excitement, due mainly to novelty, for the Boer War had ended twelve years before, and was a dim memory at our age. There was no conception at all of what the war would really be like. Our military literature, as far as we had any, belonged to the turn of the century with such books as The Defence of Duffer's Drift.

Anthony Eden, 1976

A German Diary

Frankfurt-am-Main, June 28, 1914: Archduke Francis Ferdinand has been murdered, with his wife (the Duchess of Hohenberg), by two Serbs at Sarajevo. What follows from this is not clear. You feel that a stone has begun to roll downhill and that dreadful things may be in store for Europe.

I am proposing on 1 October to start my military service instead of going to Hamburg as a commercial trainee. I'm twenty, you see, a fine age for soldiering, I don't know a better.

July 14: I travel to Würzburg, report to the 2nd Bavarian Field Artillery Regiment and get accepted.

Böhm, the German airman, has scored a world record with 24½ hours of continuous flight.

July 23: Ultimatum delivered to Serbia by Austria-Hungary. No strong action by Austria appeared to have been taken since the assassination of 28 June until suddenly this note was presented, containing ten demands which among other things were supposed to allow Austria herself to take action on Serbian soil against activities hostile to Austria. Serbia has to accept the ultimatum within 48 hours, otherwise Austria reserves the right to take military action. A world war is hanging by a thread.

July 25: Unbelievably large crowds are waiting outside the newspaper offices. News arrives in the evening that Serbia is rejecting the ultimatum. General excitement and enthusiasm, and all eyes turn towards Russia – is she going to support Serbia?

The days pass from 25 to 31 July. Incredibly exciting; the whole world is agog to see whether Germany is now going to mobilize. I've hardly got enough peace of mind left to go to the bank and do my trainee job. I play truant as though it were school and stand about all day outside the newspaper offices, feeling that war is inevitable.

Friday, July 31: State of war declared and total mobilization announced in Austria-Hungary.

Saturday, August 1: 6.30 p.m. The Kaiser orders mobilization of the Army and Navy. That word 'mobilize', it's weird, you can't grasp what it means. First mobilization day is 2 August.

Try as I may I simply can't convey the splendid spirit and wild enthusiasm that has come over us all. We feel we've been attacked, and the idea that we have to defend ourselves gives us unbelievable strength.

Russia's dirty intrigues are dragging us into this war; the Kaiser sent the Russians an ultimatum as late as 31 July. You still can't imagine what it's going to be like. Is it all real, or just a dream?

      Herbert Sulzbach

A Plea for Peace

Your Excellency, – Is there nothing that my country can do? Nothing that I can do towards stopping this dreadful war? I am sure that the President would approve any act of mine looking towards peace. – Yours ever,

      James W. Gerard, to the German Imperial Chancellor

My Diary for August 3rd, 1914, contains a most incongruous mixture of war and tennis.

The day was Bank Holiday, and a tennis tournament had been arranged at the Buxton Club. I had promised to play with my discouraged but still faithful suitor, and did not in the least want to forgo the amusement that I knew this partnership would afford me – particularly as the events reported in the newspapers seemed too incredible to be taken seriously.

'I do not know,' *I wrote in my diary,* 'how we all managed to play tennis so calmly and take quite an interest in the result. I suppose it is because we all know so little of the real meaning of war that we are so indifferent. B. and I had to owe 30. It was good handicapping as we had a very close game with everybody.'

In spite of my vague memories of the South African campaigns, Spion Kop and Magersfontein were hardly more real to me than the battles between giants and mortals in the Andrew Lang fairy-books that I began to read soon afterwards. My father had taken Edward and myself round Macclesfield in a cab on Mafeking Night, and I had a confused recollection of fireworks and bonfires and excited shouting which were never clearly distinguished in my mind from the celebrations for Edward the Seventh's postponed coronation.

Vera Brittain, 1933

Germans Invade Belgium – An Exchange

It served us right, we should have seen it coming if we hadn't been blackmailed by Edward Carson over Ulster.

Bernard Shaw

Never mind about that now. The Germans are frightfully efficient and will invade us too. We must have a *levée en masse*. We must get out our shot guns and man the hedges and ditches, but it will be the end of civilization.

H. G. Wells

Necessity knows no law, we must hack our way through.

German Imperial Chancellor Bethmann Hollweg, to the Reichstag

I held a council at 10.45 to declare war with Germany. It is a terrible catastrophe but it is not our fault. An enormous crowd collected outside the Palace; we went on the balcony both before and after dinner. When they heard that war had been declared, the excitement increased and May and I with David went on to the balcony; the cheering was terrific. Please to God it may soon be over and that He will protect dear Bertie's life.

> King George V

God heard the embattled nations shout
Gott strafe England and God save the King.
Good God, said God,
  I've got my work cut out.

> J. C. Squire

Professional Man desires to meet others from Corps Mounted Infantry. Each provide own arms and contribute hire horse. Drill and instruction after and before working hours.

> *The Times*

There was little time to think of war, because a huge charity fête was taking place.

> Vicar's Wife

I am sending thousands and thousands of men to their death . . . there is only One alone who can help.

> Tsar Nicholas II

In this war it is a question . . . of German civilization against barbarous Slavdom.

> General Count Helmuth von Moltke the Younger

And so . . . you wish to make our country the battlefield of Europe. Have you thought of that?

> The Belgian Ambassador, to the German Foreign Minister

To arms, my falcons. With faith in God let us go forward. Long live Serbia.

> Crown Prince Alexander of Serbia

The lights are going out all over Europe. They will not be lit again in our time.

> Sir Edward Grey

We are only playing Russia's game.

> John Morley

TO GERMANY

You are blind like us. Your hurt no man designed,
And no man claimed the conquest of your land.
But gropers both through fields of thought confined
We stumble and we do not understand.
You only saw your future bigly planned,
And we, the tapering paths of our own mind,
And in each other's dearest ways we stand,
And hiss and hate. And the blind fight the blind.

When it is peace, then we may view again
With new-won eyes each other's truer form
And wonder. Grown more loving-kind and warm
We'll grasp firm hands and laugh at the old pain,
When it is peace. But until peace, the storm
The darkness and the thunder and the rain.

> Charles Hamilton Sorley

His mind was full of confused images, and the sense of strain. In answer to the word 'Germany' a train of vague thoughts dragged across his brain. The pompous, middle-class vulgarity of the buildings of Berlin; the wide and restful beauty of Munich; the taste of beer, innumerable quiet, glittering cafés; *The Ring*; the swish of evening air in the face as one skis past the pines; a certain angle of the eyes in the face; long nights of drinking and singing and laughter . . . certain friends; some tunes; the quiet length of evening over the Starnbergersee.

> Rupert Brooke

AUGUST 1914

How still this quiet cornfield is to-night!
By an intenser glow the evening falls,
Bringing, not darkness, but a deeper light;
Among the stooks a partridge covey calls.

The windows glitter on the distant hill;
Beyond the hedge the sheep-bells in the fold
Stumble on sudden music and are still;
The forlorn pinewoods droop above the wold.

An endless quiet valley reaches out
Past the blue hills into the evening sky;
Over the stubble, cawing, goes a rout
Of rooks from harvest, flagging as they fly.

So beautiful it is, I never saw
So great a beauty on these English fields,
Touched by the twilight's coming into awe,
Ripe to the soul and rich with summer's yields.

> John Masefield

The Painter

The newsvendor had disappeared from the street, so I went to the coffee-house to read the newspaper there. A Colonel named Redl, on the General Staff, had betrayed the Austrian plan of campaign to the Russians the year before, and now two Pan-Slav parliamentarians had been arrested. So it began. But I was not satisfied merely to regard others as lunatics. One must try to keep one's eyes open, to see how long one remains sane oneself.

In 1914 I was twenty-eight years old, and thus liable for military service. It seemed to me better to volunteer before I was conscripted. I had no wife or child to await my happy return. I had nothing to lose or to defend. I felt melancholy at the sight of the young bank clerks, the little office workers, whom I saw hurrying with their suitcases to enlist, and yet I did not share the doom-laden mood that prevailed on the streets. The air was thick with rumours that part of the army had gone into the field wearing peacetime uniforms, with inadequate weapons and obsolete equipment. There had been no proper rearmament, and sloppiness was the rule in Austria-Hungary. Men took up arms only to die.

> Oskar Kokschka

The blood that is being shed will purge us of many hateful qualities . . . of our caste feeling, of our detestable partisanship, our gross selfishness and a hundred more. Let us thank the gods for a Wilhelm and a whole nation insane with a hatred of England, to restore us to health.

> W. H. Hudson, to Edward Thomas

The idea that we were brought up on, that Europe is the home of civilization in general – nonsense! It's a periodical slaughter-pen, with all the vices this implies. I'd as lief live in the Chicago stockyards.

> Walter Hines Page, American Ambassador to Great Britain

The Volunteer

I have been told that there may be some difficulty in finding officers for the New Army. I think I may say that my name is well-known to the younger men of this country and that if I were to take a commission at my age it might be of help. I can drill a company – I do so every evening. I have seen something of campaigning, having served as a surgeon in South Africa. I am fifty-five but I am very strong and hardy, and can make my voice audible at great distances which is useful at drill. Should you entertain my application, I should prefer a regiment which was drawn from the South of England – Sussex for choice.

> Sir Arthur Conan Doyle, to the War Office

Paris

I consider that, as in 1793, only two punishments exist, dismissal or death. You desire victory; to win it, use the most rapid, brutal, energetic and decisive methods.

> M. Messimy, Minister of War, to General Joffre

From Zurich

The transformation of the present imperialist war into a civil war is the only effective proletarian slogan, shown by the experience of the Paris Commune.

Lenin

In the autumn of 1914, when four-fifths of Europe's Socialists had taken a stand in defence of the fatherland, while one-fifth timidly bleated 'for peace', Lenin alone in the ranks of world socialism had pointed the way for others; for war! – and immediately!

Alexander Solzhenitsyn, 1976

Women of England. Do your duty. Send your son today to join our Glorious Army.

Archdeacon Wilberforce of Westminster

OH YOU YOUNG MEN

Awake, oh you young men of England,
For if, when your Country's in need,
You do not enlist in your thousands
You truly are cowards indeed.

Eric Blair (George Orwell), aged 11

From Rome

Down with the war! Down with Armaments! Long live the international brotherhood of workers.

Benito Mussolini

The Future Mahatma in Bayswater

Those Indians who are residing in the U.K. should place themselves at the disposal of the authorities . . .

We would respectfully emphasise that the one dominant idea guiding us is that of rendering such humble assistance as we may be considered capable of performing as an earnest of our desire to

share the responsibilities of membership of this great Empire, if we
would share its privileges.

M. K. Gandhi, Barrister-at-Law, to the India Office,
August 14, 1914

A Private Soldier

We crawled on our bellies to the edge of the woods. Over us
the shells were howling and whistling: splintered tree trunks and
branches flew around us. And then again grenades crashed into the
woods, hurling up clouds of stones, earth, and stifling everything in
a yellowish-green, stinking, sickening vapour. We couldn't lie there
for ever, and if we were going to be killed, it was better to be killed
outside. Then our major came up. Again we went forward. I
jumped up and ran as fast as I could, across meadows and turnip
fields, jumping over ditches, over wire and living hedges. Then I
heard someone ahead of me shouting, 'Everybody in! Everybody in
here.' A long trench lay before me; a moment later I had jumped
into it. Before me, behind me, to the left and right, others followed.
Beside me were Württembergers: under me dead and wounded
Englishmen.

Adolf Hitler, to a Munich tailor

Another von Moltke

This day is the decisive one. One whole army, stretching from Paris
to Upper Alsace, has been fighting in a battle since yesterday. If I
had to give my life today to gain the victory, I would relinquish it
with rapture, as thousands of our comrades in arms have already
done. What rivers of blood have flowed, what nameless sorrow has
overwhelmed the countless innocent whose houses and farms have
been burnt down and destroyed – I am often overcome by a sense of
horror when I think of it, and I have the feeling that I may be called
to account for all these ghastly disasters, and yet I could not have
acted differently nor changed the course of events . . .

These are hard times; countless sacrifices have already been
claimed by this war and more will be claimed. The whole world is
conspiring against us, and it seems as if all the other nations have
made it their mission to destroy Germany for ever. The few neutral
states are not sympathetic toward us. Germany has not a friend in

the world, she stands utterly alone and has only herself to depend on.

On today's outcome hangs the decision whether we shall stay where we are. In any case, it will not be much longer. The Emperor must go to France to be nearer the army; like his troops, he must enter the enemy country . . .

Things are going badly. The fighting to the east of Paris is going against us. One of our armies has had to withdraw, the others will have to follow. The war which we began with such optimism is developing differently from what we imagined. I must bear the responsibility of the outcome, standing or falling with my country. We are likely to be crushed between the East and the West, fighting on both fronts. How different it all was a few weeks ago, when we launched so brilliant a campaign – now a bitter disillusionment is setting in. And how much we shall have to pay for all that is being destroyed!

> General Count Helmuth von Moltke the Younger, to his wife

THE GREAT NIGHT

I'd often stand at the window started the day before,
stand and stare at you. It still seemed to warn me off,
the strange city, whose unconfiding landscape
gloomed as though I didn't exist. The nearest
things didn't mind if I misunderstood them. The street
would thrust itself up to the lamp, and I'd see it was strange.
A sympathisable room up there, revealed in the lamplight:
I'd begin to share: they'd notice, and close the shutters.
I'd stand. Then a child would cry, and I'd know the mothers
in the houses, what they availed, and I'd know as well
the inconsolable grounds of infinite crying.
Or else a voice would sing, and what was expected
be just a little surpassed; or an old man coughed below,
full of reproach, as if his body were in the right
against a gentler world. Or else, when an hour was striking,
I'd begin to count too late and let it escape me.
As a strange little boy, when at last they invite him to join them,
cannot catch the ball, and is quite unable
to share the game the rest are so easily playing,

but stands and gazes – whither? – I'd stand, and, all at once,
realise *you* were being friends with me, playing with me, grown-up
Night, and I'd gaze at you. While towers
were raging, and while, with its hidden fate,
a city stood round me, and undivinable mountains
camped against me, and Strangeness, in narrowing circles,
hungrily prowled round my casual flares of perception:
then, lofty Night,
you were not ashamed to recognise me. Your breathing
went over me; your smile upon all that spacious
consequence passed into me.

      Rainer Maria Rilke

The horse-shoes still ring
with the old days.
The doormen sleep on the counters
like bales of furs.

And the porter, weary as a king,
hears knocking at the iron gate,
gets up yawning like a barnyard –
they've waked the old Scythian!

So Ovid with his waning love
wove Rome with snow on his lines,
and sang of the ox-cart
in our wild wagon-trains.

      Osip Mandelstam

DECLINE
To Karl Borromäus Heinrich

Over the white pond
The wild birds have travelled on.
In the evening an icy wind blows from our stars.

Over our graves
The broken brow of the night inclines.
Under oak trees we sway in a silver boat.

Always the town's white walls resound.
Under arches of thorns,
O my brother, blind minute-hands,
We climb towards midnight.

   Georg Trakl

AT HELLBRUNN

Following once again the evening's blue lament
Along the hillside, along the vernal pond –
As if the shades of those long dead, the shades
Of prelates and of noble women hovered over them –
Their flowers are blooming already, the earnest violets
In the evening's depth, the blue wellspring's
Crystal wave purls on. So religiously
Do the oaks grow green over forgotten paths of the dead,
The golden cloud over the pond.

   Georg Trakl

GRODEK

At nightfall the autumn woods cry out
With deadly weapons and the golden plains,
The deep blue lakes, above which more darkly
Rolls the sun; the night embraces
Dying warriors, the wild lament
Of their broken mouths.
But quietly there in the willow dell
Red clouds in which an angry god resides,
The shed blood gathers, lunar coolness.
All the roads lead to blackest carrion.
Under golden twigs of the night and stars
The sister's shade now sways through the silent copse
To greet the ghosts of the heroes, the bleeding heads;
And softly the dark flutes of autumn sound in the reeds.
A prouder grief! You brazen altars,
Today a great pain feeds the hot flame of the spirit,
The grandsons yet unborn.

   Georg Trakl

ABOVE THE SILENT TOWN

Above the silent town a streak of blood!
Then from the darkness over us, a tempest
Arose and through its gusts I heard a tramping
Of armies, dim then near. An iron clatter . . .
And joyful, threatening rang a thrice-divided
Metallic high-resounding call, and rage
And force and tremor over me were loosened,
As if a sword sank flat upon my head –
A rapid rhythm drove the troops to trotting . . .
And more and more battalions and the selfsame
Stridor of fanfare-tone . . . is this the final
Uprising of the gods above this land?

      Stefan George

LIST OF CONTRIBUTORS

ADAMS, Brooks, American historian, universal rather than national in his theories, much concerned with the nature of civilization, its flaws, anxieties and future

AGATE, James, For many years theatre critic of the *Sunday Times*, and diarist

ALBERT, Prince, German husband of Queen Victoria, of immense devotion to work and responsibility, he had considerable influence on British culture, politics, reform. Believed in German political and cultural advances under Prussian leadership

ALEXANDER, Crown Prince, later King Alexander of Yugoslavia, murdered in 1934

ALEXANDER II, Tsar of Russia, the 'Liberator' whose rule saw emancipation of ten million serfs and some devolution of rural government, but whose further plans for reform were halted by his murder in 1881

ALEXANDER, Alfred, British writer, author of a biography of Verga and a book on opera

ALLIX, Jules, French communard, of lively imagination which earned him a brief internment in a lunatic asylum by his colleagues

APOLLINAIRE, Guillaume, Poet of Polish/Italian birth, educated in France, dying of influenza in 1918, serving in the French forces

ASQUITH, Margot, Second wife of Liberal Minister H. H. Asquith. She was famed for her outspoken wit

BADEN-POWELL, Robert, British general, won fame in the siege of Mafeking during the Boer War. Founder of the Boy Scout movement

BALFOUR, Arthur James, British Prime Minister, statesman, philosopher, associated today with the still controversial Balfour Declaration, pledging a 'National Home' in Palestine for the Jews

BALZAC, Honoré de, French novelist, author of *La Comédie Humaine* in some ninety volumes, giving a dramatic and comprehensive portrait of post-Napoleonic society in Paris and the provinces

BAUDELAIRE, Charles, French Symbolist poet, critic, translator and champion of Poe, poet of the Modern City, its torments, pleasures, temptations, Baudelaire comprehended the totality of people and circumstance, the squalid and noxious, the beautiful, bizarre and pitiful

BAX, E. Belfort, British socialist writer, associate of the early Fabians, an authority on European revolutionary sects and movements

BEERBOHM, Max, British artist, essayist, drama critic, story teller, wit, bridging the world of Wilde and early Shaw, and the Second World War, during which he made some notable broadcasts

BELL, Lady Florence, British essayist, novelist, playwright, writer for children, and sociologist, step-mother of Gertrude Bell

BELLOC, Hilaire, Anglo-French biographer, traveller, essayist, M.P., historian, poet, Roman Catholic pamphleteer. Not renowned for his historical accuracy. His *Cautionary Tales* continue to give pleasure. The *Path to Rome* is a fine account of a famous walk. With his friends, Chesterton, Wells and Shaw, he was part of a formidable quartet in early twentieth-century literary and political debate

BENNETT, Arnold, English novelist and critic, author of *The Old Wives' Tale*

BERNHARDT, Sarah, Leading French actress whose long career began before the 1870 war and continued after the Great War

BETHMANN-HOLLWEG, T. T. F. A., German Chancellor in 1914

BISMARCK, Prince Otto von, Prussian diplomat and statesman, first Chancellor of the German Empire, which his policies largely helped create, though with results which would have dismayed him, yet for some of them he must bear responsibility

BLACK, John George, London friend and confidant of George Gissing

BLANCH, Lesley, British autobiographer, writer on cookery, travel and historical biography

BLOK, Alexander, Russian Symbolist poet. His 'The Twelve' (1918) applauded the Revolution, in which he later lost faith

BONAPARTE, Charles Joseph, Cousin of Napoleon III, but of social, not political, distinction

BOUMAN, P. J., Dutch social historian

BOWERS, Archibald 'Jacko', British professional soldier, serving in the Boer War and the Great War, mentioned in despatches at Passchendaele and living to be a hundred

BRAILSFORD, Henry Noel, British political author, historian, journalist, classic exponent of early socialist analysis of war and empire, mostly in pre-Freudian terms of class and economics, somewhat too simple perhaps, when applied to the Great War and the appeal of dictators from left and right

BRITTAIN, Vera, British writer, feminist, pacifist, remembered for her autobiographical *Testament of Youth*

BROOKE, Rupert, English poet of widespread, popular appeal. His death from disease, on active service during the Great War, contributed to the notion of the long, pre-war Golden Age, of security, beauty, sunlit afternoons

BROWN, J. Baldwin, Quoted as 'a certain J. Baldwin Brown' in Victoria Glendinning's *A Suppressed Cry*, though with no biographical information

BURKE, Edmund, Anglo-Irish British political philosopher and politician, one of Dr Johnson's circle, and with political views still relevant. His firm common sense shattered the rhetorical abstractions evoked by the French revolutionary zealots, which he foretold would lead to a corrupt and violent dictatorship. In memorable speeches he attacked the slave trade, religious discrimination, corruption in India, and Britain's policies towards the American rebels

BURNE-JONES, Edward, British painter, friend of William Morris, with whom he worked on glass and tapestry, associate of the pre-Raphaelites

BURNS, Lucy, Pre-twentieth-century feminist, follower of Mrs Pankhurst

BUTLER, Samuel, Victorian novelist, satirist, remembered for *Erewhon* and *The Way of All Flesh*, and his pungent, witty and wide-ranging *Notebooks*. His scientific, moral and psychological speculations often foreshadowed more famous discoveries. Caustic about Victorian family life and values, he gives salt in an atmosphere sometimes overburdened with sentimentality, sententiousness and dogmatic humbug

CAMPBELL, Mrs Patrick, British actress, Bernard Shaw's first Eliza Doolittle, and helped to introduce audiences to Ibsen. A personality with malicious and trenchant tongue and intelligence, she maintained a witty and spirited correspondence with Shaw

CARLYLE, Thomas, Scottish philosopher and historian, admirer of the heroic, exemplified by Cromwell, Frederick the Great, John Paul Jones, and Danton, memorably evoked in his passionate *French Revolution*

CARUS, Karl Gustav, German philosopher, painter, art critic, writer on philosophy, psychology and much else

CAVAFY, Constantine P., Greek poet whose work is saturated with ancient Alexandria and the decline of Hellenism from external and internal causes. Admiration from E. M. Forster, W. H. Auden, Lawrence Durrell, and Rex Warner helped establish his name in Britain, together with his ironic wit, nostalgic world-weariness, and the sumptuous decadence of his backgrounds

CÉZANNE, Paul, French Post-Impressionist painter, a founder of artistic modernism, erstwhile friend of Zola, who, to his annoyance, drew on him for his novel *L'Oeuvre*

CHAMBERLAIN, Joseph, British politician, Colonial Secretary under Salisbury and Balfour, imperialist in his convictions, a social reformer with early republican views which he later discarded. Father of Neville Chamberlain

CHEKHOV, Anton P., Russian dramatist, short-story writer, doctor, with a humour and style of deceptive simplicity, actually of a subtlety which had far-reaching effects on subsequent literature

CHERTOV, Vladimir Grigoryevich, Tolstoy's secretary

CHURCHILL, Lady Randolph, Born Jennie Jerome, daughter of wealthy American, Leonard Jerome, mother of Winston Churchill. Of considerable beauty and verve, she notably assisted her son's early military, journalistic and political career

CHURCHILL, Winston Leonard Spencer, British statesman, politician, journalist, historian, biographer, amateur painter, novelist, polo-player, wit. Twice Prime Minister. Rode in the last big-scale charge, at Omdurman, of the British Cavalry. In Asquith's pre-1914 Cabinet, he has claims, with Lloyd George, to have pioneered the Welfare State

CLEMENCEAU, Georges, French doctor and statesman, Mayor of Montmartre during the 1870 War and Commune, twice Prime Minister, leader of France during the vital second part of the Great War. Philip Guedalla called him 'the last of the Jacobins'.

CLUSERET, Gustave Paul, French politician, Delegate for War under the Commune, which later tried him, mostly on fantastic charges, due to internal rivalries. Released, and vanished in the turmoil of defeat

COCTEAU, Jean, French poet, novelist, playwright, painter, draughtsman, maker of imaginative and widely-shown movies, friend of most of the famous figures in the Paris literary and artistic salons and movements

COLETTE, Sidonie Gabrielle Claudine, French actress and novelist, famed in England for *Gigi*, and for her evocative personal memories of childhood and women's emotional lives

CONRAD, Joseph, Polish-born novelist, domiciled in England, drawing on much of his experience of ships and sailors for his tales and moral values. His elaborate prose has gradually achieved classic status. *Lord Jim*, *An Outcast of the Islands*, *Victory* made intelligent, often moving films, though the atmosphere of the novels can scarcely be reproduced, charged as it is by the rare and complex personality behind it

CORNFORD, Frances, British poet, granddaughter of Charles Darwin

CORY, William Johnson, British teacher, poet, translator, educational writer

CRIPPEN, Dr H. H., Centre of a sensational murder case, following which he was hanged for murder of his wife. His story excited the imagination of many journalists and novelists. Ernest Raymond's novel *We The Accused* seems loosely based on Crippen, his wife and mistress

CURZON, George Nathaniel, British statesman, Viceroy of India, Foreign Secretary, famed for his sumptuous and haughty style which, in India, obscured his genuine concern for Indian art, culture and welfare

DALTON, Hugh, British Socialist politician, served in Churchill's war-time coalition, and Clement Attlee's post-war Labour Cabinet

DARWIN, Bernard, British international golfer, biographer, journalist

DAUDET, Alphonse, French novelist, short-story writer, creator of *Tartarin of Tarascon* and of a play *L'Arlésienne*

DAVIDSON, John, Scottish poet, playwright, for a time schoolmaster

DELANE, Charles Thaddeus, British journalist, as editor of *The Times*, 1841–77, he must have seemed an unofficial part of government, when the paper was considered the 'Thunderer'

DELESCLUZE, Louis Charles, French communard, Jacobin in outlook, finally meeting a famous death on the barricades, in top hat, frock coat, red sash, black trousers, with cane in hand

DHINGRA, Indian nationalist and terrorist

DICKENS, Charles, British novelist, editor, philanthropist. His lapses into sentimentality have been condemned, not least by Lenin, but his mastery of language and imagery, his humour and dark symbolism, affected Tolstoy, Dostoevsky, Kafka, Conrad, Wittgenstein, Strindberg, Brecht, Proust, Orwell and an immense public

DISRAELI, Benjamin, British statesman, twice Prime Minister, novelist, dandy. Witty and colourful – 'thank God for something warm,' he said of his host's champagne – romantic yet shrewd, a founder of modern Conservatism, admirer of traditional institutions, suspicious of overpowerful and inorganic political institutions, he is still a subject for debate and speculation. He fascinated or horrified his contemporaries. His fiction survives through its style, wit and glitter, though *Sybil* revealed in grim and indignant detail the 'Two Nations' between which Victorian Britain was divided

DOSTOEVSKY, Fedor Mikail, Russian novelist of extraordinary psychological and moral complexity, and of towering reputation. Later of extreme orthodox political and religious views. As a young man he survived a sentence of death for conspiracy, then Siberian exile, described in *The House of the Dead*. It has been observed that his major work is preoccupied with the Fall of Man

DOYLE, Sir Arthur Conan, Anglo-Irish doctor, spiritualist, legal reformer, quixotic in his approach to many social wrongs and miscarriages of justice, writer of historical and scientific romances and detective fiction, and chronicler of much of the Boer and Great Wars

DUCROT, French general in 1870 war. Given supreme command by the Emperor after the wounding of Marshal MacMahon, soon superseded by de Wimpffen, then assisted in the defence of Paris

DUMAS, Alexandre, French playwright, author of *La Dame aux Camélias*, son of the creator of *The Three Musketeers*

DUNCAN, Isadora, American dancer, who made a resolute effort to free the dance from the lengthy traditions of Classical Ballet

EDEN, Anthony (Lord Avon), British statesman, Foreign Secretary in the 1930s, and again in Churchill's war cabinet, Prime Minister at the start of the Suez Crisis. Served in the Great War, on the Western Front

ELIOT, George (Mary Anne Evans), British novelist, with *Middlemarch* often held her masterpiece, and with an intellect and breadth of knowledge unusual amongst her contemporaries

ELLIS, Peter Beresford, Novelist, historian, biographer, with works on the Cornish language and the Great Fire of London

ENGELS, Friedrich, Wealthy businessman, associate and supporter of Karl Marx, many of whose works he translated and edited, and with whom he wrote the Communist Manifesto, 1848. His own books included the substantial *The Condition of the Working Class in England*

ENSOR, James, Belgian painter and engraver, an independent spirit who had to overcome much initial public and critical hostility. 'Avant-garde', his work is yet saturated with the spirit of Bosch and Breughel!

EUGÉNIE, Empress of the French, daughter of a Spanish general, and with

Scottish blood. Of great beauty, never very popular amongst the French who blamed her, wrongly, for the outbreak of the 1870 war: during which she was briefly Regent, her husband, Napoleon, being at the Front. She died in Madrid, aged 94

FERRÉ, Theophile, French communard, served on the Police Commission, ordered execution of hostages, including the Archbishop of Paris. Executed, smoking a cigar, after the defeat

FISCHER, Ernst, Austrian art and literary critic, for some years a Marxist, serving the Comintern in Stalin's Moscow

FOCH, Marshal Ferdinand, French general and theorist, Allied Supreme Commander in 1918

FONTANE, Theodor, Prussian novelist, described by Michael Hamburger as 'much less ambiguously on the side of sweetness and light than Nietzsche, Stefan George, Rilke, Thomas Mann, or even Goethe'

FORBES, Archibald, Pioneer war-correspondent, covered Crimean and Franco-Prussian wars

FORD, Ford Madox, English novelist, editor and poet, born Ford Madox Hueffer. Influential man of letters, collaborated with Joseph Conrad on three novels. 'Moderates of any type I have always found insupportable.'

FRANZ-JOSEF, Penultimate Habsburg Emperor, 1848–1916. He presided over national disasters with a monumental dignity not yet quite forgotten

FREDERICK, Crown Prince of Prussia, Later Emperor Frederick. His death from cancer after a few months' rule removed a liberal and humane personality, with ideas more akin to those of his father-in-law, Prince Albert, than to those of Bismarck. The succession passed to his son, Wilhelm II, gifted, volatile, but nervous, conceited and of poor judgment of men, events and issues

FREUD, Dr Sigmund, Viennese founder of psycho-analysis, developed modern theories of the unconscious, dreams, infantile sexuality, and the concealed motives beneath art, religion, human plans, symbolism: coincidence, chance, neurosis. His findings startled many who might have found some of his distinctions between appearance and reality implicit in Shakespeare, and asserted by Dr Johnson

FULLER, J. F. C., British general, military theorist, historian, of controversial politics but with extensive knowledge of warfare

GAUGUIN, Paul, French painter, an early Impressionist until removal to the South Seas gave him access to different techniques, fiercer colours, simpler lives. Like that of his one-time friend Van Gogh, his work is cherished by a vast international public

GEORGE V, King of Great Britain, Stolid, insular, philistine, conventional, he yet expressed much national common sense, professional responsibility and human concern. Alert to preserve the Crown's remaining rights, he intervened, or interfered, more often in public affairs than might be supposed, very seldom without good reason

GEORGE, Stefan, German poet, admirer of Nietzsche and himself a cult figure in pre-Hitler days. Mistaking his love of leadership, summer fields, open air values and young men for sympathy with themselves, the Nazis vainly tried to enlist his support

GERARD, James W., American lawyer and diplomat, ambassador to Germany in 1914

GISSING, George, British realistic novelist and man of letters. His life of great suffering and hardship produced such considerable works as *New Grub Street* and *The Nether World*

GLADSTONE, William Ewart, British Liberal politician and statesman. Four times Prime Minister, a dominating personality in Victorian politics at home and abroad. A vigorous reforming influence, practical and effective, as against the utopian theories of many London-based continental exiles – Kropotkin and Marx amongst them – in old age he made a prolonged and humane attempt to solve the Irish problem, a failure, but heroic. In later years he was known as G.O.M., 'Grand Old Man', though his detractors transcribed it as 'God's Only Mistake'

GOGH, Vincent Van, Dutch Expressionist painter. Selling nothing in his complex lifetime, he created a warmth of colour and human feeling that now ensures him a huge popularity even amongst those unconcerned with art

GONCOURT, Edmund and Jules de, Joint authors of early realistic nineteenth-century novels but better known today for their journal, with its vivid accounts of social life in Paris and its literary, artistic and political celebrities

GORKY, Maxim, Russian novelist, short-story writer, playwright, exemplar of Socialist Realism for contemporary Marxists, and for the Russian State its foremost orthodox writer

GOULD, Sabine Baring, Devonshire parson, antiquarian, man of letters, creator of some thirty books, of 'Onward Christian Soldiers', and fifteen children

GREY, Edward (later, Lord Grey of Fallodon), Liberal politician and statesman, Foreign Secretary in 1914, blamed by some for ambiguities in foreign policy which led Germany to believe that Britain might remain neutral in the event of war, thus encouraging German bellicosity

GUEDALLA, Philip, English biographer, historian and essayist

GUTMAN, Robert, Musicologist, author of a widely-read, critical biography of Wagner

HAGGARD, Henry Rider, English journalist, agriculturalist, colonial administrator, romantic novelist. His bestselling *She* was admired by Jung

HARDY, Thomas, Famous for his 'Wessex' novels and poetry, his *Tess of the D'Urbervilles* and *Far from the Madding Crowd* reached a further audience through the cinema. For some critics, his verse – quirky, personal, observant, impervious to fashion – makes him one of the first of the moderns

HARLEY, Rodney, Minor British novelist, whose 'Hilda' is quoted in Victoria Glendinning's *A Suppressed Cry*

HARRISON, Robert Arthur, British headmaster, who taught this editor at Marlborough House School, Hawkhurst, 1930–4

HÉBERT, Jacques René, French revolutionary terrorist: falling foul of Danton, Robespierre and Saint-Just, he was guillotined in 1794, swiftly followed by all three

HERZEN, Alexander, Russian political journalist, novelist, publisher of the *Russian Free Press* from his base in London. Author of an absorbing autobiography, he was consistently sceptical of the idealistic goals and utopias that attracted and bemused many of his famous contemporaries

HESSE, Hermann, German novelist and poet, superb at describing the anxieties, hesitations, joys and rebuffs of adolescence, and particularly well-known for the psychological implications of his novel *Steppenwolf*

HEYM, Georg, German poet, whose 'Der Krieg' (1911, the year before his death), in its imagery and descriptions anticipated many of the horrors of the Great War

HINGLEY, Ronald, British academic, biographer and critic, an authority on Russian history, society, literature

HITLER, Adolf, Austrian born, of artistic and intellectual pretentions and pretentiousness, rescued from a drab existence by service in the German army during the Great War. Leading the post-war National Socialist party, he eventually succeeded Hindenburg as Head of State. As dictator, he eliminated all opposition with a mass-brutality rivalled only by Lenin and Stalin. A violent nationalist, racialist, anti-Semite, and of mental powers and military insight still unresolved by historians, he led Germany into the Second World War and with Heinrich Himmler and the SS, presided over the 'Final Solution', disposing of racial minorities, and dissidents with gas, rope, torture, overwork. A lover of Wagner, admirer of Nietzsche and, for some years, of Mussolini, a curious mixture of cripple and, for so many, magician, his end, in flame and ruin, might not have wholly disappointed him

HODDIS, Jakob Van, German Expressionist poet

HOFMANNSTHAL, Hugo von, Austrian poet and critic, famous too for his librettos for the operas of Richard Strauss, notably 'Der Rosenkavalier'

HOOPER, George, British authority on military affairs, specifically on the Franco-Prussian war

HORNE, Alistair, British military historian, author of works on Napoleon I, the Great War struggle for Verdun, the Siege of Paris and the Commune, and the French collapse, 1940

HOWARTH, Thomas Edward Brodie, British historian, educational writer and biographer of King Louis-Philippe

HUDSON, W. H., American writer, born in Argentina, remembered for his novel *Green Mansions* (1904)

HUGHES, M. V. 'Mollie', British schoolteacher, author of several autobiographical works, excelling in description of London and provincial life and lives

HUGO, Victor, French Romantic poet, novelist, playwright, hater of Napoleon III, whom he stigmatized as 'Napoleon the Little', under whose rule he lived in exile, in Jersey

IBSEN, Henrick, Norwegian dramatist and poet, mingled realism and symbolism, found a British champion in George Bernard Shaw and directly affected Shaw's own work

JACOB, Alexandre, French anarchist and bandit leader, robbing churches and country houses. Deported in 1905 for 150 robberies, released 1929

JAEGER, Gustav, Nineteenth-century German physician

JAMES, Henry, American novelist, short-story writer and playwright, whose profound merits the British and American public were slow to recognize. Long domiciled in England, he became a British citizen during a grim period of the Great War

JAURÉS, Jean, French politician and writer with a forceful generosity of personality and thought which has ensured his reputation long surviving him. Founder of the Socialist paper *L'Humanité*, defender of Dreyfus, he was no Marxist, but perhaps harked back to the more generous traits of the Revolution. Murdered, 1914, for his anti-war efforts to promote a Franco-German general strike

JEROME, Jerome K., British humorist, novelist and playwright

JOYCE, James, Irish poet, novelist, playwright, short-story writer and linguist. His monumental *Ulysses* and unique *Finnegans Wake* presented problems to later experimental novelists, seldom very satisfactorily solved. He died too soon to appreciate the fact that his remark that the worst point about the Second World War was that it would prevent people reading *Finnegans Wake* would scarcely be appreciated by the victims of gas-chamber, rope, torture, starvation and battle

JULLIAN, Phillipe, French painter, writer and authority on *Art Nouveau*

JUNG, Carl Gustav, Swiss psycho-analyst, psycho-therapist, writer, one-time associate of Freud, with theories of archetypes and collective unconscious which have had considerable appeal throughout the world. Some of his work is condemned as more mystical than scientific by opponents; his early support of the Nazis was subsequently withdrawn

KELVIN, William Thompson, Scottish scientist and inventor, pioneer of thermodynamics, a founder member of the Order of Merit

KHLEBNIKOV, Velemir (christened Viktor), Russian Symbolist and Futurist poet, died 1922. His dependence on sound makes his work almost impossible to translate

KILVERT, Francis, British Anglican parson, author of a famous Diary, posthumously published, and justly enjoying much popularity amongst general readers and students of Victorian country life, manners and outlook

KING-HALL, Magdalen, Prolific British novelist, social historian and journalist

KINGSLEY, Charles, British novelist, Anglican clergyman and historian. His early beliefs in Christian Socialism and social reform he later abandoned. *The Water Babies*, a story for children, may now be his best-remembered book

KIPLING, Rudyard, British novelist, poet, short-story writer and journalist. Famous for his youthful tales of India and his ballads of military life. These, with their vigorous common speech, were to influence Brecht. The variety of technique in his verse is extraordinary, as it is in his stories. His imperialism, once mistaken for vulgar jingoism, actually insisted on responsibility, useful work, selflessness, and inter-racial and religious respect. Few successors have written better for children

KOKOSHKA, Oskar, Austrian Expressionist painter, British citizen from

1947. From the start he derided conventional notions of beauty and form and, as writer, teacher and artist, he created a 'School of Seeing' at Salzburg, to heighten perception, and awareness. He was 'profoundly influenced by the vigour and spatial freedom of Baroque art, by the passionate and intellectual honesty of a great architect, Adolf Loos, and of a political writer of genius, Karl Kraus'.

KOLLONTAI, Alexandra, Russian Marxist reformer, educationalist, the only woman member of Lenin's Cabinet, courageously feminist in a movement which, ostensibly revolutionary and socialist, was blatantly masculine. She also refutes the remark made in an Arthur Koestler novel that one can see what's wrong with the Left by the ugliness of its women

KRAUS, Karl, Viennese satirist and poet, author of 'The Last Days of Mankind'. His use of language and topical insights are still scarcely approached by any succeeding journalist

KROPOTKIN, Prince Peter, Russian anarchist philosopher, whose 'Mutual Aid' excited several generations of political and social idealists. He renounced his career, lands and position for anarchism, science and reform, and lived mostly in London. He returned to Russia in 1917, surprisingly supporting the Kerensky offensive. Hostile to the Bolsheviks. Anarchists were allowed to attend his funeral in 1921, but were then rounded up and anarchism proscribed. Author of the idiosyncratic *French Revolution*

LABOUCHERE, Henry, British journalist, founder of 'Truth'

LAFORGUE, Jules, French poet, whose ironic lyricism and precision were deeply admired by T. S. Eliot and, through him, affected British and American 'modernism'

LATEY, Maurice, BBC editor, political and historical journalist, with specialized knowledge of despotic regimes

LAWRENCE, David Herbert, British novelist, poet, short-story writer, traveller, critic and painter: of passionate vision, scarcely rivalled for intensity of feeling for nature, human relationships, sunlit landscapes. His doctrines of possessive masculine sexuality, 'dark gods' of loins, of blood – instinct and earthy, organic existence and communities find less favour, partly due to their association with Fascist and Nazi blood and soil notions and, for Bertrand Russell, Lawrence's ideas on sex, society and behaviour 'led straight to Auschwitz'

LENIN, Russian Bolshevik leader, overcame Kerensky and the Mensheviks in 1917, subsequently holding elections, which the Bolsheviks lost. By force he established a one-party dictatorial state which has lasted into the present. Discussion remains whether the brutalities, corruption, inefficiencies and moral squalor should be traced to Stalin, or whether they were from the start inherent in Lenin's system and thought. A man of outstanding ability and obduracy, his influence on the twentieth century has, however interpreted, been profound

LEO, Alan, British astrological consultant and journalist, editor of the journal 'Modern Astrology', from 1895, and of the book, *Esoteric Astrology*. Member of Blavatsky's Theosophical Society. Much of his copious work remains in print

LESLIE, Anita, British autobiographer, biographer of Rodin, Madame Tussaud, Leonard Jerome, Jennie Jerome (Lady Randolph Churchill) and others

LICHENSTEIN, Alfred, German Expressionist poet killed in the Great War

LORD, Walter, American writer, authority on the American Civil War, song-writer, journalist

LOWE, Harold Godfrey, Fifth Officer of the *Titanic*, the sinking of which he survived

LUEGER, Karl, Austrian politician, Mayor of Vienna, whose tough methods and skilful use of flags, music and marches impressed the young Hitler

LUXEMBURG, Rosa, German Marxist politician and writer, with pronounced reservations against Lenin's ruthless and authoritarian methods. Imprisoned for her opposition to the Great War, about which she wrote some moving passages. Murdered with her friend and colleague, Karl Liebknecht, by the Right, following their abortive 'Spartacist' revolt in Berlin

MACEMBA, Chief, Tribal ruler who bravely, though vainly, attempted to resist brutal German colonial expansion in Africa

McGONAGALL, William, Scottish writer, who commented on topical events in verse of endearing badness

MACHADOS, Antonio, Spanish poet, son of a collector of Andalusian folk-song. His own work is saturated with images and moods of Andalusia and Castille, and his reputation remains high in Spain

MacNAB, Maurice, Parisian left-wing satirist and song-writer, associated with the beginnings of European Cabaret

MALMESBURY, James Harvard Harris, Earl of, British politician, Foreign Secretary, friend of Napoleon III

MANDELSTAM, Osip, Outstanding Russian poet, who vanished in Stalin's camps. His life, with its achievements, tribulations, friends, enemies, the brave and the cowardly, is movingly chronicled by his widow, Nadezhda, and is available in English in two volumes

MANN, Heinrich, German novelist, brother of Thomas, who, with Romain Rolland, courageously opposed the Great War. Best remembered for *The Blue Angel*, he is unfairly disregarded in Britain, few of his many books being translated

MANN, Thomas, German novelist, essayist, short-story writer and critic. Nobel Prize winner, author of *The Magic Mountain*, *Buddenbrooks* and many other works

MANNING, Cardinal Henry Edward, Leading personality in Victorian ecclesiastical and social life and Roman Catholic politics, remembered too for his support for prison and social reform and for his relations, ambiguous, sometimes harsh, with Cardinal Newman

MANSFIELD, Katherine, New Zealand short-story writer and critic, married to John Middleton Murry

MARINETTI, Emilio Filippo Tommaso, Italian writer, largely working in France; a founding member of Futurism and Dadaism

MARLY, Diana de, British journalist and biographer

MARX, Eleanor 'Tussy', Daughter of Karl, Socialist union organiser and lecturer, translator of *Madame Bovary*, acted in first, and amateur, production of Ibsen's *The Doll's House*, with Bernard Shaw as Krogstadt. Her husband, Edward Aveling, has some traits of Shaw's Dubedat in *The Doctor's Dilemma*

MARX, Karl, German-born economist, historian and political publicist, whose writing, notably *Kapital* gave a theoretical basis to communist revolutions and states throughout the world, since the Communist Manifesto of 1848. Foretelling inevitable world revolutions, he failed to envisage the rise of Fascism and Nazism. Though scarcely an original thinker, his theories of class-war and the materialist conception of historical development have won consent from generations of radicals, mostly at second hand. John Plamenatz has pointed out the dependence of much of his social theory on accurate statistics for proof, which were unavailable to Marx. A. J. P. Taylor has written 'Marx's generalizations about history can never be shown to be either true or false. They are merely curious.' The scientific philosopher, Karl Popper, dismisses Marxism as sham science, with Marx – along with Freud and Jung – a rhetoricist with findings incapable of proof, in a world less deterministic than he, together with many nineteenth-century thinkers, had supposed

MASEFIELD, John, British poet, novelist, playwright, autobiographer and writer for children. His status as 'modern' poet was superseded by that of T. S. Eliot and Ezra Pound, but his reputation survives on his ballads, lyrics and verse narratives in traditional styles, with sea and pastoral themes – the Chaucerian 'Reynard the Fox', and the seafaring drama 'Dauber' with its vivid characters and powerful descriptions of the sea's moods, its furies and tranquillity. His books on both world wars, particularly concerning Gallipoli and Dunkirk, continue to be moving; children can still delight in *The Midnight Folk*; his tragedies *Pompey the Great* and *The Tragedy of Nan* get an occasional performance; and his recollections of pre-nineteenth-century rural and seafaring life remain absorbing

MASON, A. E. W., Liberal M.P., journalist, romantic novelist – *The Four Feathers* has made successful films. He played Major Plechanoff in the first production of Shaw's *Arms and the Man*, in 1894

MAUGHAM, W. Somerset, British novelist, playwright, short-story writer, man of letters, of vast popularity. Much of the middle-aged British concept of the Far East must derive from Maugham's expertly crafted stories, novels and films, limited though his vision and language become in comparison with Joseph Conrad

MEARNS, Andrew, British pamphleteer, sociologist, Secretary of the London Congregational Union

MESSIMY, French politician, Minister of War at the outbreak of the Great War

MEW, Charlotte, Poet, short-story writer, essayist, contributor to *The Yellow Book*. She lacked self-confidence, and lived a troubled life

MICHEL, Louise, French revolutionary, 'the Red Virgin' of the Paris Commune, deported to New Caledonia in 1871

MILL, John Stuart, Regarded throughout the world as representative of British liberal values, with *On Liberty* probably his most influential work, though *On the Subjection of Women* is currently being discussed as an early feminist plea. On his initiative, Parliament held the first debate about female suffrage

MILNER, Lord, British Imperialist statesman, and South African proconsul

MOLTKE, Field-Marshal Helmuth von, Prussian commander in 1870. Reputed to have smiled only twice in his life: at his mother-in-law's funeral, and at a claim that Stockholm was impregnable. His son, Von Moltke the younger, of too philosophical a disposition to be a decisive leader, was chosen by the Kaiser to command the invasion of France in 1914, more for his name than for his abilities

MOORE, Dorothea, British author, best known for her writings for children

MOORE, George, Irish novelist, playwright, art critic. *Esther Waters* (1894) is one of his best-known novels

MORGENSTERN, Christian, German poet. 'Naturalistic, patriotic, Nietzschean, Rilkean, ironic, sentimental – each in turn – Morgenstern, despite all these variations in style, is primarily known today for his humorous poetry, which all but defies translation.' (Arthur S. Wensinger.)

MORLEY, John, British Liberal politician, writer, biographer of Gladstone. Pacifist convictions forced him to resign from the Cabinet in protest against British entry into the Great War in 1914

MORRIS, William, British poet, painter, designer, craftsman, printer and friend of the pre-Raphaelites. A socialist considered by Shaw as 'the saint of the century', along with Kropotkin, follower of Ruskin in striving to bring art and beauty to the impoverished industrial masses. Writer of visionary outlines of life as it could and should be

MUSSOLINI, Benito, Italian journalist, one-time socialist agitator, founder of the Fascist Corporate State, dictator of Italy, 1922–43

MYERS, Frederick William Harvey, Cambridge classical don, poet, essayist, co-founder of the Society of Psychical Research in 1882

NANSEN, Fridtjof, Norwegian polar explorer, sportsman, scientist, writer, humanitarian. Helped the peaceful separation of Norway from Sweden in 1905; the first Norwegian ambassador to Britain; helped inspire the League of Nations; organized famine relief in post-1918 Russia, and the repatriation of prisoners after the Greek-Turkish war in 1922. Founder of the Nansen Passport for stateless people

NAPOLEON III, Louis Napoleon Bonaparte, nephew of Napoleon I, and one of the great nineteenth-century adventurers, was captured in youth by the Austrians while fighting with Italian Nationalists. Escaping, he was later imprisoned 'for life' after a second unsuccessful coup against Louis Philippe. He escaped, disguised as a workman. His obdurate self-belief eventually carried him to the Presidency of the Second Republic, thence, by a dramatic coup d'état, to the imperial throne. He assisted the establishment of independent Italy, and of Romania, fought with Britain the Crimean war, was 'the inventor of the ironclad' (Hugh Thomas) and, with Haussmann, the designer of modern Paris. His social and political ideas and hedonistic outlook were more generous and advanced than those of his detractors – Marx and Bismarck amongst them. Disraeli introduced him into a novel as 'Prince Florizel'. His regime was too personal for its own good, and his good sense became increasingly impaired by ill-health. The final disaster has made him, until recently, a 'non-person' in French history, and his remains, together with those of his wife and son, remain in England. Like de Gaulle, he seems to represent a recurring element in French politics, contemptuous of parliamentary debate, appealing both to the humane and vulgar instincts of the crowd, mistrustful of colleagues, with personal courage and dignity balanced by periods of bad judgment

NECHAEV, Sergei, Mysterious Russian terrorist, believing that revolution justified all fraud, violence and betrayal, inclined more towards anarchism and Bakunin than to Marx. His precise importance is undecided and Russian opinion today is wary of him. He may have influenced Lenin, his methods of organized terror are shown in Dostoevsky's *The Devils*, he himself identified as Verkhovensky

NEUMANN, Alfred, German historical novelist, author of a trilogy about Napoleon III and the Paris Commune

NICHOLAS II, Last Russian Tsar, mediocre, weak and obstinate. Unable to cope with the Great War, murdered by revolutionaries in 1918

NIETZSCHE, Friedrich, German poet and philosopher, served in the Franco-Prussian war, attempted to substitute a dynamic metaphysic for Christianity which he condemned for its devitalizing ethics and herd values. Admired, but probably misunderstood, by Hitler and Mussolini

NORTHCLIFFE, Lord (Alfred Charles William Harmsworth) Pioneer of cheap popular newspapers, co-founder of the *Daily Mail*, owner of *The Times*, 1908, a savage and unscrupulous propagandist during the Great War. Hugh Walpole described him as 'rather like a wicked hippo in training'

OBERDANK, William, Italian nationalist, hanged in 1882 for planning to murder Franz-Josef during a state visit

OLLIVIER, Émile, French politician and historian. Former republican, but Head of the French Imperial government at the start of the Franco-Prussian war which destroyed his political career

ORWELL, George, British novelist, essayist, political journalist, whose obstinate independence of mind, loathing of the pretentious and hypocritical, obsession with purity of language, scourged the Left and ridiculed the Right, and any who believed that political and social ideas could not be contaminated by the moral squalor of those who held them. *Animal Farm* and *Nineteen Eighty-Four* are read throughout the world, but his essays give a more rounded understanding of him

PAGE, Walter Hines, American politician and diplomat, ambassador to London at the start of the Great War

PALÉOLOGUE, Georges Maurice, French diplomat and author

PANKHURST, Emmeline, British suffragette leader

PARASKA, Larin, Leading Finnish female poet and singer, particularly of folk-song. She died in 1904

PÉGUY, Charles, French socialist poet, dramatist, founder (1900) of the journal *Cahiers de la Quinzaine*, in which much of his own work appears. Killed in the Great War

PEROVSKAYA, Sophia, Russian nihilist hanged for her part in the murder of Tsar Alexander II. Like many nihilists, from a comfortable background and of idealistic disposition

POUND, Ezra, American poet, critic, translator, composer, editor, domiciled first in England, then Paris, finally settling in Italy where he ardently supported Mussolini, praised Hitler's *Mein Kampf*, stated (1941) that Hitler had taught the Germans 'manners'. Author of the controversial Cantos, and of versions of Chinese and Provençal verse, champion of the early T. S. Eliot, James Joyce, Ernest Hemingway, Scott Fitzgerald, Tagore, Robert Frost and other writers, composers, painters and sculptors, particularly Henri Gaudier-Brzeska. His work on Eliot's 'The Waste Land' was a major literary contribution, and W. B. Yeats confessed a debt to him, Pound urging him to develop a sterner poetic style, 'cold and passionate as the dawn'

PRIESTLEY, John Boynton, British novelist, essayist, playwright, critic and general man of letters. His autobiographical *Margin Released* has some of the best, though under-rated, descriptions of active service in the Great War

PROUST, Marcel, French novelist and critic, whose vast *A la Recherche du temps perdu* is regarded as one of the masterpieces of modern European imaginative literature

QUINET, Edgar, French historian and professor, author of *The Revolution*, in which he attacked the growing cult of the Jacobin and Hébertist terrorists

RHODES, Cecil, British millionaire businessman and imperialist politician, founder of Rhodesia, now Zimbabwe, and a prime representative of nineteenth-century developments in British Southern Africa with its mixture of commercial expansion, racial ideology and strategic planning

RIGAULT, Raoul, French terrorist, Public Prosecutor under the Commune, responsible for many killings, before, in the White Terror, being 'shot while trying to escape'

RILKE, Rainer Maria, Austrian poet, one of the most acclaimed European poets before and after the Great War, and whose letters give an extraordinarily personal picture of the early twentieth century, notably in Paris and Germany

ROBESPIERRE, Maximilien Marie Isidore, French Revolutionary politician, foremost among the Jacobins, identified with the last and direst stage of the Terror. Has been called 'the first modern dictator', probably wrongly. He remains a phenomenon of considerable fascination. Outwardly, and on reasoned evidence, a mediocrity, he yet somehow survives as a formidable personality, who overcame the dynamic Danton, and for a while dominated the Assembly, and was idealized by Paris, and was regarded abroad as master of France. A deputy was once convinced that Robespierre was looking at him, and reflected in horror, 'He'll be imagining I was thinking about something.' He is fixed in Carlyle's stormy pages as 'the sea-green Incorruptible', though conceivably, save in terms of money and comfort, he was morally more corrupt than most, in his self-deception. In sudden crisis he proved virtually incapable of defending himself, and, like Mussolini, was overthrown within hours as a public nuisance

ROCHEFORT, Henri, French aristocrat, journalist and vehement republican, viciously attacking the last years of the Second Empire in *La Lanterne* – a man of wit and erudition. Briefly involved in the Commune, he was later transported; eventually escaping to Australia, he died in obscurity. An autobiography appeared in 1895

ROSSETTI, Christina, British poet, sister of Dante Gabriel. Her colourful, indeed pre-Raphael-like 'Goblin Market' was widely read: religious reflections and considerable melancholy affect her later work

ROZHESTVENSKY, Petrovitch, Russian admiral, totally defeated by the Japanese at Tsu-Shima in 1905, which dramatically announced Japan's entry into the modern world

RUSKIN, John, British artist, art critic and lecturer whose views on the nature and purposes of art and life influenced several generations of thinkers, teachers, politicians, artists and writers, as different as Proust and Gandhi

SAINT-JUST, Louis-Antoine de, French Jacobin politician and terrorist, associate of Robespierre, whose views he shared, perhaps more ruthlessly, and with whom he was guillotined in July 1794

SALA, George Augustus, British journalist, novelist and travel writer. He covered the Franco-Prussian war for the *Daily Telegraph*, as he had the American Civil War

SALISBURY, Third Viscount, British Conservative statesman, often called 'the Great'. Three times Prime Minister between 1885 and 1902 – the first to be simultaneously Foreign Secretary

SAND, George (Aurora Lucile Dupin), French novelist, socialist and feminist, who had celebrated friendships with Alfred de Musset, Chopin and Flaubert. Her letters and memoirs are today more interesting, perhaps, than her fiction

SAZONOV, Yegor, Russian Social Revolutionary Party member. Given a life sentence for murdering the Chief Minister, Plehve, the government fearing to execute him on account of popular hatred of the victim. Sazonov committed suicide in 1911, a gesture against prison conditions

SCHLIEFFEN, Field Marshal Count Alfred von, Served in Franco-Prussian war, became Chief of the German General Staff, and prepared the famous Plan for the invasion of France, which was only partly followed in the unsuccessful drive for Paris in 1914

SCHÖNERER, Georg von, Austrian nationalist and anti-semitic politician, prominent in Vienna during Hitler's youth

SCHREINER, Olive, South African novelist, famous for *The Story of an African Farm*, also for her friendships, notably with Havelock Ellis

SCHWEITZER, Albert, Alsatian medical missionary, theologian, musicologist, philosopher and historian

SCOTT, Captain Robert Falcon, British polar explorer, whose death near the South Pole still arouses sympathy and controversy

SEEBOHM, Winnie, Daughter of banker-historian Frederick Seebohm, of Hitchin, England; an early woman student at Cambridge University; died at 22; the subject of Victoria Glendinning's *A Suppressed Cry*

SHAFTESBURY, Seventh Earl of, Leading nineteenth-century British social reformer, philanthropist, educationalist and politician, who achieved outstanding good on behalf of lunatics, lodging-house tenants, children, factory workers, the poor and illiterate, despite parliamentary and religious opposition. A high Tory, he hated socialism, as an anarchic and destructive process. Socialists, often respecting him as a man, condemned his methods as designed to prop up and restore a political set-up essentially selfish and unjust

SHAW, George Bernard, Irish playwright, novelist, Fabian socialist, music and drama critic, champion of Ibsen and Wagner. Much of his work, with its lively wit and flashing, sometimes flashy, interruptions by ideas and teaching, still holds the world stage. An admirer of Samuel Butler, and of the French Naturalist, Lamarck, Shaw's theories of creative evolution and the Life Force, are important in his major plays and prove slightly more acceptable today than much of his political philosophy. In later life, impatient with British parliamentary debate, which he considered a procrastinating obstruction to vital social and economic reform, he became a supporter of the ruthless and authoritarian – of Stalin, Mussolini and, to a lesser degree, Hitler. Himself of unusual kindliness and generosity – he attempted to help Oscar Wilde at the time of his downfall, when many friends and colleagues deserted him – he seems overinfluenced by the witty, unscrupulous, managerial and hard Caesar of his *Caesar and Cleopatra*. The elements of crankiness, clownishness and vanity in his make-up enlivened him as an author but sometimes handicapped him as a thinker of influence. 'England had conquered Ireland; so that there was nothing for it but to come over and conquer England.'

SICKERT, Walter, British Impressionist painter, influenced by Pissarro; associated with the Camden Town Group and the London Group; lover of music halls from which he took many themes for his work

SIMS, George Robert, Specialist in Edwardian and late-Victorian London, with books including *Off the Track in London*, and *London by Night*

SITWELL, Sacheverell, British poet, art historian, essayist, traveller and social historian

SMITH, Edward J., Captain of the *Titanic*, whose fate he shared. The presence on board of Bruce Ismay, his Managing Director, may have been a handicap, even an interference, seriously impairing his judgment

SMYTHE, Ethel, British composer, largely of operas and chamber music, whose one-act opera, 'The Wreckers', achieved considerable critical acclaim. A vigorous personality, she suffered a short imprisonment for her support of the suffragettes, the March she composed for them is seldom played. A tireless, sometimes tiresome, devotee of Virginia Woolf. Her autobiography deserves attention

SOLZHENITSYN, Alexander, Russian novelist. Fought in Red Army against

Hitler, subsequently imprisoned by the Stalinist State in dreadful conditions, described in his fiction and the mammoth *The Gulag Archipelago*. An outspoken critic of the Communist regime on political and religious grounds, he later left Russia for North America. Author of such novels as *The First Circle* and *August 1914*. Awarded the Nobel Prize for Literature in 1970

SOREL, Georges, French Syndicalist, believing in violent revolution led by trade unions. A professed disciple of Marx and admirer of Nietzsche, he in his turn excited many who would turn to Nazism and Fascism

SORLEY, Charles Hamilton, British poet, killed in the Great War, his letters and poems being published posthumously

SPENCE, Lewis, British authority on folk-lore. Prolific author

SQUIRE, John C., British poet and editor, known too for his cricket team which he led for many years with enthusiastic eccentricity

STADLER, Ernst, German poet, often called Expressionist though much of his work is not. Wrote a number of poems describing the poorer quarters of England, particularly London. A Christian mystic, translator of Péguy, he wrote on Shakespeare, and many of the political, sexual, religious and social themes prominent in pre-war Europe. Killed in the Great War

STENDHAL (Marie Henri Beyle), French officer under Napoleon, travel writer, critic and novelist. Author of *La Chartreuse de parme* and *Le Rouge et le noir*

STEPHEN, J. K., British writer of light, often satirical, verse

STEPHEN, Leslie, Prominent biographer, man of letters, alpine climber, editor of the *Cornhill Magazine*, writer on philosophical and religious themes, first editor of the *Dictionary of National Biography*, father of Virginia Woolf and Vanessa Bell

STEPUN, Fedor, Baltic writer who had deep sympathies with Russian culture. Studied in Germany, founded the review *Logos*, worked in Russian adult education, friend of many European writers, and in his autobiography gave a broad picture of pre-revolutionary Russia

STEVENSON, Robert Louis, Scottish romantic novelist and poet

SULZBACH, Herbert, Fought in German army during the Great War, refugee from Hitler in 1937, officer in the British army in 1945, later Cultural Officer at the West German Embassy, London. One of the three holders of the *Croix de paix de l'Europe*, a Franco-German peace award

SWINBURNE, Algernon Charles, British poet, friend of Rossetti, Watts, Duncan, Landor, a passionate, rhetorical, romantic writer, using colour and feeling as often for their own sake than for strong supports of a theme

SWINNERTON, Frank, British novelist, critic, publisher's adviser. *Nocturne* is his most widely-read novel, and his autobiography, together with *The Georgian Literary Scene*, give an interesting account of the lives and preoccupations of some sixty years of English writers

SYMONS, Arthur William, British poet, critic, essayist, translator, admirer of the French Symbolists, particularly Baudelaire and Verlaine. He had a large part in introducing such writers to Britain, though premature illness arrested his own writing, permanently, thirty years before his death in 1948

TAYLOR, A. J. P., British historian, whose judgments are usually stimulating and provocative, and sometimes unpopular. Author of some thirty books, including ones on Bismarck, the Habsburg Empire, the Great War, the origins of the Second World War, and general English and European history

TENNYSON, Alfred, Lord, British poet and playwright, Queen Victoria's Laureate, of lyric and descriptive powers seldom surpassed in native literature. His total work shows an astonishing profusion of talent and banality, genius and the commonplace, realism and romanticism, raw patriotism and awareness of the moral, social and intellectual issues of nineteenth-century Britain and Europe

TERRY, Ellen, British actress, for many years associated with Sir Henry Irving and his productions of Shakespeare. She had a long correspondence with Bernard Shaw, and was the mother of Edward Gordon Craig. Her marriage to the painter G. W. Watts was not a success

THIERS, Adolphe, French statesman, politician, historian of the French revolution, and of the Consulate and First Empire. A Prime Minister under Louis Philippe. Supported Louis Napoleon, whom he seriously under-estimated, in 1848. In political eclipse during the Second Empire, but took the lead when the Republic was proclaimed after Sedan, and took responsibility for suppressing the Commune, and signing the peace treaty with the new German Empire

TOLSTOY, Leo N., Russian novelist, teacher, moralist, and tractarian whose writings have never ceased to be read throughout the world. His monumental *War and Peace* made an outstanding Russian film

TOYNBEE, Philip, British novelist, poet and literary journalist. Son of the historian, Arnold Toynbee

TRAKL, Georg, Austrian poet, described by Arthur S. Wensinger as 'a lyricist of the stamp and nearly the stature of Friedrich Hölderlin . . . he produces a rotting and changing autumnal world – a Christian world, moribund, fragmentary, and ineffably melancholy, dissolving into dream and insanity.' He has affinities with Baudelaire, Rimbaud, Verlaine, Maeterlinck, Heym, Novalis, Hölderlin, but with a vision very much his own. Committed suicide on active service during the Great War

TREITSCHKE, Heinrich von, German nationalist historian and politician, whose admiration of force and war helped to prepare German intellectual support for the Great War

TREVELYAN, George Macaulay, Cambridge liberal historian both of Great Britain and Italy

TRINQUET, French communard, served on Police Commission and subsequently deported to New Caledonia

TROLLOPE, Anthony, Prolific British novelist, inventor of 'Barchester' – still of unflagging popularity – and the subject of a number of recent studies of his literary and sociological significance

TUCHMAN, Barbara, American historian, author of, amongst other works,

August 1914, *The Proud Tower*, *A Distant Mirror*, a study of the fourteenth century

TURGENEV, Ivan, Russian novelist and playwright, essayist. His play *A Month in the Country*, and novel, *Fathers and Sons*, amongst other works, have been recognized for style, sensitivity and wit throughout the world. Professor John Bayley has lately written that his novels now please no one. To this, there are exceptions

UNDERWOOD, Peter, British journalist, authority on the psychic and the occult, author of a dictionary of the supernatural, a life of Boris Karloff, *The Ghosts of Borley*, and much else

VACHELL, H. A., British popular novelist, whose public school story *The Hill*, 1905, is still read, not only by Harrovians

VAILLANT, Auguste, French anarchist, guillotined for throwing a bomb into the Chamber of Deputies, which killed no one. His period witnessed much fear of anarchist bombs and assaults. He must not be confused with Edward Vaillant, the communard

VERLAINE, Paul, French lyric and Symbolist poet, one of the 'last of the Bohemians', whose purity of diction made him a dominant 'Nineties' figure and an important one today

VICTORIA, Queen of Great Britain, Empress of India. Longest reigning of all British monarchs. Her journals of her Highland life, her letters and conversation, often derided, show a decided uncompromising personality of common sense, prejudice, self-confidence and awareness of her own royal privileges. On Louis Napoleon's election as President of the Second Republic, she proved more sophisticated than Thiers and the French professional politicians. 'It will . . . perhaps be more difficult to get rid of him again than one at *first* may imagine.' After the fall of the Empire, she befriended Eugénie and Napoleon, remaining on close terms with the former until her own death. She, like Eugénie, believed in the innocence of Captain Dreyfus

VICTORIA, Crown Princess of Prussia, Later Empress of Germany. Daughter of Queen Victoria and Prince Albert. She inherited her father's intellectual tastes, liberal outlook and wide reading, which her husband's premature death and the antipathies between herself and her eldest son, Wilhelm II, were denied Germany when they were most needed

WAGENER, Herman, Prussian senior civil servant, friend of Bismarck

WAGNER, Orlando, British private school headmaster, quoted by R. A. Harrison

WAGNER, Richard, German composer, still controversial, whose music, drama and artistic theories had pronounced effect on music and literature

WARD, Mrs Humphry, English novelist, granddaughter of Dr Arnold of Rugby. She instigated play-centres and welfare schemes for children and the handicapped, and opposed women's suffrage

WEBB, Beatrice, British Fabian Socialist, associated, with her husband Sidney, George Bernard Shaw, Hubert Bland, H. G. Wells and others, with the early fortunes of the British parliamentary Labour Party and methodical programmes for social reform

WELLS, Herbert George, British novelist, short-story writer, journalist and sociologist, whose imaginative combination of scientific speculation, utopian prophecy, fantasy and realism gave 'Wellsian' a universal significance before the Second World War. His passionate belief in education and the benefits to be expected from science invited a reputation for reckless optimism and gullibility, disproved by more tragic elements in his thought, shown in such works as *The Time Machine* and *The Island of Dr Moreau*

WILDE, Oscar Fingall O'Flahertie Wills, Irish playwright, story-teller, poet, wit, man of letters

WILHELM I, King of Prussia, first Emperor of the German Empire, whose support was useful and sometimes essential to Bismarck·in his plans for Prussian supremacy in Germany and eventual German unity and the overthrow of Austrian leadership in German affairs

WILHELM II, Third and last of the modern German Emperors. Despite a useless arm he made an impressive ceremonial head of state, but unfortunately demanded a role much fuller, for which he was constitutionally entitled. His mercurial temperament and theoretical posturings did much to continue the dislike and fear of Germany initiated by Bismarck. The outbreak of the Great War swiftly reduced him to a cipher controlled by the Military. German defeat, leading to revolution moved him into exile and obscurity. He survived until 1941, with interests in archaeology, tree-cutting, and the works of P. G. Wodehouse. Kipling's 'If' is said to have been his favourite verse

WIMPFFEN, General de, Commanded the French army at Sedan, thus forced to accept the capitulation terms after the disaster

WODEHOUSE, Pelham Grènville, British novelist and short-story writer whose popularity sometimes disguises his comic and stylistic inventiveness

WOLSELEY, Garnet Joseph, Field Marshal, British soldier and military reformer, victor of Tel el Kebir in 1882, pacified the Red River rebels in Canada in 1870, tried vainly to save Gordon at Khartoum. For years, 'all Sir Garnet' meant that everything was secure and in order. No favourite of Queen Victoria

WOOLF, Leonard, British colonial civil servant, later a tireless editor and committee-man for British and international social democracy: political journalist, novelist, and with his wife, Virginia, publisher, founder of the Hogarth Press

WOOLF, Virginia, One of the most discussed of twentieth-century British novelists; critic and diarist. Her freshness of observation and kinetic technique have given her work, after a slow start, a wide readership, at least throughout the English-speaking world. *To The Lighthouse*, *Mrs Dalloway*, *Between the Acts*, and *The Waves*, amongst the novels, and the literary essays in *The Common Reader* are prominent. The ardours and complexities of serious writing emerge, often painfully, from the diaries and letters

ZELDIN, Theodore, British historian, author of *A History of Modern*

France, in which political history is balanced by a rare exposition of social history and detail

ZEMPIRIK, Inspector, Police official in nineteenth-century Trieste, then part of the Habsburg Empire

ZOLA, Émile, Prodigious French Naturalist novelist and journalist, who won additional fame, admiration and abuse, by his dynamic defence of Captain Alfred Dreyfus in the notorious 'Affair'

ZWEIG, Stefan, Austrian novelist, short-story writer, biographer and auto-biographer. His *Marie Antoinette* long agitated countless adolescents in Europe and America

ACKNOWLEDGMENTS

An anthology demands considerable rather tedious work of research, follow-up, lay-out, from various people, only one of whom gets any attention. My gratitude is due to the editorial and design staff of Jonathan Cape, notably, once more, Valerie Buckingham. Also, for useful help from James Greene and Frederick Grubb. From my old friend Michael Hamburger, whose knowledge of European literature far exceeds my own, I plunder almost beyond legitimate bounds, as I do the work of the late Blair Leishman.

The pictures are reproduced by kind permission of the following sources: p. 1, The Mansell Collection; pp. 13, 87, 123, 153, Mary Evans Picture Library; p. 211 from the Robert Harding Picture Library Ltd, reproduced by permission of the Tate Gallery, London.

The author and publishers are indebted to the copyright holders for permission to reproduce material as follows:

ALFRED ALEXANDER: extract from *The Hanging of William Oberdank* reprinted by permission of London Magazine Editions

GUILLAUME APOLLINAIRE: extract from *Selected Poems*, © Éditions Gallimard 1920, reprinted by permission of Éditions Gallimard

ROBERT BALDICK (trs.): extracts from *Pages from the Goncourt Journals*, © O.U.P. 1978, reprinted by permission of Librairie Ernest Flammarion

MAX BEERBOHM: extract taken from *A Peep Into the Past*, Heinemann, 1972, reprinted by permission of Mrs. Eva Reichmann

HILAIRE BELLOC: extracts from *Collected Verse* reprinted by permission of Gerald Duckworth & Co. Ltd

SARAH BERNHARDT: extracts from *My Double Life* reprinted by permission of Peter Owen Ltd

LESLEY BLANCH: extract from *The Wilder Shores of Love* reprinted by permission of John Murray (Publishers) Ltd

VERA BRITTAIN: extracts from *Testament of Youth* are included with the permission of The Putnam Publishing Group.

MRS. PATRICK CAMPBELL: extract from *My Life and Some Letters* reprinted by permission of Hutchinson Publishing Group Ltd

C.P. CAVAFY: "Desires," copyright © 1961 by Rae Dalven. Reprinted from *The Complete Poems of C.P. Cavafy*, translated by Rae Dalven, by permission of Harcourt Brace Jovanovich, Inc.; "Voices" and "Candles" from *The Complete Poems of C.P. Cavafy*, translated and copyright © 1961 by Rae Dalven. Reprinted by permission of Harcourt Brace Jovanovich, Inc.; "The God Forsakes Antony," copyright 1948, 1976 by Rae Dalven. Reprinted from *The Complete Poems of C.P. Cavafy*, translated by Rae Dalven, by permission of Harcourt Brace Jovanovich, Inc.

WINSTON CHURCHILL: extract on page 109 from Winston Churchill, *My Early Life*, copyright 1930 Charles Scribner's Sons; copyright renewed 1958 Winston Churchill. Reprinted with the permission of Charles Scribner's Sons.

JEAN COCTEAU: extracts from *Edwardians in Love* by Anita Leslie reprinted by permission of Hutchinson Publishing Group Ltd extracts from *1001 Mornings* reprinted by permission of Peter Owen Ltd

FRANCES CORNFORD: poem from *Mountains and Molehills*, 1934, reprinted by permission of Cambridge University Press

H.H. CRIPPEN: extract from *Crippen, the Mild Murderer* by Tom Cullen reprinted by permission of the Bodley Head Ltd

HUGH DALTON: extract taken from *Call Back Yesterday,* published by Frederick Muller, 1953

BERNARD DARWIN: extract from *W.G. Grace* reprinted by permission of Gerald Duckworth & Co. Ltd

ANTHONY EDEN: extracts from *Another World 1897–1917* reprinted by permission of the Countess of Avon

FRIEDRICH ENGELS: extract from *The Marx–Engels Letters*, ed. Fritz Raddatz, reprinted by permission of Weidenfeld & Nicolson Ltd

THEODOR FONTANE: extract from *Gold and Iron: Bismarck, Bleichroder and the Building of the German Empire* by Fritz Stern. Copyright © 1977 by Fritz Stern. By permission of Alfred A. Knopf.

J.F.C. FULLER: extract from *Decisive Battles of the Western World*, published by Eyre & Spottiswoode, reprinted by permission of David Higham Associates Ltd

STEFAN GEORGE: extracts from *Stefan George: Poems*, trs. by Carol North Valhope and Ernst Morwitz. Copyright 1943 by Pantheon Books, a Division of Random House. Reprinted by permission of the publisher.

GONCOURT JOURNAL: *see* Baldick, Robert

HERMANN HESSE: extract from *Peter Camenzind*, trs. by
                                   W.G. Strachey, reprinted by permis-
                                   sion of Peter Owen Ltd

GEORG HEYM: "And the Horns of Summer Fall
                                   Silent" from *German Poetry
                                   1910–1975*. Copyright © 1976, 1977
                                   by Michael Hamburger. Reprinted by
                                   permission of Persea Books, Inc.,
                                   225 Lafayette Street, New York,
                                   N.Y. 10012

RONALD HINGLEY: extract from *A New Life of Chekhov,*
                                   1976, reprinted by permission of Ox-
                                   ford University Press

JAKOB VAN HODDIS: from *German Poetry 1910–1975*, Per-
                                   sea Books, New York, 1981, re-
                                   printed by permission of the
                                   translator, Michael Hamburger

HUGO VON HOFMANNSTHAL: extract on p. 148 from *Poems and
                                   Verse Plays,* Bollingen Series XXX-
                                   II, 2, Pantheon Books, Inc., New
                                   York, 1961, and Routledge & Kegan
                                   Paul, 1961, reprinted by permission of
                                   the translator, Michael Hamburger
                                   and S. Fischer Verlag, Frankfurt.

ALISTAIR HORNE: extract from *The Terrible Year* re-
                                   printed by permission of Macmillan
                                   Publishers Ltd

M. V. HUGHES: extracts from *A London Family
                                   1870–1900*, 1947, reprinted by per-
                                   mission of Oxford University Press

GUSTAV JAEGER: extract from *Life on Man* by T. Roseb-
                                   ury reprinted by permission of Secker
                                   & Warburg

FRANCIS KILVERT: extracts from *Kilvert's Diary*, ed.
                                   William Plomer, reprinted by permis-
                                   sion of Mrs. Sheila Hooper and
                                   Jonathan Cape Ltd

RUDYARD KIPLING: extract on p. 168 (middle) from *Let-
                                   ters of Travel* reprinted by permission
                                   of Macmillan Publishers Ltd; extracts
                                   on pp. 116–17, 131–3, 167, 168 (top)

from *The Definitive Edition of Rudyard Kipling's Verse* reprinted by permission of the National Trust

VIKTOR KHLEBNIKOV: poem reprinted by permission of the translator, James Greene

OSKAR KOKOSHKA: extract from *Oskar Kokoshka–Mein Leben* © 1971 reprinted by permission of F. Bruckmann K G, Publishers, Munich

ANITA LESLIE: extracts from *Edwardians in Love* reprinted by permission of Hutchinson Publishing Group Ltd

ALFRED LICHENSTEIN: "Return of the Village Lad" and "Ash Wednesday" from *German Poetry 1910–1975*. Copyright 1976, 1977 by Michael Hamburger. Reprinted by permission of Persea Books, Inc., 225 Lafayette Street, New York, N.Y. 10012.

OSIP MANDELSTAM: extracts on pp. 240 (middle), 240–1, 262 from *Osip Mandelstam: Selected Poems,* trs. by Clarence Brown and W. S. Merwin. English translation copyright © 1973 by Clarence Brown and W. S. Merwin. Reprinted with permission of Atheneum Publishers; extracts on pp. 218, 240 (top), 241 (middle) from *Poems,* trs. by James Greene, reprinted by permission of Granada Publishing Ltd

THOMAS MANN: extracts from *Stories of Three Decades* by Thomas Mann, translated by H.T. Lowe-Porter. Copyright 1936 by Alfred A. Knopf. By permission of the publisher.

ELEANOR MARX: letter to Olive Schreiner from *Olive Schreiner* by Ruth First and Anne Scott, 1980, reprinted by permission of Andre Deutsch Ltd

JOHN MASEFIELD: excerpt from "August 1914." Reprinted with permission of Macmillan Publishing Company from *Poems* by John Masefield. Copyright 1914 by Macmillan Publishing Company, renewed 1942 by John Masefield.

CHARLOTTE MEW: extract from *Collected Poems* reprinted by permission of Gerald Duckworth & Co. Ltd

LOUISE MICHEL: extract from *Prison Anthology* by A. L. Stock and R. Reynolds, published by Hutchinson Publishing Group Ltd

JOHN STUART MILL: extracts from *Early Draft of Autobiography,* ed. Jack Stillinger, reprinted by permission of the University of Illinois Press.

J. MIDDLETON MURRY: extract from *Selected Criticism* reprinted by permission of the Society of Authors as the literary representative of the Estate of J. Middleton Murry

ALFRED NEUMANN: extract from *Man of December* reprinted by permission of Hutchinson Publishing Group Ltd

FRIEDRICH NIETZSCHE: extracts from *Nietzsche* by Ronald Hayman reprinted by permission of Weidenfeld & Nicolson Ltd

SOPHIA PEROVSKAYA: extract taken from *Prison Anthology* by A. L. Stock and R. Reynolds, published by Hutchinson Publishing Group Ltd

EZRA POUND: extract from *Collected Shorter Poems* reprinted by permission of Faber and Faber Ltd

J. B. PRIESTLEY: extract from *Margin Released* reprinted by permission of William Heinemann Ltd

MARCEL PROUST: extracts from *Letters of Marcel Proust,* trs. and ed. by Mina Curtiss, reprinted by permission of Mina Curtiss and Chatto & Windus

RAINER MARIA RILKE: poems on pp. 197–8, 198, 198–9, 261–2 from *Poems 1906–26*, trs. by J. B. Leishman, reprinted by permission of St. John's College, Oxford and the Hogarth Press; poem on pp. 244–5 from *Fifty Selected Poems*, trs. by C. F. MacIntyre, © 1940, 1968 by C. F. MacIntyre, reprinted by permission of the University of California Press

ARTHUR RIMBAUD: extracts taken from *The Drunken Boat: 36 Poems of Arthur Rimbaud*, trs. by Brain Hill, published by Rupert Hart-Davis Ltd

YEGOR SAZONOV: extract taken from *Prison Anthology* by A. L. Stock and R. Reynolds, published by Hutchinson Publishing Group Ltd

SACHEVERELL SITWELL: extracts from *For Want of the Golden City*, published by Thames and Hudson, reprinted by permission of David Higham Associates Ltd

ETHEL SMYTHE: extract from *Streaks of Life* reprinted by permission of Letcher & Son

ALEXANDER SOLZHENITSYN: Reprinted by permission of Farrar, Straus & Giroux, Inc. from *Lenin in Zurich* by Alexander Solzhenitsyn, translated by H. T. Willetts. Translation copyright © 1976 by Farrar, Straus & Giroux, Inc.

J. C. SQUIRE: extracts from *Collected Poems* reprinted by permission Raglan Squire.

ERNST STADLER: "Children in Front of a London Soup Kitchen" from *German Poetry 1910–1975*. Copyright © 1976, 1977 by Michael Hamburger. Reprinted by permission of Persea Books, Inc., 225 Lafayette Street, New York, N.Y. 10012.

STENDHAL: extract from *Rome, Naples and Flo-*

rence, trs. by Richard N. Coe, reprinted by permission of John Calder (Publishers) Ltd

HERBERT SULZBACH: extract from *With the German Guns* reprinted by permission of Frederick Warne (Publishers) Ltd

FRANK SWINNERTON: extract from *An Autobiography* reprinted by permission of Hutchinson Publishing Group Ltd

ARTHUR SYMONS: extract taken from *Playgoing* by James Agate, published by Hutchinson Publishing Group Ltd

A. J. P. TAYLOR: extract from *The Course of German History* reprinted by permission of Hamish Hamilton Ltd

LEO TOLSTOY: extract on p. 141 from *The Kreutzer Sonata,* trs. by Aylmer Maude, 1924, reprinted by permission of Oxford University Press

GEORGE TRAKL: "Decline," "At Hellbrunn," and "Grodek" from *German Poetry 1910–1975.* Copyright © 1976, 1977 by Michael Hamburger. Reprinted by permission of Persea Books, Inc., 225 Lafayette Street, New York, N.Y. 10012.

PETER UNDERWOOD: extract from *Haunted London* reprinted by permission of Harrap Ltd

BEATRICE WEBB: extracts from *Diary Vol. I* reprinted by permission of the London School of Economics and Political Science

VIRGINIA WOOLF: extracts from *Books and Portraits* by Virginia Woolf. Copyright © 1977 by Mary Lyon. Reprinted by permission of Harcourt Brace Jovanovich, Inc.

THEODORE ZELDIN: extracts taken from *France 1848–1945,* published by Oxford University Press, reprinted by permission of the author

INSPECTOR ZEMPIREK: extract from *The Hanging of William Oberdank* by Alfred Alexander reprinted by permission of London Magazine Editions

ÉMILE ZOLA: extract from *Nana*, trs. by Charles Duff, reprinted by permission of William Heinemann Ltd

STEFAN ZWEIG: extract from *The World of Yesterday*, published by Cassell in 1943, reprinted by permission of Williams Verlag A G

The publishers have endeavoured to trace all copyright holders of extracts used. If, however, appropriate acknowledgment has not been made please write to the publishers.

BIBLIOGRAPHY

AGATE, James, *Playgoing*, Jarrolds, 1927
ALDICK, Richard D., *Victorian Studies in Scarlet*, Dent, 1972
ALEXANDER, Alfred, *The Hanging of William Oberdank*, London Magazine Editions, 1977
Alexandra Magazine, The, London, 1864–5
Annals of Our Time, ed. Joseph Irving, Macmillan, 1876
APOLLINAIRE, Guillaume, *see* Barnstone, Willis, and Bernard, Oliver
APPIGNANESI, Lisa, *The Cabaret*, Studio Vista, 1976
ARANSON, Theo, *The Fall of the Third Napoleon*, Cassell, 1970
ARNOLD, Matthew, *Culture and Anarchy*, Smith, Elder & Co., 1869
ARTHUR, Herbert, *All the Sinners*, John Long, 1931
AULARD, A., *The Jacobin Club*, Paris, 1889–97
    Political History of the French Revolution, Paris, 1901
AVERY, G., *Nineteenth-century Children: Heroes and Heroines in English Children's Stories*, Hodder and Stoughton, 1965
BADEN-POWELL, Robert, *Scouting for Boys*, London, 1908
    Yarns for Scouts, London
BAKUNIN, Mikhail, *God and the State*, Paris, 1905 edition
BALDICK, Robert (ed.), *Pages from the Goncourt Journals*, Oxford, 1978 edition
    The Siege of Paris, Batsford, 1964
BALDWIN, Michael, *The Kaiser and his Times*, Cresset-Press, 1964
BALZAC, Honoré de, *Miscellaneous Works*, Paris, 1870–2
BARING-GOULD, S., *Curious Myths of the Middle Ages*, Longmans, Green, 1892
BARNSTONE, Willis (ed.), *Modern European Poetry*, Bantam Books, 1966
BATTISCOMBE, Georgina, *Christina Rossetti*, Constable, 1981
BAUDELAIRE, Charles, *Les Fleurs du mal*, Paris, 1857
    Selected Poems, trs. G. A. Wagner, Falcon Press, 1946
    Works, Paris, 1868

BEERBOHM, Max, *A Peep into the Past*, New York, 1923
BELL, Lady Florence, *At the Works*, Edward Arnold, 1907
BELLOC, Hilaire, *Collected Verse*, Duckworth, 1954
    Danton, Bell, 1899
    The Path to Rome, George Allen, 1902
BENCE-JONES, Mark, *Palaces of the Raj*, Allen and Unwin, 1973
BENNETT, Arnold, *The Journals of Arnold Bennett*, Penguin, 1954
BERGONZI, Bernard, *The Turn of the Century*, Macmillan, 1973
BERNARD, Oliver (ed.), *Apollinaire: Selected Poems*, Penguin, 1965
BERNHARDT, Sarah, *My Double Life*, Peter Owen, 1977 edition
BISMARCK, Prince Otto von, *Reflections and Reminiscences*, Smith, Elder and Co., 1898
BLAKESTON, Oswell, *Some Essential Information*, Kaleidoscope, 1975
BLAMIRES, Henry, *Word Unheard*, Methuen, 1969
BLANCH, Lesley, *The Wilder Shores of Love,* John Murray, 1954
BLOK, Alexander, *see* Cohen, J. M.
BLUMENBERG, Werner, *Karl Marx*, N. L. B., 1972
BOUMAN, P. J., *Revolution of the Lonely*, McGraw Hill, 1951
BOWERS, A., *Diary*, unpublished
BRAILSFORD, H. N., *The War of Steel and Gold*, G. Bell, 1914
British Medical Journal, 1868
BRITTAIN, Vera, *Testament of Youth*, Victor Gollancz, 1933
BROOKE, Rupert, *Collected Poems*, Sidgwick and Jackson, 1918
    'An Unusual Young Man', *New Statesman*, 1914
BRYANT, Sir Arthur, *English Saga 1840–1940*, Collins with Eyre & Spottiswoode, 1940
BÜLOW, Prince von, *Memoires*, Berlin, 1930
BUSCH, Moritz, *Our Chancellor, Sketches for a Historical Picture*, London, 1884
BYRNE, Patrick F., *Witchcraft in Ireland*, Mercier Press, 1967
CAMPBELL, Mrs Patrick, *My Life and Some Letters*, Hutchinson, 1922
CAMUS, Albert, *The Rebel*, Hamish Hamilton, 1953
CARR, E. H., *Bakunin*, London, 1937
CARUS, K. G., *Pysche*, Germany, 1846
CAVAFY, C. P., *The Complete Poems of C. P. Cavafy*, trs. Rae Dalven, Hogarth Press, 1961
CECIL, Algernon, *Queen Victoria and her Prime Ministers*, Eyre & Spottiswoode, 1953
Century Magazine, The, 1881
CÉZANNE, Paul, *see* Friedenthal, Richard
CHADWICK, Owen, *The Secularization of the European Mind in the 19th Century*, Cambridge, 1976
CHEKHOV, Anton, *Letters on the Short Story, the Drama, and other Literary Topics*, Moscow, 1893
    Sakhalin Island, Moscow, 1893
    The Wood Demon, Moscow, 1889
CHITTY, Susan, *The Beast and the Monk* (life of Charles Kingsby), Hodder and Stoughton, 1974

CHURCHILL, Sir Winston S., *My Early Life*, Macmillan, 1930
   The World Crisis, Thornton Butterworth, 1923–31
COHEN, J. M., *Poetry of this Age*, Arrow Books, 1959
COLETTE, *The Commonweal*, Vol. 5, 1888
   The Thousand and One Mornings, Peter Owen, 1977
CONQUEST, Robert, *We and They*, Maurice Temple Smith, 1980
CONRAD, Joseph, *Heart of Darkness*, J. M. Dent, 1902
   Notes on Life and Letters, J. M. Dent, 1921
COOK, Sir Edward, *Delane of the Times*, Constable, 1916
CORLEY, T. A. B., *Democratic Despot: a Life of Napoleon III*, Frederick
   Muller, 1958
COSMAN, Carol, Keefe, Joan and Weaver, Kathleen (eds), *Penguin Book
   of Women Poets*, Allen Lane, 1978
COURTHION, Pierre, *Courbet, Related by Himself and his Friends*, Geneva,
   1948
CRANKSHAW, Edward, *Bismarck*, Macmillan, 1981
   The Shadow of the Winter Palace, Macmillan, 1976
CULLEN, Tom, *Crippen, the Mild Murderer*, Bodley Head, 1977
CURTIS, E. N., *Saint-Just, Colleague of Robespierre*, New York, 1925
CURTISS, Mina, (ed.), *Letters of Marcel Proust*, Chatto and Windus, 1950
DALTON, Hugh, *Call Back Yesterday*, Frederick Muller, 1953
DARWIN, Bernard, *W. G. Grace*, Duckworth, 1934
DAUDET, Alphonse, *Memories of a Man of Letters*, Paris, 1880
   Notes on Life, Paris, 1899
DAVIDSON, John, *Ballads and Songs*, Grant Richards, 1894
DAVIES, Margaret Llewellyn (ed.), *Life as We Have Known It*, Virago, 1977
DENT, Edward J., *Opera*, Penguin, 1940
DICKENS, Charles, *Bleak House*, J. M. Dent, 1907
   Hard Times, J. M. Dent, 1908
   Nicholas Nickleby, J. M. Dent, 1907
   The Pickwick Papers, J. M. Dent, 1908
DICKSON, Lovat, *H. G. Wells: His Turbulent Life and Times*, Macmillan,
   1969
DISRAELI, Benjamin, *Lothair*, Longmans, Green, 1870
DOBRÉE, Bonamy, *Rudyard Kipling, Realist or Fatalist*, Oxford, 1967
DOSTOEVSKY, F. M., *The Brothers Karamazov*, St Petersburg, 1880
   Writer's Diary, St Petersburg, 1873
DOYLE, Sir Arthur Conan, *The Great Boer War*, Smith, Elder, 1900
   The Return of Sherlock Holmes, George Newnes, 1905
   A Study in Scarlet, Ward Lock, 1888
DUNCAN, Isadora, *My Life*, Victor Gollancz, 1928
EDEL, Leon, *Henry James: the Treacherous Years 1895–1900*, Hart-Davis,
   1972
EDEN, Anthony, *Another World 1897–1917*, Allen Lane, 1976
EDWARDS, Stewart, *The Paris Commune of 1871*, Eyre & Spottiswoode,
   1971
ELIOT, George, *Daniel Deronda*, Wm Blackwood and Sons, 1876
   Middlemarch, Wm Blackwood and Sons, 1871

ELLIS, Peter Beresford, *H. Rider Haggard*, Routledge & Kegan Paul, 1978
ENGELS, Frederick, *The Marx-Engels Letters*, Weidenfeld and Nicolson, 1981
EUGÉNIE, Empress, *Lettres Familières*, Paris, 1935
EVANS, George Evans, *The Pattern Under the Plough*, Faber and Faber, 1966
FARWELL, Brian, *The Great Boer War*, Allen Lane, 1977
Figaro, Le, 1871
FINLAYSON, Geoffrey B. A. M., *The Seventh Earl of Shaftesbury*, Eyre Methuen, 1981
FIRST, Ruth and Scott, Anne, *Olive Schreiner*, Andre Deutsch, 1980
FISCHER, Ernst, *An Opposing Man*, Allen Lane, 1974
FISHMAN, William J., *East End Jewish Radicals 1875–1914*, Duckworth
FLAUBERT, Gustav, *Correspondence*, Paris, 1926–30
FORBES, Archibald, *Despatches for the Daily News*, 1870–1
      Life of Napoleon III, Chatto and Windus, 1898
FORD, Ford Madox, *Return to Yesterday*, *The Freewoman*, Victor Gollancz, 1931
FREDERICK III, *War Diaries*, Stanley Paul, 1895
FREDERICK, Empress, *Letters*, Macmillan, 1928
FREUD, Sigmund, *Psychopathology of Everyday Life*, Pelican, 1938
FRIEDENTHAL, Richard (ed.), *Letters of the Great Artists*, Thames and Hudson, 1963
FULLER, J. F. C., *The Decisive Battles of the Western World*, Eyre & Spottiswoode, 1954
FYVEL, T. R., *George Orwell: a Memoir*, Secker and Warburg, 1982
Gaelic-American, The
GEORGE, Stefan, *Poems*, trs. Carol North Valhope and Ernst Morwitz, Kegan Paul, Trench, Trubner, 1944
GERARD, James W., *My Four Years in Germany*, Hodder and Stoughton, 1917
GILBERT, Elliot L., *The Good Kipling*, Manchester University Press, 1972
GISSING, George, *In The Year of Jubilee*, Lawrence and Bullen, 1894
      The Whirlpool, Lawrence and Bullen, 1897
GLENDINNING, Victoria, *A Suppressed Cry*, Routledge & Kegan Paul, 1969
GOGH, Vincent van, *The Complete Letters of Vincent van Gogh*, Thames and Hudson, 1958
Goncourt Journal, The, see Baldick, Robert
GOOCH, G. P., *The Second Empire*, Longmans, Green, 1960
GORKY, Maxim, *Fragments from my Diary*, P. Allan, 1924
Graphic Magazine, The
GREEN, Martin, *The Von Richtofen Sisters*, Weidenfeld and Nicolson, 1974
GUEDALLA, Philip, *The Second Empire*, Constable, 1922
GUTMAN, Robert, *Richard Wagner, the Man, his Mind and his Music*, Secker and Warburg, 1968
HAESAERTS, Paul, *James Ensor*, Thames and Hudson, 1959
HAIGHT, Gordon S., *George Eliot*, Oxford, 1968
HAMBURGER, Michael, *From Prophecy to Exorcism*, Longmans, 1965

(ed.), *German Poetry 1910–1975*, Carcanet Press, Manchester, 1976
  The Truth of Poetry, Weidenfeld and Nicolson, 1969
HAMILTON, Nigel, *The Brothers Mann*, Secker and Warburg, 1978
HARDY, Thomas, *The Mayor of Casterbridge*, Macmillan, 1886
  Selected Poems, ed. David Wright, Penguin, 1978
HARE, Richard, *Portraits of Russian Revolutionaries*, London, 1959
HARRISON, R. A., *How Was That, Sir?*, I.A.P.S., 1975
HART-DAVIS, Rupert, *Selected Essays of Oscar Wilde*, Hart-Davis, 1962
HAUSRATH, H., *Life and Works of Heinrich von Treitshke*, London, 1914
HAYMAN, Ronald, *Nietzsche: a critical life*, Weidenfeld and Nicolson, 1980
HELLER, Erich, *The Disinherited Mind*, Bowes and Bowes, 1952
HERZEN, Alexander, *My Past and Thoughts*, Chatto and Windus, 1924–7
HESSE, Hermann, *Peter Camenzind*, trs. W. G. Strachan, Peter Owen,
  1961
HIGGINS, D. S., *Rider Haggard, the Great Story-Teller*, Cassell, 1982
HILLIER, Bevis, *Dead Funny*, Ash and Grant, 1974
HINGLEY, Ronald, *A New Life of Chekhov*, Oxford, 1976
HOFMANNSTAHL, Hugo von, *Collected Works*, Berlin, 1924
  Selected Prose, ed. and trs. Tania and James Stern, Bollingen Series,
  New York, 1952
HOOPER, George, *The Campaign of Sedan*, G. Bell, 1916
HORNE, Alistair, *The Fall of Paris*, Macmillan, 1965
  The Terrible Year, Macmillan, 1971
HOUGH, Richard, *The Fleet that had to Die*, Hamish Hamilton, 1958
HOWARD, Michael, *The Franco-Prussian War*, Hart-Davis, 1961
HOWARTH, T. E. B., *Citizen-King: the Life of Louis Philippe*, Eyre &
  Spottiswoode, 1961
HOWE, Ellic, *Urania's Children*, William Kimber, 1967
HOYER, Liv Nansen, *Nansen*, Longmans, Green, 1957
HUGHES, M. V., *A London Family 1870–1900*, Oxford, 1981 edition
HUGO, Victor, *The Terrible Year* , Paris, 1872
HULSE, James W., *Revolutionists in London*, Oxford, 1970
HYDE, H. Montgomery, *Henry James at Home*, Methuen, 1969
IBSEN, Henrik, *Letters*, New York, 1908
IVES, George, *Man Bites Man*, Landesman, 1980
JACKSON, J. Hampden, *Clemenceau and the Third Republic*, Hodder and
  Stoughton, 1946
  Jaurés, Hodder and Stoughton, 1943
JAMES, Henry, *The Ambassadors*, Methuen, 1903
  The Notebooks of Henry James, ed. F. O. Matthiessen and K. B.
  Murdock, Brazillier, O.U.P., 1947
  The Portrait of a Lady, Macmillan, 1881
  Portraits of Places, Macmillan, 1883
  The Princess Casamassima, Macmillan, 1886
JELLINEK, Frank, *The Paris Commune of 1871*, Victor Gollancz, 1936
JEROME, Jennie, *The Reminiscences of Lady Randolph Churchill*, Edward
  Arnold, 1908
JEROME, Jerome K., *Three Men in a Boat*, J. W. Arrowsmith, 1889

JOLL, James, *Europe since 1870: an International History*, Weidenfeld and Nicolson, 1973

JONES, Ernest, *Sigmund Freud: Life and Work*, Hogarth Press, 1953–7

JUNG, C. G., *Memories, Dreams, Reflections*, ed. Aniela Jaffé, Collins with Routledge & Kegan Paul, 1963

KAPP, Yvonne, *Eleanor Marx*, Vol. 2, Virago, 1979

KEATING, Peter, *Into Unknown England*, Fontana, 1976

KENNER, Hugh, *The Pound Era*, Faber, 1972

KILVERT, Rev. Francis, *Diary*, ed. William Plomer, Jonathan Cape, 1976 edition

KING-HALL, Magdalen, *The Story of the Nursery*, Routledge & Kegan Paul, 1958

KIPLING, Rudyard, *The Definitive Edition of Rudyard Kipling's Verse*, Eyre Methuen
  Letters of Travel, Macmillan, 1908
  On the City Wall, Macmillan, 1888

KOKOSHKA, Oskar, *My Life*, Thames and Hudson, 1974

KOLLONTAI, Alexandra, *International Socialist Conferences of Working Women 1907–1910*, Moscow, 1918

KORNGOLD, Ralph, *Robespierre, First Modern Dictator*, Macmillan, 1937

KOTELIANSKI, S. S. and Tomlinson, P., *The Life and Letters of Anton Chekhov*, Cassell, 1925

KRAUS, Karl, *Die Fackel*, Vienna, 1899–1936

KROPOTKIN, Prince Peter, *The Conquest of Bread*, Chapman and Hall, 1906
  Mutual Aid, Heinemann, 1902

KURTZ, Harold, *The Empress Eugénie*, Hamish Hamilton, 1964

LABOUCHERE, Henry, *Diary of the Besieged Resident in Paris*, London, 1871

Lanterne, La, Paris, 1867–9

LATEY, Maurice, *Tyranny: a Study in the Abuse of Power*, Macmillan, 1969

LAWRENCE, D. H., *Collected Works*, Vol. 15, Berlin, 1925
  The Letters of D. H. Lawrence, Heinemann, 1932

LENIN, *War Theses*, Zurich, 1914

LESLIE, Anita, *Edwardians in Love*, Hutchinson, 1972

L'ÉTANG, Hugh, *The Pathology of Leadership*, Heinemann, 1969

LOCKHART, J. G., and Woodhouse, C. M., *Cecil Rhodes*, Duckworth, 1933

LORD, Walter, *A Night to Remember*, Longmans, Green, 1956

LUXEMBURG, Rosa, *Organizational Questions of Russian Social Democracy*, Neue Zeit, Stuttgart, 1904

McGONAGALL, William, *Last Poetic Gems*, Duckworth, 1980

MACKENZIE, Norman and Jeanne, *The Time Traveller: the Life of H. G. Wells*, Weidenfeld and Nicolson, 1971

MAGEE, Bryan, *Aspects of Wagner*, Alan Ross, 1968

MALMESBURY, Lord, *Memoirs of an ex-Minister*, Longmans, Green, 1884

MANDELSTAM, Osip, *Selected Poems*, trs. Clarence Brown and W. S. Merwin, Oxford, 1973
  Selected Poems, trs. David McDuff, Rivers Press, 1973
  Poems, trs. James Greene, Paul Elek, 1977

MANN, Heinrich, *Geist und Tat*, Berlin, 1911

MANN, Thomas, *Stories of Three Decades*, Secker and Warburg, 1946
Manners and Rules of Good Society by a Member of the Aristocracy, London, 1890
MANSFIELD, Katherine, *Letters and Journals*, Penguin, 1977
Manual of Verse for Victorian Children, London, undated
MARCUS, Geoffrey, *The Maiden Voyage*, Allen and Unwin, 1969
MARINETTI, Filippo Tommaso, *Futurism*, Zurich, 1911
    Manifesto on the Variety Theatre
MARKET, Jean, *Clemenceau*, Paris, 1936
MARLOWE, John, *Milner, Apostle of Empire*, Hamish Hamilton, 1976
MARLY, Diana de, *Worth, Father of Haute Couture*, Elm Tree Books, 1980
MARTIN, E. W., *Country Life in England*, MacDonald, 1966
MARTIN, Ralph G., *Lady Randolph Churchill*, Cassell, 1966
MARX, Karl, *The Civil War in France*, London, 1871
    Letters to Dr Kugelmann 1862–74, Martin Lawrence, 1934
    Marx-Engels Letters, Weidenfeld and Nicolson, 1981
    The Paris Commune of 1871, Sidgwick and Jackson, 1971 edition
MASEFIELD, John, *Collected Poems*, Heinemann, 1941 edition
MASON, A. E. W., *The Four Feathers*, John Murray, 1902
MASUR, Gerhard, *Prophets of Yesterday*, Weidenfeld and Nicolson, 1963
MATHIEZ, Albert, *The French Revolution*, Paris, 1922
MAUGHAM, W. Somerset, *The Explorer*, Heinemann, 1908
MEW, Charlotte, *Collected Poems*, Duckworth, 1953
MILL, John Stuart, *Early Draft of Autobiography*, ed. Jack Stillinger, University of Illinois, 1961
    On Liberty, 1859
MOLTKE, Count Helmuth von, the Elder, *The Franco-Prussian War of 1870–1*, Osgood, McIlvaine, 1891
MOORMAN, Mary, *George Macaulay Trevelyan: a Memoir*, Hamish Hamilton, 1980
MOORS, Dorothy, *Terry the Girl Guide*, Nisbet, 1912
MORRIS, William, *Collected Works*, ed. Mary Morris, London, 1910–15
MUNRO, H. H., *see* Saki
MURRY, J. Middleton, *Selected Criticism*, Oxford, 1960
MUSSOLINI, Benito, *Avanti*, 1911–14
NANSEN, Fridtjof, *In Northern Mists*, Heinemann, 1932
NAPOLEON III, *Letters, Revue des Deux-mondes, 1930*
    Life of Julius Caesar, Paris, 1865
NECHAEV Sergei, *The Revolutionary's Catechism*, Geneva, 1869
NEUMANN, Alfred, *Man of December*, Hutchinson, 1936
NEWSOME, D., *Godliness and Good Learning*, London, 1891
NICOLSON, Nigel, *Portrait of a Marriage*, Weidenfeld and Nicolson, 1973
NIETZSCHE, Friedrich, *Complete Works*, ed. Oscar Lévy, J. N. Foulis, 1909–13
    Letters 1864–71 and *Letters 1872–4*
NORDERN, Pierre, *Conan Doyle*, John Murray, 1966
O'SHEA, J. A., *An Iron-Bound City*, London, 1886
PAGE, Walter Hines, Despatch to Washington, August 1914

PALÉOLOGUE, Georges Maurice, *Diary*, Paris, 1947
   Intimate Conversations with the Empress Eugénie, Thornton Butter-
   worth, 1928
Pall Mall Gazette, 1870
PAYNE, Robert, *The Wanton Nymph*, Heinemann, 1951
   Zero, Wingate, 1951
PÉGUY, Charles, 'L'Argent', *Cahiers de la quinzaine*, Paris, 1901
PORTER, Cathy, *Alexandra Kollontai*, Virago, 1980
PORTER, Donald, *The Refugee Question in mid-Victorian Politics*, Cam-
   bridge, 1980
POUND, Ezra, *Selected Poems*, ed. T. S. Eliot, Faber and Faber, 1928
POWELL, Enoch, *Joseph Chamberlain*, Thames and Hudson, 1977
PRAWDIN, Michael, *The Unmentionable Nechaev*, Allen and Unwin, 1961
PREBBLE, John, *The High Guiders*, Secker and Warburg, 1956
PRICE, M. Philips, *My Three Revolutions*, Allen and Unwin, 1970
PRIESTLEY, J. B., *Margin Released*, Heinemann, 1964
PROUST, Marcel, *Les Plaisirs et les jours*, Paris, 1896
   Letters of Marcel Proust, ed. Mina Curtiss, Chatto and Windus, 1950
Punch
PYNCHON, Thomas, *V*, Jonathan Cape, 1961
QUERLIN, Marise, *Princess Mathilde*, Lausanne, 1966
RAY, Robin (ed.), *Time for Lovers*, Weidenfeld and Nicolson, 1975
REES, Barbara, *The Victorian Lady*, Gordon and Cremonesi, 1978
REWALD, John, *Paul Cézanne, Correspondence*, Paris, 1937
REYNOLDS, E. E., *Nansen*, Geoffrey Bles, 1932
REYNOLDS, Reginald and Stock, A. L., Prison Anthology, Jarrolds, 1938
RICHTER, Werner, *Bismarck*, Macdonald, 1964
RILKE, Rainer Maria, *Fifty Selected Poems*, trs. C. F. MacIntyre, Univer-
   sity of California, 1940
   Poems 1906–26, trs. J. B. Leishman, Hogarth Press, 1957
RIMBAUD, Arthur, *The Drunken Boat: 36 Poems of Arthur Rimbaud*, trs.
   Brian Hill, Hart-Davis, 1952
   Selected Verse Poems of Arthur Rimbaud, trs. Norman Cameron,
   Hogarth Press, 1942
ROBBINS, Ian, *Tuesday 4 August 1914*, Oxford, 1970
ROSE, Kenneth, *King George V*, Weidenfeld and Nicolson, 1983
ROSEBURY, Theodor, *Life on Man*, Secker and Warburg, 1969
ROSSETTI, Christina, *Complete Works*, ed. William Rossetti, London, 1904
ROTHNEY, John, *Bonapartism after Sedan*, Cornell University, 1969
RUSKIN, John, *Slade Lectures 1870–9*
SAKI (H. H. Munro), *The Best of Saki*, ed. Graham Greene, Guild Books,
   1950
SALA, George Augustus, *Paris Herself Again*, London, 1880
SAND, George, *Letters*, ed. E. V. Lucas, London, 1930
SCHLIEFFEN, Count Alfred von, *Western War Plan*, 1891–1906
SCHREINER, Olive, *The Story of an African Farm*, Hutchinson, 1893
SCHWEITZER, Albert, *The Quest of the Historical Jesus*, A. and C. Black,
   1910

SENCOURT, Robert, *Napoleon III: The Modern Emperor*, Ernest Benn, 1933

SHAW, George Bernard, *Man and Superman*, Constable, 1906

SIMS, George Robert, *Off the Track in London*, Jarrolds, 1910

SITWELL, Sacheverell, *For Want of the Golden City*, Thames and Hudson, 1973

SMITH, Senator W. A., *Report on the* Titanic, Washington, 1912

SMYTHE, Ethel, *Streaks of Life*, Longmans, Green

SOLZHENITSYN, Alexander, *Lenin in Zurich*, Bodley Head, 1976

SOREL, Georges, *Reflections on Violence*, Paris, 1908

SORLEY, Charles Hamilton, *Marlborough and other Poems*, Cambridge, 1932

SPENCE, Lewis, *The Minor Traditions of British Mythology*, Rider, 1948
    Myth and Ritual in Dance, Game and Rhyme, Watts, 1947

SQUIRE, J. C., *Collected Poems*, Macmillan, 1959

STEIN, Fritz, *Gold and Iron*, Knopf, 1977

STEINER, George (ed.), *Poem into Poem*, Penguin, 1970

STENDHAL, *Rome, Naples and Florence*, John Calder, 1959

STEPHEN, F. K., *The Cambridge Review*, 1891

STEPHEN, Leslie, *The Decay of Murder*: 'The Cornhill', 1869

STEPUN, Fedor, *Vergangenes und Unvergängliches*, Munich, 1947

STEVENSON, Robert Louis, *Letters*, ed. Lloyd Osbourne, Methuen, 1914

STOCK, A. L., *see* Reynolds, Reginald

SULZBACH, Herbert, *With the German Guns*, Frederick Warne, 1981 edition

SWINNERTON, Frank, *An Autobiography*, Hutchinson, 1937

SYMONS, Arthur, *London: a Book of Aspects*, London, 1909
    Silhouettes, Mathews and Lane, 1892

TALMON, J. L., *The Origins of Totalitarian Democracy*, Secker and Warburg, 1952

TAYLOR, A. J. P., *Bismarck*, Hamish Hamilton, 1955
    The Course of German History, Hamish Hamilton, 1945
    Europe: Grandeur and Decline, Penguin in association with Hamish Hamilton, 1967
    The Struggle for Mastery in Europe 1848–1918, Oxford, 1954

TENNYSON, Alfred, Lord, *Poems*, Oxford, 1912
    The Princess, E. Moxon, 1847
    Works, Macmillan, 1911

TERRY, Ellen, Letter to George Bernard Shaw, 1896

THOMPSON, J. M., *The French Revolution*, Blackwell, 1944
    Leaders of the French Revolution, Blackwell, 1929
    Louis Napoleon and the Second Empire, Blackwell, 1954
    Robespierre, Blackwell, 1935

TINDALL, Gillian, *The Born Exile: George Gissing*, Harcourt Brace Jovanovich, 1974

TOLSTOY, Leo N., *Anna Karenina*, trs. Louise and Aylmer Maude, Oxford, 1939

Diary
The Kreutzer Sonata, Humphrey Milford, 1924
What I Believe, World's Classics, 1921
What is Art?, O.U.P., 1930
for *Letters*, *see* Troyat, Henri
TOMLINSON, Charles, *Verses from Fyodur Tyutcher*, Oxford, 1960
TOYNBEE, Philip, *Two Brothers*, Chatto and Windus, 1964
TREVELYAN, G. M., *Edward Bowen*, 'The Harrovian', 1901
TROLLOPE, Anthony, *An Autobiography*, Wm Blackwood and Sons, 1883
    Dr Wortle's School, Chapman and Hall, 1881
    The Duke's Children, Chapman and Hall, 1880
    The Eustace Diamonds, London, 1873
    The Prime Minister, London, 1876
TROYAT, Henri, *Tolstoy*, trs. Nancy Amphoux, Penguin, 1970
TUCHMAN, Barbara, *The Proud Tower*, Hamish Hamilton, 1966
TURGENEV, Ivan S., *Virgin Soil*, trs. Constance Garnett
UNDERWOOD, Peter, *Haunted London*, Harrap, 1973
VACHELL, H. A., *The Hill*, John Murray, 1905
VANSITTART, Peter, *Dictators*, Studio Vista, 1973
    Worlds and Underworlds, Peter Owen, 1974
VELLAY, C. (ed.), *The Complete Works of Saint-Just*, Paris, 1908
VICTORIA, Queen, *Letters*, ed. Viscount Esher and George Buckle, London, 1907–30
WADE, Wyn Craig, *The Titanic*, Weidenfeld and Nicolson, 1979
WAGNER, Richard, *My Life*, London, 1911
WALVIN, James, *A Child's World*, Penguin, 1982
WARD, Mrs Humphrey, *A Writer's Recollections*, Collins, 1918
WEBB, Beatrice, *My Apprenticeship*, London, 1926
    Diary, Much of it unpublished, in the Passfield Papers, London School of Economics; Vol. 1, ed. Margaret Cole, Longmans, Green, 1952
WELLS, H. G., *Anticipations of the Reaction of Mechanical and Scientific Progress upon Human Life and Thought*, Chapman and Hall, 1901
    Boon, T. Fisher Unwin, 1906–15
    This Misery of Boots, Fabian Society, 1907
    The New Machiavelli, John Lane, 1911
    'The Rediscovery of the Unique', *Fortnightly Review*, 1891
    The Time Machine, Heinemann, 1895
    Tono-Bungay, Macmillan, 1909
    The War of the Worlds, Heinemann, 1898
    The Work, Wealth and Happiness of Mankind, Heinemann, 1932
WEST, Rebecca, *Black Lamb and Grey Falcon*, Macmillan, 1942
WILDE, OSCAR, O'F. W., *De Profundis*, Methuen, 1905
    The Decay of Lying, Osgood, McIlvaine, 1894
    Essays, *see* Hart-Davis, Rupert
    'The Soul of Man under Socialism', *Fortnightly Review*, 1891
WILSON, D. A., *Life of Carlyle*, Kegan Paul, 1923–34
WODEHOUSE, P. G., *Mike and Psmith*, Herbert Jenkins, 1953 edition

WOHL, Anthony S. (ed.), *The Bitter Cry of Outcast London*, Leicester University, 1970

WOLSELEY, Field Marshal Viscount, *The Story of a Soldier's Life*, Constable, 1903

WOOLF, Leonard, *Beginning Again*, Hogarth Press, 1964

WOOLF, Virginia, *Books and Portraits*, Hogarth Press, 1977

Young Ladies' Journal, The

ZELDIN, Theodore, *France 1848–1945*, Oxford, 1974

ZOLA, Émile, *The Downfall*, Chatto and Windus, 1896

   Nana, Heinemann, 1953

ZWEIG, Stefan, *The World of Yesterday*, Cassell, 1943

INDEX

(*Note*: Arrangement of sub-headings under personal names is
chronological)